CONTENTS

Cover Photograph courtesy of Bill Currie.

Pastime Publications Ltd gratefully acknowledge the assistance of The Scottish Tourist Board, Area Tourist Boards and others in compiling this guide.

Published by Pastime Publications Ltd., 6 York Place, Edinburgh EH1 3EP.
Tel: 0131-556 1105.

First published by The Scottish Tourist Board 1970.
UK & Worldwide Distribution by AA Publishing Ltd.
Typesetting by Servis Filmsetting Ltd.
Printed and bound by Offset Print Veneta

ADVERTISERS' INDEX
DISPLAY ADVERTISEMENTS

(ALSO SEE COLOUR ADVERTS)

CLASSIFIED ADVERTISEMENTS
HOTELS & GUEST HOUSES

ABERDEENSHIRE
Aberdeen — 29

ANGUS
Carnoustie — 29
Dundee — 29
Forfar — 29
Kirriemuir — 29
Montrose — 29

ARGYLL
Dalmally — 29
Dunoon — 29
Oban — 30
Taynuilt — 30

AYRSHIRE
Ayr — 30
Kilmarnock — 30
Sorn — 30

DUMFRIESSHIRE
Annan — 30
Crocketford — 30
Dumfries — 30
Moffat — 31

FIFE
Auchtermuchty — 31
Crail — 31
Dunfermline — 31

INVERNESS-SHIRE
Beauly — 31
Kincraig — 31
Whitebridge — 31

KINCARDINESHIRE
Banchory — 31

KIRKCUDBRIGHTSHIRE
Castle Douglas — 32
Dalbeattie — 32
Kippford — 32

PEEBLESSHIRE
Peebles — 32

PERTHSHIRE
Aberfeldy — 32
Callander — 32
Kinloch Rannoch — 32
Perth — 32
Pitlochry — 33

ROXBURGHSHIRE
Hawick — 33

SELKIRKSHIRE
Galashiels — 33

SUTHERLAND
Brora — 33
Lairg — 33

SCOTLAND'S ISLANDS
Islay — 33
Orkney — 33

SELF CATERING

ABERDEENSHIRE
Aboyne — 34
Inverurie — 34

ARGYLL
Dalavich — 34
Dalmally — 34

BERWICKSHIRE
Coldingham — 34

DUMFRIESSHIRE
Dumfries — 34

INVERNESS-SHIRE
Aviemore — 34
Boat of Garten — .35
Invergarry — 35

PEEBLESSHIRE
West Linton — 35

PERTHSHIRE
Aberfeldy — 35

ROSS-SHIRE
Lochcarron — 35

SUTHERLAND
Helmsdale — 35

WIGTOWNSHIRE
Cairnryan — 35

5 PALL MALL, LONDON, S.W.1.
Telephone 0171-839 2423

Open till 6 p.m. weekdays and 4 p.m. Saturdays

Only 3 minutes walk from Piccadilly Circus & Trafalgar Square

Until you can visit us, our full colour Magazine will give you a glimpse of what is in store
Free on request

A B E R D E E N S H I R E

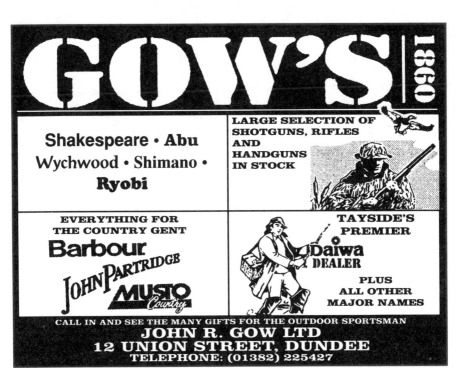

AYR SEA ANGLING CENTRE

Come fishing aboard the fully equipped purpose built sea angling boats.
"MARION B" and "KINGFISHER"
Professional skippers to
attend and advise. 3, 4
and 6 hour trips.
Daily sailings from
Ayr Harbour.

PARTIES AND INDIVIDUALS
Novices and experienced anglers all welcome.
PHONE TICH or TONY MEDINA on AYR (01292) 285297 or write 10 Britannia Place, Ayr.

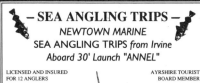

— SEA ANGLING TRIPS —

NEWTOWN MARINE
SEA ANGLING TRIPS *from Irvine*
Aboard 30' Launch "ANNEL"

LICENSED AND INSURED
FOR 12 ANGLERS

AYRSHIRE TOURIST
BOARD MEMBER

FROM IRVINE
ABOARD 30' LAUNCH "ANNEL'

4 hr., 6 hr. and 8 hr. trips available all year round.

TACKLE FOR HIRE, TUITION
GIVEN IF REQUIRED.

BAIT MAY BE ORDERED.

DIVING TRIPS ALSO CATERED FOR.

FREE HOT DRINKS AVAILABLE ON BOARD.

TO RESERVE YOUR TRIP:

TELEPHONE: NORRY MASON ON 01563 71629
(24 Hour Answering Service).
BOAT: 0374 700614.

SELF CATERING HOLIDAYS ON THE BERWICKSHIRE COAST

Secluded Holiday Cottages and Chalets centred on private Trout Loch in wooded country estate close to sea. Shops and sandy beach 2 miles. An ideal centre for anglers, naturalists and walkers or for touring the Borders, Edinburgh and Northumberland.

Write or phone for brochure

Dr and Mrs E.J. Wise
West Loch House,
Coldingham, Berwickshire
Tel: (018907) 71270

Northburn

Situated on the Historic 'Fort Point' Headland and on Scotland's only Marine Reserve, NORTHBURN HOLIDAY HOME PARK, EYEMOUTH has commanding views and the BEST THAT BERWICKSHIRE HAS TO OFFER.

Northburn is a popular centre for sub-aqua sports, sea angling, bird watching and coastal walks. Beach and harbour a short walk. Scottish Tourist Board 'Excellent' Award, holiday homes are fully equipped, touring caravans welcome.

FOR FREE BROCHURE CALL NOW 018907 51050

Northburn Holiday Home Park, Fort Road, Eyemouth TD14 5BE.

14

**D
U
M
F
R
I
E
S
S
H
I
R
E**

**D
U
N
B
A
R
T
O
N
S
H
I
R
E**

**F
I
F
E**

TURN TO PAGE 58 FOR GAME FISHING GAZETTEER

I
N
V
E
R
N
E
S
S

K
I
N
C
A
R
D
I
N
E
S
H
I
R
E

K
I
R
K
C
U
D
B
R
I
G
H
T
S
H
I
R
E

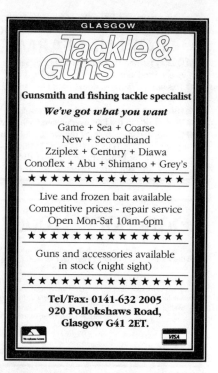

TRADES DESCRIPTION ACT

The accommodation mentioned in this holiday guide has not been inspected, and the publishers rely on information provided. The publishers have every confidence in their advertisers but cannot be held responsible for the accuracy of the descriptions published.

STAKIS
DUNKELD

DUNKELD HOUSE RESORT HOTEL

PERTHSHIRE

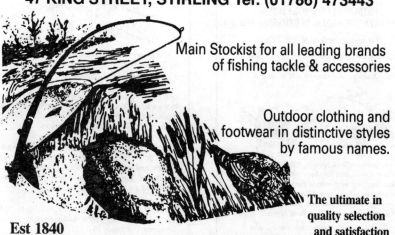

STIRLINGSHIRE SUTHERLAND

TURN TO PAGE 137 FOR COARSE FISHING GAZETTEER

TORWOOD HOUSE HOTEL

Galloway Leisure Sport
Glenluce, Newton Stewart, Wigtownshire DG8 OPB.
Tel: (01581) 300469.   Fax: (01581) 300258

EXCLUSIVE FISHERIES

Loch Dernaglar - Pike Loch	£3.50/Day	£15.00/Week
Barnbarroch Coarse Fishery	£3.50/Day	£15.00/Week
Torwood Tench Fishery	£3.50/Day	£15.00/Week

HOME OF THE SCOTTISH TENCH RECORD

Torwood Coarse Fishery	£3.50/Day	£15.00/Week
Torwood Trout Loch	£6.00/Day	£30.00/Week

CATCH & RELEASE, BROWN & RAINBOW TROUT

Ardwell Trout Loch	£12.00/Day	£48.00/Week

Brown & Brook Trout - price includes boat

Sea & Salmon fishing available

BAIT & TACKLE

Bait For Sale   Boats Available

Tackle bought and sold and for hire.

Accommodation (20% Fishing Permit discount for residents)

Anglers Special. 3 days accommodation and coarse fishing, all for £30 based on minimum 2 persons sharing.

Parties/Clubs. Special rates will be discussed with pleasure. Groups of 11 or more, organiser free.

Self Catering. £150-£250 per week - sleeping 4-6.

Normal Hotel Accommodation. £16.50-£30.00 per person/day.

Snacks, suppers, a la Carte Restaurant.

Flexible Bar!!

Clay pigeon and other shooting available.

WIGTOWNSHIRE

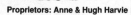
TURN TO PAGE 157 FOR SEA ANGLING INFORMATION

28

	Type of accommodation	Type of Fishing	Permits available	Drying facilities	Freezing facilities	Price p.p. B/B or B.B.E.M.	Special features

Michael Waller & Margaret Cockburn, School of Casting, Salmon & Trout Fishing, Station House, Clovenfords, Galashiels TD1 3LU. Tel: (089695) 293.

Weekly fly fishing courses for novice and experienced fishers. The oldest established school with a fine reputation for the teaching of casting and fishing. Full equipment hire including waders. A wonderful holiday by mountain and moorland.

HOTELS & GUESTS HOUSES

ABERDEENSHIRE
Aberdeen

	Type of accommodation	Type of Fishing	Permits available	Drying facilities	Freezing facilities	Price p.p. B/B or B.B.E.M.	Special features
Stephen Taylor (Mr.), Water Wheel Inn, 203 North Deeside Road, Bieldside, Aberdeen. Tel: (01224) 861659.	Inn 4 Crowns	River Dee River Don	No	Yes	Yes	On Appl.	25 luxury rooms – each has ensuite facilities, TV, hair dryer, trouser press, telephone, tea/coffee facilities.

ANGUS
Carnoustie

	Type of accommodation	Type of Fishing	Permits available	Drying facilities	Freezing facilities	Price p.p. B/B or B.B.E.M.	Special features
Glencoe Hotel, Links Parade, Carnoustie. Tel: (01241) 853273.	Hotel 3 Crowns	Sea River	Yes	Yes	Yes	B.&B. from £30.	Tayside is an excellent location for the keen fisherman. The Glencoe Hotel is your ideal base.

Dundee

Rosalind Butcher (Mrs.), Ashley House, 15 Monifieth Road, Broughty Ferry DD5 2RN. Tel: (01382) 776109.	House 2 Crowns	Ask	Ask	Yes	Yes	B.&B. from £17–£18	Small family-run bed & breakfast on bus route to Dundee. Ensuite facilities. TV. Radio, Clock, Heating, Elec. blankets, Tea/coffee fac.

Forfar

D. Douglas (Mr.), Chapelbank House Hotel, 69 East High Street, Forfar. Tel: (01307) 463151.	Hotel 4 Crowns High. Comm.	Fly	Ask	Yes	Yes	On Appl.	Town house only mins. away from lochs and Rivers Tay and Esk. 4 ensuite luxury bedrooms.

Kirriemuir

Airlie Arms Hotel, Kirriemuir. Tel: (01575) 572847.	Hotel 3 Crowns	Loch & river	Ask	Yes	Yes	B. & B.: £19.50–£24.50	Excellent loch and river fishing for salmon, sea trout and trout.

Montrose

G. Reid (Mr.), Corner House Hotel, 131 High Street, Montrose. Tel: (01674) 673126.	Hotel 3 Crowns Commended	River & Sea	No	Yes	Yes	B.&B. from £20.	Free house. Sizzling steaks, home baking. Friendly. Ensuite Bed & Breakfast.

ARGYLL
Dalmally

A.J. Burke (Mr.), "Orchy Bank", Dalmally PA33 1AS. Tel: (01838) 200370.	Guest House Listed Commended	Salmon Trout Pike	Yes	Yes	Yes	B.&B.: £17.00 B.B.E.M.: £26.00	Two miles from Loch Awe on bank of River Orchy.

Dunoon

M.J. Greig (Mr.), Royal Marine Hotel, Hunter's Quay, Dunoon PA23 8HJ. Tel: (01369) 5810	Hotel 3 Crowns Commended	Ghillie service	Yes	Yes	Yes	D.B.B. from £30.	Warm welcome. Good food. Friendly staff. Beautiful area. Great Fishing.

	Type of accommodation	Type of Fishing	Permits available	Drying facilities	Freezing facilities	Price p.p. B/B or B.B.E.M.	Special features
Oban Anne C. Donn (Mrs.), Palace Hotel, George Street, Oban. Tel/Fax: (01631) 62294.	Hotel 2 Crowns	Coarse Fly Sea	Locally	Yes	Yes	B.&B.: £17.50–£25.	Warm and friendly welcome. Overlooking Oban Bay. Ensuite rooms.
Taynuilt Taychreggan Hotel, Kilchrenan, by Taynuilt PA35 1HQ. Tel: (018663) 221/366. Fax: (018663) 244.	Hotel 4 Crowns Commended	Brown/ Rainbow Trout. Pike Char Salmon	Yes	Yes	Yes	B. & B. from £30. D.B.&B. from £67.	Own boats with ghillie. Open all year. Award winning dining room. On shores of Loch Awe. Bargain breaks available.
AYRSHIRE **Ayr** R. Henderson (Mr.), Savoy Park Hotel, 16 Racecourse Road, Ayr. Tel: (01292) 266112.	Hotel 4 Crowns	Sea/ River	Ask	Yes	Yes	B.&B. from £35. B.B.E.M. from £45.	Traditional family-run hotel. Close to town centre. Ample free parking. A real home from home.
Elms Court Hotel, Miller Road, Ayr. Tel: (01292) 264191.	Hotel 4 Crowns Commended	Various	No	Yes	Yes	D.B.&B.: £45.	Well situated in Ayr town. Extensive parking. Attractive lounge bar. Excellent food served.
Sheila Campbell, Parson's Lodge, 15 Main Street, Patna, Ayr. Tel: (01292) 531306.	Lodge Commended Listed	Trout Salmon	Yes	Yes	Yes	B. & B. from £12.50. B.B.E.M. from £19.50.	3 mins. from River Doon. Licensed restaurant on premises. CTV and tea/coffee facilities in all rooms.
Kilmarnock David & Judith Dye, Burnside Hotel, 18 London Road, Kilmarnock KA3 7AQ. Tel: (01563) 22952.	Hotel 3 Crowns Commended	All	Locally	Yes	Yes	B.&B. from £15.	"Fore" economy and comfort. Excellent area for fishing.
SORN P. Poole (Mrs.), Templandshaw Farm, Sorn, Mauchline KA5 6NF. Tel: (01290) 551543.	F'house	River Trout Salmon	Yes	Yes	Yes	B. & B. £12 B.B.E.M. £19	Pets Welcome. Small self catering flat also available (sleeps 2).
DUMFRIESSHIRE **Annan** Adam T. Gribbon Powfoot Golf Hotel, Links Avenue, Powfoot, Annan. Tel: (01461) 700254. Fax: (01461) 700288.	Hotel	Game Coarse	Yes	Yes	Yes	B. & B. from £44. E. M.: £13.	Excellent game fishing on River Annan. Coarse fishing near hotel.
Crocketford Anthony B. Mullan (Mr.), Galloway Arms Hotel, Crocketford. Tel: (01556) 690248.	Hotel	All	Yes	Yes	Yes	B. & B. from £20	Group rates available on request.
Dumfries H.M. McFeat (Mr.), Carrutherstown Hotel, Carrutherstown. Tel: (01387) 84 268.	Hotel	River Loch Coarse Sea	Ask	Yes	Yes	B.&B.: £15	Centrally situated for access to all types of fishing.

	Type of accommodation	Type of Fishing	Permits available	Drying facilities	Freezing facilities	Price p.p. B/B or B.B.E.M.	Special features
M.E. Hamlet (Mrs.), Cowans, Kirkgunzeon, Dumfries DG2 8JY. Tel: (01387) 760284	Guest House	Coarse	Yes	No	Yes	B.&B. from £13.50	Coarse fishing: carp, tench, roach on own loch.
Heather Owens Abbey Arms, 1 The Square, New Abbey, Dumfries. Tel: (01387) 850489.	Lic. Hotel	River Loch	Locally	Yes	Yes	B.&B.: £20. D.B.&B.: £26.	Family run, situated in quiet unspoilt village.

Moffat

Peter Hesketh (Mr.), The Moffat Fishery, Moffat DG10 9QL. Tel: (01683) 21068.

Fishing for all the family, everyday of the year (except Christmas Day). Also 5 acre fly-only fishery stocked with large brown, brook and rainbow trout. Smokehouse and game shop, mail order and smoking service.

FIFE
Auchtermuchty

	Type of accommodation	Type of Fishing	Permits available	Drying facilities	Freezing facilities	Price p.p. B/B or B.B.E.M.	Special features
Van Beusekom (Mr.), Forest Hills Hotel, Auchtermuchty. Tel: (01337) 828318.	Hotel 3 Crowns	Fly. Trout - Rainbow, Brown. Salmon.	No	Yes	Yes	On Appl.	All rooms with facilities. Free use of leisure centre. 25% discount on production of this advert.

Crail

Healy (Mr. & Mrs.), Croma Hotel, Crail. Tel: (01333) 450239.	Hotel	Sea/ Stream fishing	No	Yes	Yes	On Appl.	Licensed lounge bar. Half mile from harbour. 4 miles from Anstruther where boats leave for deep sea fishing.

Dunfermline

V. Pegg (Mr.), Halfway House Hotel, Kingseat, by Dunfermline. Tel: (01383) 731661.	Hotel 3 Crowns Commended	Trout	Locally	Yes	Yes	B. & B.: £18.50 (sharing)	Hotel overlooks Loch Fitty and close to Loch Leven.

INVERNESS-SHIRE
Beauly

Iain Campbell (Mr.), Caledonian Hotel, Beauly. Tel: (01463) 782278.	Hotel 2 Crowns	Trout Salmon	Yes	Yes	Yes	B.B.E.M.: £295 weekly inc. pack lunch	Boat engine included – "Fish a loch a day for your stay"

Kincraig

L.E. Rainbow (Mrs.), Ossian Hotel, Kincraig, Kingussie PH21 1NA. Tel: (01540) 651242.	Lic. Hotel 4 Crowns Commended	Trout & salmon on loch & river	Bank/ boat permits	Yes	Yes	B. & B. from £18.00–£28.50	Family-run hotel. Beautiful lochside village. Good food and wines.

Whitebridge

Ian Milward (Mr.), Knockie Lodge, Whitebridge IV1 2UP. Tel: (0145 486) 276.	Hotel 3 Crowns Deluxe	Brown Trout Fly only.	N/A	Yes	Yes	B. & B.: £50	Family run hotel in magnificent setting on hills above Loch Ness.

KINCARDINESHIRE
Banchory

D. Jaffray (Mr.), Banchory Lodge Hotel, Banchory. Tel: (01330) 822625	Hotel 4 Crowns Highly Comm	Salmon	No	Yes	Yes	D.B. & B.: £80.00	Feb 1 to mid-April bait allowed; April to Sept, fly fishing salmon, sea trout

Please mention this Pastime Publications guide 31

	Type of accommodation	Type of Fishing	Permits available	Drying facilities	Freezing facilities	Price p.p. B/B or B.B.E.M.	Special features
KIRKCUDBRIGHTSHIRE							
Castle Douglas							
E. Montgomery (Mr.), The Market Inn Hotel, 6/7 Queen Street, Castle Douglas. Tel: (01556) 502105.	Hotel 2 Crowns	Coarse Game	Yes	Yes	Yes	B.&B.: £21.00	Family-run hotel, warm welcome to all our guests.
N. Swain (Mr.), Kenmure Arms Hotel, High Street, New Galloway, Castle Douglas. Tel: (016 442) 240.	Lic. Hotel	Coarse: Trout Pike etc.	Yes	Yes	Yes	B.&B. from £13.50. D.B.&B. from £20.50	Loch Ken 2 mins. Boat and rod hire. Open all year. Fridges for baits, freezer for catches.
Dalbeattie							
Joan Thompson (Mrs.), Clonyard House Hotel, Colvend, Dalbeattie. Tel: (01556) 630372.	Hotel 4 Crowns Commended	Coarse Salmon Trout Sea	Yes	Yes	Yes	B.&B. from £35.	Open all year. Restaurant and bar meals. Winter breaks £33 B.B.&E.M.
Kippford							
J. Muir (Mrs.), Rosemount On Sea Front, Kippford, by Dalbeatttie. Tel: (01556) 620214.	Guest House 2 Crowns Commended	Cod Trout	Locally	Yes	Yes	B.&B. From: £17.50–£20	We extend a warm welcome to all our guests. Ideal base for the keen fisherman.
PEEBLESSHIRE							
Peebles							
Norman Kerr (Mr.), Kingsmuir Hotel, Springhill Road, Peebles EH45 9EP. Tel: (01721) 720151.	Hotel 3 Crowns Commended	River Tweed Trout (Spring). Salmon (Autumn).	Hotel will arrange	Yes	Yes	B. &B.: £27–£37 E.M.: £5–£11	Family run hotel, all rooms ensuite. Traditional Scottish cooking using fresh local produce.
PERTHSHIRE							
Aberfeldy							
Alan Schofield (Mr.), Fortingall House, Fortingall, by Aberfeldy PH15 2NQ. Tel: (01887) 830367.	Hotel 3 Crowns Commended	Trout Salmon	Yes	Yes	Yes	B.&B.: £22–£28. E.M. from £8	Ideal centre for River Tay and River Lyon.
Callander							
Thompson (Mrs.), East Mains House, Manse Lane, Bridgend, Callander FK17 8AG. Tel: (01877) 330535.	Guest House 2 Crowns Commended	Various	Locally	Yes	Yes	B.&B.: £18.	Spacious guest house, 2 mins walk from River Teith. 10% discount for bookings for 7 days or more.
Kinloch Rannoch							
Jennifer Skeaping (Mrs.), Bunrannoch House, Kinloch Rannoch PH16. Tel: (01882) 632407.	Guest House Approved	Coarse	Yes	Yes	Yes	B.&B. from £16. D.B&B. from £27.	Good food, a warm welcome and relaxing atmosphere ensures that you will want to return.
Perth							
White Horse Inn, 5 North William Street, Perth. Tel: (01738) 28479.	Hotel	Salmon Sea trout Roach	Yes	No	Yes	B. & B.: £20 B.B.E.M.: £30	
Burrelton Park Inn, High Street, Burrelton PH13 9NX. Tel: 0182 87 206.	3 Crowns Commended	Salmon Trout	Yes	Yes	Yes	B.&B.: Twin – £45. Single – £30	20% off on production of this advert. Excellent value.

32

	Type of accommodation	Type of Fishing	Permits available	Drying facilities	Freezing facilities	Price p.p. B/B or B.B.E.M.	Special features
Pitlochry C.A. Toremar (Mr.), Bunrannoch Hotel, Kinloch Rannoch, by Pitlochry. Tel: (01882) 632367	Hotel	Trout Salmon	Yes	Yes	Yes	B.&B. from £22.50–£26.00	Public bar, lounge bar. All rooms with Sky-TV.
ROXBURGHSHIRE **Hawick** Forbes J. Neish (Mr.), Elm House Hotel, 17 North Bridge Street, Hawick. Tel: (01450) 372866.	Hotel 3 Crowns Commended	Loch & River	Yes	Yes	Yes	B.&B.: £20. B.B.E.M.: £30.	Quiet family run hotel.
SELKIRKSHIRE **Galashiels** C.W. Scott (Mrs.), Abbotsford Arms Hotel, 63 Stirling Street, Galashiels. Tel: (01896) 752517.	Hotel 3 Crowns Commended	Trout Salmon	Yes	Yes	Yes	On Appl.	Family run hotel with excellent food. Function room available. Live music in public bar.
SUTHERLAND **Brora** John & Ishbel Clarkson, Tigh Fada, Golf Road, Brora KW9 6QS. Tel: (01408) 621332.	House 2 Crowns Commended	Game Sea Angling	Locally	Yes	Yes	B.&B. £16–£20	Home from home for fishers with fishers! Overlooking golf course. Reduced weekly rates.
Lairg P. Panchard, Altnaharra Hotel, by Lairg IV27 4UE. Tel: (0154981) 222	Hotel	Loch	Yes	Yes	Yes	On Appl.	Special handicapped seat in boat.
Spencer (Mr.), Sutherland Arms Hotel, Lairg IV27 4AJ. Tel: (01549) 40 2291.	Hotel	Wild brown trout - fly only. Salmon.	Yes	Yes	Yes	On Appl.	Fully inclusive fly fishing holidays available. Details on request.
SCOTTISH ISLANDS **Islay** Paul Fogerty (Mr.), Marine Hotel, Shore Street, Bowmore PA43 7LB. Tel: (01496) 810324.	Hotel 5 Crowns (pending)	Trout fly	Ask	Yes	Yes	B.&B.: £32.50	Centrally situated overlooking Loch Indaal. Ideal base for touring. Ample parking. Wonderful bedrooms – all ensuite.
Orkney A. MacDonald (Mr.), Merkister Hotel, Loch Harray KW17 2LF. Tel: (0185677) 366.	Hotel 3 Crowns Commended	Wild brown trout & sea trout	N/A	Yes	Yes	B.&B.: £20–£29.50. D.B.&B.: £35–£41.50	Excellent boats with Guinrude motors. Own pier 100 yards from hotel.
D. Davidson (Mr. & Mrs.), Barony Hotel, Birsay, Orkney KW17 2LS. Tel: (01856) 721327.	Hotel 3 Crowns Commended	Brown Trout	N/A	Yes	Yes	B.&B.: £28. B.B.E.M.: £40.	Lochside hotel, on Boardhouse Loch for brown trout fishing.

SELF CATERING

	Type of accommodation	Type of Fishing	Permits available	Drying facilities	Freezing facilities	Price per unit	Special features
ABERDEENSHIRE **Aboyne** Mrs. Bruce, Glen Tanar Estate, Brooks House, Glen Tanar, Aboyne AB34 5EU. Tel: (013398) 86451.	Cottages 3 Crowns Commended - 5 Crowns Highly Comm	Salmon Sea/ Rainbow Trout	Day or weekly	Yes	Yes	From £130	Carefully restored traditional cottages set in beautiful countryside on a private estate.
Inverurie J.M. Uren (Mr.), Write to: Priory Farm, Appledore Road, Tenterden, Kent. Tel: (01322) 384646 (01580) 764161.	Lodge 3 Crowns	Salmon Sea Trout Brown Trout	Daily or weekly.	Yes	Yes	£211.50–£300	2 miles of one bank of River Don with 10 named pools.
ARGYLL **Dalavich** S.A.Watts (Mrs.), Write to: The Old Rectory, Alphamstone, Bures, Suffolk CO8 5HH. Tel: (01787) 269 340	2 Houses 3 Crowns Approved	Fly Salmon, Trout. Coarse - Pike, Trout etc.	Yes	Yes	Ask	From £150 (2 people inc. Elec & linen)	2 lochs – boat hire on both shore fishing. Awe short walking distance – shore and boats. Avich short drive – fly only.
Dalmally Jonathan Soar (Mr.), Sonachan House, Portsonachan, by Dalmally PA33 1BN. Tel: (018663) 240. Fax: (018663) 241.	Flats (6) House (1) Chalets (3) C'vans (4) 4 Crowns Comm. to Highly Comm.	Brown & Rainbow Trout. Pike, Perch, Char. Salmon, Sea Trout.	On site	On site	On site	£115–£450	Lochside mansion. Free shore fishing. Boats, bikes, cruises. Beautiful gardens.
BERWICKSHIRE **Coldingham** E.J. Wise (Dr.), Westloch House, Coldingham TD14 5QE. Tel: (018907) 71270.	Cottages Chalets 2–4 Crowns Commended	Fly fishing - brown & rainbow trout	Ask	Yes	Yes	£130–£270	Cottages and chalets centred on loch in wooded coastal estate.
DUMFRIESSHIRE **Dumfries** J. Millar (Mrs.), Write to: Glensone, Southwick, Dumfries DG2 8AW. Tel: (01387) 780215.	Farmhouse 4 Crowns Approved		near by	Yes		£250–£400	Peaceful, scenic, excellent accommodation. Time to unwind, ramble, picnics, cycle, tour.
INVERNESS-SHIRE **Aviemore** C. Webb (Mr.), Pine Bank Chalets, Dalfaber Road, Aviemore PH22 1PX. Tel: (01479) 810000	Log cabins Apartments Hol. Homes 1–5 crown De-luxe	Loch River	Yes	Yes	Yes	£161–£525	Quality chalets nestling in mountain setting by Spey River – all amenities.

	Type of accommodation	Type of Fishing	Permits available	Drying facilities	Freezing facilities	Price per unit	Special features
Boat of Garten J. Laurie (Mr.), Write to: 5 Barnton Avenue West, Edinburgh EH4 6DF. Tel: 0131–312 8010.	Bungalow Pending	River Loch	Yes	Yes	Yes	From £100 p.w.	Ideally located in quiet village. Walking distance to River Spey.
Invergarry Jean Ellice (Miss), Taigh-an-Lianach, Aberchalder Estate, Invergarry PA35 4HN. Tel: (01809) 501287.	Flat Cottage House	Salmon Trout	Yes	Yes	Yes	Flat £90 Cottage £145 House £600	Both flat and cottage overlook the river.
PEEBLESSHIRE **West Linton** C.M. Kilpatrick (Mrs.), Slipperfield House, West Linton EH46 7AA. Tel: (01968) 660401.	2 Cottages 4 Crowns Commended	Pte. fly fishing for trout	Ask	Yes	Yes	From £200	Boat fishing on 7 acre loch in beautiful surroundings.
PERTHSHIRE **Aberfeldy** M. McDiarmid (Mrs.), Castle Menzies Farm, Aberfeldy PH15 2LT. Tel: (01887) 820260.	Cottages 4 Crowns Commended	Trout Salmon	Ask	Yes	Yes	£150–£350	3 stone built cottages beside River Tay. 2 miles west of Aberfeldy.
ROSS-SHIRE **Lochcarron** Ewen MacPherson (Mrs.), Attadale, Strathcarron IV54 8YX. Tel: (015202) 722217	Cottages 3 Crowns Highly Comm	Stocked hill loch	Yes	Yes	Yes	£165–£320	40 acre hill loch stocked with brown trout. Boats, rods for hire.
SUTHERLAND **Helmsdale** Victoria Reeves or Sally MacKinnon, Deible Cottage, Suisgill Estate, nr. Helmsdale KW8 6ID. Tel: (01234) 781112 or (01431) 831246.	*Cottage	Trout Salmon	On Appl.	Ask	Ask	From £180 (sleeps 6)	Stunning location. Warm and comfortable cottage – the best of fishing.
WIGTOWNSHIRE **Cairnryan** Charles Dobson (Mr.), Cairnryan Caravan & Chalet Park, Cairnryan, nr. Stranraer DG9 8QX. Tel: (01581) 200231. Fax: (01581) 200207.	C'vans Chalets	Sea & trout fishing	Yes	Yes	Yes	From: £60–£180.	Facilities include pub/ restaurant, swimming pool, billiards, shop. Superb location.

SCOTLAND – ANGLING FOR ALL SEASONS
BY
JIM MCLANAGHAN

Big fish mean hard work

Very few things in the natural world are not affected by the seasons as they change throughout our man-made calendar. It would be nice to think that we understand all of how the seasons affect our angling but that would merely be wishful thinking, although by keeping records and exchanging information we can get a rough idea of where and when our angling prospects are best in Scottish waters.

Whereas our freshwater brethren are tied by strict close seasons, the Scottish sea angler has no such barriers and by being prepared to move around he can usually find sport throughout the entire year. Such a calendar would obviously be a huge benefit to the holidaymaker hoping for a few hours or days afloat but what would it look like? No two years are ever the same in fish catching terms but as a rough guide a typical year would probably look something like this.

Angling can be excellent in Scotland – even in a snow storm

WINTER: JANUARY-APRIL

Cod and shore angling are scenes which, for most, epitomise the winter angling picture and whilst this still holds true, new venues are constantly being opened up.

Balcary must inevitably be Scotland's premier winter shore mark with catches of huge double figure cod ensuring its rightful place. Flat fish can play their part also and the Clyde can always be relied on for bags of these plus occasional codling. Further north the rock marks at Arbroath and Aberdeen also produce some fine bags of codling.

A new venue which is producing a few cod and spurdogs from the shore is Loch Etive near Oban. This has access to some deep water very close inshore, ideal for casting. Boat fishing in this area will also produce these species and I suspect there may be a few more species further up the loch like common skate.

Boat fishing also relies on cod as its mainstay but once again, over the past few years a new venue has started up - Scrabster in the very north. No stranger to sea angling, or good catches, but a venue for some huge - world record size - porbeagle sharks. So popular has this venue become for winter sharks that boats can be booked a year in advance! These big fish are sought mainly through February to April.

With anglers realising the potential for previously "out of season" catches, some very early big skate are being sought and boated from Mull and they will be available in other locations too, no doubt.

A fine pair of Pollack

SUMMER: MAY-AUGUST

This is really the transitional period when summer species start to slow up and angling will pick up all round the coasts. Boat angling in the south west will start to produce summer cod for the Solway and Clyde and the skate and tope will be the target from all ports on the Solway and up to Girvan, which is very underfished.

The Clyde and Outer Islands such as Skye and the Hebrides will start to produce cod, pollack, tope, skate and for anyone fishing a wreck the potential for huge conger is always present. For some reason blue sharks have never figured in Scottish catches but I am certain that for some dedicated anglers who are prepared to motor 10 miles, or maybe less, from one of our outer islands, the rewards would be huge. A good rubby dubby and a slight breeze and I feel the Scottish Blue Shark Record could topple, several times, They are there.

The north and east of the country also pick up with cod being the mainstay of the catches with ling, plaice and pollack also filling bags.

It is no coincidence that most sea angling festivals are held around this period, on average at least one per week. The visiting angler can get details of these from The Scottish Federation of Sea Anglers - address elsewhere in this publication - and can utilise the festivals to get a boat place. They do not need to be members. The Federation produces a superb booklet detailing all the festivals and contact numbers who can also give details for local catches and baits.

AUTUMN: SEPTEMBER-DECEMBER

This is my favourite angling period when the seas are alive with all species and the shore and boat angler can enjoy sport of the highest calibre. Every species in the record list will be targeted and tope can be taken right through till December. Cod as always will be a prime catch and at today's prices a welcome addition for the table. This is also the time of the year when most species are within reach of the shore angler, from the huge skate at Lochaline pier to tope from Portpatrick and the very sporting pollack - what a bonanza! For the dedicated angler, mullet and bass can be tempted from power station outlets and some harbours. Bass are always present at the Solway and the extreme opposite end of the country at Thurso and several areas between as yet to be discovered.

There are still some festivals running as late as November, such as the Highland and Islands Cod Championship at Thurso, which indicates that there is enough potential for the late visitor or dedicated competitor.

One fish which has shown up in the last year or so, the halibut, tends to be very elusive indeed but it is a species well worth hunting. Strong gear and very good gaffs are a must as a huge fish was lost recently at the boat when it wrecked the gaff. The main areas for a trial hunt must obviously be Thurso and the Pentland Firth, Shetland, Orkney and the west coast and Islands. There is potential enough for anyone.

As the year draws to a close and the nights take over, that most hardy of creatures, the winter cod angler appears. On cold beaches with spluttering lamps he takes advantage of the inshore cod feeding in the surf and many good catches are taken each winter, a scene which can be repeated from almost any beach and promontory - but rock angling is best left till daylight hours.

With boats available in most parts all year round, the sea angler in Scotland has a 12 month season and with one of the most underfished coastlines in Europe it can certainly offer Angling for All Season.

A CHECKLIST FOR SCOTTISH GAMEFISHING

BY

BILL CURRIE

A good spring salmon from the Spey near Grantown

I have often been lucky in my fishing in Scotland, fishing an unknown water and finding it excellent. Sometimes freak weather and water conditions give you a memorable day or two of great sport after which the question asked by the perceptive fishers is, 'What went right?' While luck is an important feature of fishing, it is still prudent to plan fishing in Scotland and plan it carefully. You cannot expect excellent fishing at random. I belong to the class of fisher who plans his sport with as much information as he can get, but, of course, nobody would ever close the door to trying the new place, the unexpected water or the unusual fly which might lead to an unexpected patch of good fishing which, as it were, comes unasked to cheer us up.

One of the great strengths of *Scotland for Fishing* is that, over the years, it has built up what planning experts would call an excellent information base from which to start. Here you will find places, sources and costs of permit, local infor-mation and tips from the expert. Having that to hand gets you several steps up the ladder of good planning. What no book can really tell you, however, is how to use this information to its best effect in your planning. You have to bring to the planning operation questions of your own and you need to sift the information according to the kind of holiday fishing you want to find. What you need is a kind of checklist which sorts out the great array of facts available so that you might end up with a well planned fishing trip in a country which has a huge range of sport to offer.

While it is true that Scottish fishing is like a seamless robe, with trout loch fishing blending into river fishing, with trout rods catching sea trout and sea trout fishers catching salmon from time to time, it is useful in planning fishing to separate trout from sea trout and salmon. Not the least reason for doing this is that generally trout fishing is very widely available and is cheap, sea trout

A 22 pounder from the Dee

fishing is much more highly seasonal and is rather special and costs more, while salmon fishing operates in a different gear, as it were, and requires not only the most careful planning of the three types of fishing, but also costs substantially more than trout or sea trout fishing. The questions on any checklist will, therefore be different for these different fish, and while not ruling out crossovers, it is wise to ask a trout question to get a trout answer.

Salmon Fishers' Questions

1. Where shall I go for early Spring fishing?

Your choice will be from the east and north-flowing rivers of Scotland. In recent seasons we have seen the early spring runs in February and March falter and even fail on rivers which ten years ago would have been reliable. The middle and lower Dee, for example, has been poor in February and March, but the cold winters we have had recently

may have had something to do with this, since the Dee now has no estuary nets to intercept the salmon runs (although nearby coastal netting still takes a considerable toll). On the Tweed there is a slightly better scene. The 1994 spring brought to its fishers twice as many salmon as in 1993, bringing the early spring runs back towards normal. These fish, however, were largely taken on the river between Kelso and the sea. Fishers on the middle river had to wait until mid-April to get some sport. The Tay had a slow start in 1994 but picked up hearteningly in April. The pattern being set in 1994 was that of a late season, but one with some reasonable numbers of salmon in it when the weather began to improve. In the last three years February fish have been hard to find everywhere.

The best of the spring fishing in 1994 was undoubtedly the March and April fishings on the North Esk. This small river has an extraordinary yield of spring fish even in years when the main

A May salmon from the Dee, Aberdeenshire

spring rivers are weak. It is a remarkable water, strongly managed by the netting interests which also control much of the rod fishing and manage the re-stocking programme. It is good to see a small river like this keeping strong when neighbouring larger waters are toiling to maintain levels of stock. The Dee has been very slow to start for about three years now, as has the Spey. This last river, however, has a high degree of expectancy associated with it this year. In July 1993 the estuary nets, which took up to 5,000 salmon and sea trout from the water in a season, were taken off. This means that the Spey will have spring and (particularly) summer fish in good numbers in its waters, if the runs materialise. Compare it with its neighbour the smaller Deveron, which in 1993 had the best summer salmon fishing for 20 years. There are bright patches and high hopes for this whole north east area.

2. Where are the Best Summer and Autumn Locations?

Summer salmon seem to be responding to the new agreements restricting netting off Greenland and on the high seas. In June-July 1993 the northern rivers, Thurso, Halladale, Naver, Borgie had some very good sport. There is a new pattern emerging in this region. If I were planning a trip to Sutherland in the early summer I would do two things, plan early to get access to a fishery and pray for rain about mid-June.

It is almost impossible to give a checklist of all the possibilities for Scottish west coast summer salmon. Largely, sport there depends on water conditions. Summer runs tend to be late, coming in August and September in many cases. Take the case of the Ayrshire rivers, which have had two or three good summers recently. The Doon fishings had a surge in July 1993 and a steady run of good numbers in September and October. The Stinchar behaved similarly. Round in the Solway, the Nith has had improving summer runs of sea trout and salmon recently and good October fishing.

The star of the autumn salmon fishings, of course, is the Tweed. For a few seasons now there has been a pattern of rainfall which has left the upper river low and the lower river has held the bulk of the salmon run, where anglers have made hay. Given a wet September and early October, however, we can expect the middle and upper river, the part between Melrose and Peebles (and above), to do well in October and November. In recent seasons the Ettrick has shone as an autumn fishery also. Remember, fishings on the Tweed and its tributaries is hard to get unless you plan the trip well ahead.

Sea Trout Fishers' Questions

The sea trout runs are wonderful events in the game fishing year. They begin in late May on most rivers and reach their peak at different times on east and west coasts. The Spey, one of the best sea trout rivers in Scotland, fishes well in mid-June to mid-July, but has sport earlier and later. The best areas are in the middle and upper middle regions and the visitor ticket fishings at Grantown-upon-Spey are probably as good waters for sea trout as anywhere in the land. Fish up to seven pounds will be taken, but expect three pounders. Fish in the dusk and dark for best results. Dee sea trout have also shone in recent years. The sometimes startlingly good South Esk has its best fishing from the end of June to mid-August. The nice thing about sea trout is that they run a great variety of rivers when people want to be on holiday! The bad news about sea trout is social; getting into good runs which keep you out for half the night leaves you hardly ready for family fun the following day.

Our sea trout on the west coast also run into the large river and loch systems which have brought so much sport in the past. These lochs have suffered all sorts of declines in the recent past. Shiel is in a poor state these days, but Maree showed good form in August and September 1993 with good numbers of fish in the two pound class showing as

Drifting Loch Choire, Sutherland for brown trout

well as finnoch, the immature fish which will provide the larger sized fish in later years.

Going down to another favourite sea trout area, the Solway, the River Nith has been improving as a summer sea trout river recently with some big fish returning in June and July. The Border Esk has had some decline, but in 1993 showed some signs of strong recovery. Its best days are late June and July, but in the upper river, above Langholm, the sport can run right on to the end of August, given water.

Trout Fishers' Questions
There is a spectrum of trout fishing sport in Scotland and at one end there is connoisseurs' sport with delicate dry fly fishing in April, May and June, and at the other, there is high summer and September sport with family trout fishing on lochs in the west highlands and Hebrides. These forms of fishing are worlds apart. The difficult, but very rewarding trout of Tweed and Tay in the late Spring are nobody's fools. They can be large, two pounds or over, but they are not easy. The Don, once our very best spring trout fishery, still produces sport but it has been slow in recent years, but again a return to better early summer sport has been noticed recently. The river has very clearly defined upper and lower characteristics. The upper river is streamy and small, the lower river is rather slow in places, but harbours some large trout.

On the better salmon rivers, trout fishing is often not good. The Dee is hardly worth a thought for its trout, but the Spey in its middle and upper waters, even above Loch Insh, has some great sport to offer. Several of our rivers have trout Protection orders on them, allowing easier access to the fishing, but regulating the numbers of rods and the methods of fishing. This has brought trout fishing into its own on waters where sport in the past could be spoiled by too many rods jostling for sport. Under the new regulations, proprietors are now stocking more and cherishing their beats more. There are Orders on Tweed, Tay, and most of the Spey. We are all sure our trout fishings will radically improve under this form of management.

Loch trout are so prolific and so varied in Scotland that it is difficult to do a checklist for them at all. In my own mind I divide them into small hill lochs, mostly in the North-West Highlands and the Hebrides, where you can have delightful family days drifting lochs in moorland and hill scenery. My dream lochs include those in Western Sutherland where you can walk over the moor to your fishing and drift under romantic hills for good brownies. Mind you, I very much like the Hebridean lochs too. Often they are over shell sand and are right beside the sea. Their trout can be memorable. there are so many trout lochs, in the Outer Hebrides in particular, that it is hard to decide where to go. I did read a remark by a loch fishing expert recently who noted that there were any number of excellent trout lochs in Lewis and Harris, and all that was missing was anglers to fish them. What a temptation!

Planning a fishing holiday in Scotland, or just going up north for a day or two to escape is a wonderful use of time out. Even elemental planning will make it much more worth while than just driving north and hoping for the best. Hotels and good bed and breakfast places can often help with the fishing arrangements. In some hotels trout fishing on local lochs is included with the tariff. In all your planning, as I have already said, never rule out that Scottish fishing will suddenly surprise you with a bonus. There will be a good sea trout unexpectedly taking your flies on a river or a loch. The wind, water and temperatures might suddenly come right and fish, once thought difficult to catch, will go mad. You can pray for it, if you like, but I have never found it easy to say when this kind of luck will arise. My advice is to plan well and keep hoping. This is the essential route to good Scottish fishing, of which there is plenty.

Useful addresses in
Scottish Sport Fisheries

Scottish Tourist Board
23 Ravelston Terrace,
Edinburgh EH4 3EU.
Tel: 0131-332 2433.

Department of Agriculture & Fisheries for Scotland
Pentland House, 47 Robb's Loan, Edinburgh EH14 1TY
Tel: 0131-244 6015.

Inspector of Salmon Fisheries
Pentland House (Room 407), 47 Robb's Loan, Edinburgh EH14 1TW.
Tel: 0131-244 6227.

S.O.A.F.D.
Officer in Charge, Freshwater Fisheries Laboratory, Faskally, Pitlochry PH16 5LB.
Tel: (01796) 472060.
Fax: (01796) 473523.

S.O.A.F.D. Marine Laboratory
P.O. Box 101, Victoria Road, Aberdeen AB9 8DB.
Tel: (01224) 876544.

Secretary, Scottish River Purification Boards Association
1 South Street,
Perth PH2 8NJ.
Tel: (01738) 27989.

Scottish Sports Council
Caledonia House, South Gyle, Edinburgh EH12 9DQ.
Tel: 0131-317 7200.

Scottish Natural Heritage
12 Hope Terrace,
Edinburgh EH9 2AS.
Tel: 0131-447 4784.

Forest Enterprise
Dawn McNiven, Information Officer, 231 Corstorphine Road, Edinburgh EH12 7AT.
Tel: 0131-334 0303.

Scottish Hydro-Electric plc
16 Rothesay Terrace,
Edinburgh EH3 7SE.
Tel: 0131-225 1361.

Scottish Anglers' National Association
Administrative Office, Caledonia House, South Gyle, Edinburgh EH12 9DQ.
Tel: 0131-339 8808.

Central Scotland Anglers' Association
Secretary, Kevin Burns, 53 Fernieside Crescent, Edinburgh EH17 7HS.
Tel: 0131-664 4685.

Esk Valley Angling Association
Secretary, Kevin Burns, 53 Fernieside Crescent, Edinburgh EH17 7HS.
Tel: 0131-664 4685.

Federation of Highland Angling Clubs
Secretary, W. Brown, Coruisk, Strathpeffer, Ross-shire IV14 9BD.
Tel: (01997) 421446.

Department of Forestry and Natural Resources
University of Edinburgh, Kings Buildings, Mayfield Road, Edinburgh EH9 3JU.
Tel: 0131-650 1000.

Institute of Aquaculture
University of Stirling, Stirling FK9 4LA.
Tel: (01786) 473171.

The Effects of POLLUTION may take years to disappear from a river

REPORT ALL CASES IMMEDIATELY

Keep samples of dead fish
Please telephone

Forth River Purification Board
TEL: 0131 441 4691
or your local Police Office

46

GAME ANGLING CLUBS

CLUB	SECRETARY
Aberfeldy Angling Club	G. MacDougall, 60 Moness Crescent, Aberfeldy, Perthshire. Tel: (01887) 820653
Airdrie Angling Club	Jimmy Potter, Sharp Avenue, Coatbridge, Lanarkshire.
Badenoch Angling Association	J. Dallas, The Mills, Kingussie, Inverness-shire.
Berwick & District Angling Association	D. Cowan, 3 Church Street, Berwick TD15 1EE. Tel: (01289) 330145
Blairgowrie, Rattray & District Angling Association	W. Matthew, 4 Mitchell Square, Blairgowrie, Perthshire. Tel: (01250) 873679
Brechin Angling Club	W.G. Balfour, 9 Cookston Crescent, Brechin DD9. Tel: (01356) 622753.
Castle Douglas & District Angling Association	Ian Bandall, Tommy's Sports Shop, Castle Douglas, Kirkcudbrightshire. Tel: (01556) 502851
Chatton Angling Association	D. Boyle, 12 West End, Chatton, Alnwick, Northumberland NE66 5PP. Tel: (016685) 388.
Coldstream & District Angling Association	Mr. H.F. Bell, 12 Priory Hill, Coldstream. Tel: (01890) 882171.
Cramond Angling Club	E. McCrindle, 15A London Street, Edinburgh. Tel: 0131–556 0318.
Dalbeattie Angling Association	J. Moran, 12 Church Crescent, Dalbeattie DG5 4BA. Tel: (01556) 502292.
Devon Angling Association	R. Breingan, 33 Redwell Place, Alloa, Clackmannanshire FK10 2BT. Tel: (01259) 215185
Dumfries & Galloway Angling Association	D. Byers, 4 Bloomfield, Edinburgh Road, Dumfries DG1 1SG. Tel: (01387) 53850
Dunkeld & Birnam Angling Association	Mr. K.L. Scott, "Mandaya", Highfield Place, Bankfoot, Perthshire PH1 4AX. Tel: (01738) 787448.
Dunoon & District Angling Club	A.H. Young, "Ashgrove", 28 Royal Crescent, Dunoon PA23 7AH. Tel: (01369) 5732
Eaglesham Angling Association,	Alan Wylie, Tel: (013552) 45073.
Earlston Angling Association	C.T. Austin, 23 Summerfield, Earlston, Berwickshire TD4 6DP.
Eckford Angling Association	The Buccleuch Estates Ltd., Estate Office, Bowhill, Selkirk. Tel: (01750) 20753.
Elgin & District Angling Association	W. Mulholland, 9 Conon Crescent, Elgin, Moray.
Esk & Liddle Fisheries	G.L. Lewis, The Buccleuch Estates Ltd, Ewesbank, Langholm, Dumfriesshire DG13 0ND.
Esk Valley Angling Improvement Association	K. Burns, 53 Fernieside Crescent, Edinburgh.
Eye Water Angling Club,	W.S. Gillie, 2 Tod's Court, Eyemouth, Berwickshire. Tel: (018907) 50038

Ford & Etal Estates Fishing Club	W.M. Bell, Heatherslaw, Cornhill on Tweed. Tel: (0189 082) 221	**Kyles of Bute Angling Club**	R. Newton, Viewfield Cottage, Tighnabruaich, Argyll.
Fyvie Angling Association	J.D. Pirie, Prenton, South Road, Oldmeldrum, Aberdeenshire AB51 0AB.	**Ladykirk & Norham Angling Association**	Mr. R.G. Wharton, 8 St. Cuthbert's Square, Norham. Berwick-upon-Tweed TD15 2LE. Tel: (01289) 382467
Galashiels Angling Association	Mr. S. Grzybowski, 3 St. Andrew Street, Galashiels. Tel: (01896) 55712.	**Lairg Angling Club**	J.M. Ross, St. Murie, Church Hill Road, Lairg, Sutherland IV27 4BL. Tel: (01549) 2010
Goil Angling Club,	Mr. Ian Given, Bonnyrigg', 25 Churchill Drive, Bishopton, Renfrew. Tel: (01505) 863531.	**Larbert & Stenhousemuir Angling Club**	A. Paterson, 6 Wheatlands Avenue, Bonnybridge, Stirlingshire.
Gordon Fishing Club	J. Fairgrieve, Burnbrae Eden Road, Gordon.	**Lauderdale Angling Association**	D.M. Milligan, Gifford Cottage, Main Street, Gifford, Haddington EH41 4QH.
Greenlaw Angling Club	J. Purves, 9 Wester Row, Greenlaw, Berwickshire TD10 6XE.	**Lochgilphead & District Angling Club**	Inter Sport, Lochnell Street, Lochgilphead, Argyll.
Hawick Angling Club	R. Kohler, 8 Twirlees Terrace, Hawick, TD9 9LP. Tel: (01450) 73903.	**Loch Keose & Associated Waters**	M. Morrison, Handa, 18 Keose Glebe, Lochs, Isle of Lewis Tel: (0185 183) 334
Inverness Angling Club	G.M. Smith, 50 Nevis Park, Inverness.		
Jedforest Angling Club	J.T. Renilson, 72 Howdenburn Court, Jedburgh TD8 6PX. Tel: (01835) 862681.	**Loch Lomond Angling Improvement Association**	Clements Chartered Accountants, 29 St. Vincent Place, Glasgow. Tel: 0141–221 0068.
Kelso Angling Association	Euan Robson, 33 Tweedsyde Park, Kelso TD5 7RF. Tel: (01573) 225279.	**Loch Rannoch Conservation Association**	E.M. Beattie, 2 Schiehallion Place, Kinloch Rannoch. Tel: (01882) 632261.
Killin, Breadalbane Angling Club,	J.H. Rough, J.R. News, Main Street, Killin, Perthshire. Tel: (01567) 820362.	**Melrose & District Angling Association**	T. McLeish, Planetree Cottage, Newstead, Melrose. Tel: (0189 682) 2232
Kilmaurs Angling Club	D. Dunn, 22 Habbieauld Road, Kilmaurs, Ayrshire. Tel: (01563) 23846.	**Morebattle Angling Club**	Mr. D.Y. Gray, 17 Mainsfield Avenue, Morebattle. Tel: (01573) 440528.
Kintyre Fish Protection & Angling Club	Mr. MacMillan, Banbreck', Kilkerran Road, Campbeltown.		

New Galloway Angling Association	A. Cairnie, Carsons Knowe, New Galloway.	**Selkirk & District Angling Association**	Mr. A. Murray, 40 Raeburn Meadows, Selkirk. Tel: (01750) 21534
Peeblesshire Trout Fishing Association	D.G. Fyfe, 39 High Street, Peebles. Tel: (01721) 720131	**Stanley & District Angling Club**	Stewart Grant, 7 Murray Place, Stanley, Perth.
Peeblesshire Salmon Fishing Association	Blackwood & Smith W.S., 39 High Street, Peebles.	**Stormont Angling Club**	The Factor, Scone Estates Office, Scone Palace, Perth.
Perth & District Anglers' Association	G.D. Nicholls, 30 Wallace Crescent, Perth.	**Stranraer & District Angling Association**	J. Nimmo, Inchparks Schoolhouse, Stranraer DG9 8RR. Tel: (01776) 4568
Pitlochry Angling Club	R. Harriman, Sunnyknowe, Nursing Home Brae, Pitlochry, Perthshire. Tel: (01796) 2484	**Strathmore Angling Improvement Association**	Mrs. M. C. Milne, 1, West Park Gardens, Dundee DD2 1NY. Tel: (01382) 67711
Rannoch & District Angling Club	J. Brown, The Square, Kinloch Rannoch, Perthshire. Tel: (01882) 632268	**Turriff Angling Association**	I. Masson, 6 Castle Street, Turriff AB53 7BJ.
River Almond Angling Association	H. Meikle, 23 Glen Terrace, Deans, Livingston, West Lothian.	**Upper Annandale Angling Association**	A. Dickson, Braehead, Woodfoot, Beattock, Dumfriesshire DG10 9PL. Tel: (016833) 592.
St. Andrews Angling Club	Secretary, 54 St. Nicholas Street, St. Andrews, Fife. Tel: (01334) 76347	**Upper Nithsdale Angling Club**	K. Mclean, Pollock & McLean, Solicitors, 61 High Street, Sanquhar DG4 6DT. Tel: (01659) 50241
St. Boswells Newtown & District Angling Association	Ian M. Horn, Fern Lodge, 6 Grantsfield, Maxton, Melrose. Tel: (01835) 22559.	**Walton Anging Club,**	Simon Cocker. Tel: Hamilton 283800.
St. Marys Loch Angling Association	J. Miller, 25 Abbotsford Court, Colinton Road, Edinburgh EH10 5EH. Tel: 0131–447 4187.	**Whiteadder Angling Association**	R. Baker, Milburn House, Duns, Berwickshire. Tel: (01361) 883086

FINDING THE BIG BROWNIES
BY
LESLEY CRAWFORD

Lesley Crawford offers advice on finding those big wild brown trout known to lurk in many a Highland loch.....

To catch a big wild brown, that is anything over 1lb 8oz, takes patience, a fair amount of skill and just a modicum of luck in being in the right place at the right time. Those larger trout have grown big because they have been adroit enough to dominate the best feeding and shelter areas within a loch and in doing so they have developed a more cautious approach than some of their smaller brethren. Nevertheless they are by no ,means uncatchable and can still be taken given the right tactics and conditions.

To begin with it pays to do a little background research to ensure that there are indeed some larger trout amongst the fish population. Local knowledge and any available guides on your chosen water should be carefully absorbed but do not always believe the hearsay, good or bad. Sometimes you will be told "Oh that loch is full of trout but they are all tiddlers" or "Used to have some big trout in it but not now" or "Big bottom feeders you won't catch them!"......More often than not none of these statements are correct, there are almost always one or two takeable specimen fish somewhere. The best plan is to go and look carefully at your selected loch, not actually to spot the big trout for they never seem to rise when you want them to, rather you 'recce' the whole water system. Look particularly at the number of spawning burns. A considerable number of streams, or lochs interlinked by small rivers, will often lead to copious spawning and numerous small trout, whereas lochs with poor natural spawning may have a less dense fish population but the fish may grow much larger without the competition for food. Also have a look at the loch shape and contours, lochs in shallow fertile hollows with plenty of indentations are generally more productive then deep, icy cold peat waters lying in exposed windswept areas. Check out the actual food availability by having a look at what invertebrate life resides in and around the water. In particular be on the look out for the more alkaline loving shrimp for 'Gammarus' will almost always indicate a fertile water where trout are likely to grow to a good size. Lochs with plenty of shrimp, caddis, snail, beetles and nymphs are usually productive and watch out for any hatches of sedge, olives and mayfly as these insects will encourage fish both to feed and to grow.

Having ascertained something of the fertility of the loch it's important to get to know where the favoured lies of the trout are. If you can withstand the onslaught of biting midges it is of great benefit to study the loch during a flat calm for you should see most of the trout's best feeding spots. Looking at the rise forms will sometimes tell you a lot and sometimes very little, a specimen trout can take a fly with an almighty splash or the most gentle of sips! In general, weedbeds, amongst boulders, edges of points and bays are the places to look for big trout; bare sand and very exposed water without shelter are places to avoid.

This study of the water should not take very long and next you must decide on your tactics in trying to attract those bigger trout out from their lairs. There are a number of theories for doing this, you can fish at night when the more cautious specimens come into the shallows to feed, or fish with a sunk line and a lure to 'get down to the bigger fish' or alternatively you can fish a big static dry fly on a floating line. I have tried all of these tactics with varying degrees of success and failure. Unfortunately there is no sure fire answer as any strategy is always influenced by the weather conditions, for example a dry fly can be a great attractor of big fish but on a very bright day they cannot see it! Equally some of our lochs are very shallow particularly in Caithness, and sunk line fishing means you hit bottom more often than the fish. Evening fishing offers great sport but fishing and wading in complete darkness takes a fair degree of nerve, I find it all too easy to trip over rocks and heather! However something I would always advocate is getting your fly over the specimen fish when they are ACTIVELY FEEDING so you must follow the movements of all aquatic life closely. Say for example it is late August or September, a time when the stickleback shoals are profuse in the shallows. Almost invariably there will be a big trout lurking nearby gobbling up this tiny source of protein with relish, get your fly in his way and you may well be surprisingly successful. Or try during May or September when there is often a concentration of small freshwater snails in shallower areas or look out for the plentiful Highland mayfly hatch which occurs from about mid June to early August. One of the best attractors of bigger trout is the humble cow dung fly for when these greeny brown flies are blown off the bank from the surrounding fields from about May on, they stir all fish into great activity. A rise to the cow dung fly is about the nearest thing I have seen to a feeding frenzy in the wild brown trout as it seems to have a 'domino' effect with the smaller fish exciting the larger ones into feeding as they splash and slash on the surface.

Interestingly I have not caught bigger trout on exact representations of what they are busily feeding on, rather I have been successful by following the course of nature year and stalking specimens when they are most likely to be on the take. By putting my fly into the path of a feeding fish I simply intercept his movements. Abundance is the key word in getting those larger fish to feed voraciously and throw caution to the wind, so if you see LOTS of sticklebacks, masses of snails or 'cow dungs' by the dozen get out there amongst them for who knows what big sleek shadows lurk nearby.

A specimen trout of 3lbs 2oz caught on the Soldier Palmer

THE EVENING RISE
BY
ALAN SPENCE

One of the great delights of angling, nay even of life itself, is the evening rise of trout. An occasion that does have its peaks and troughs, its successes and failures, experience shows that trout are not necessarily easier to catch during the course of this event than they are at other times. In fact accompanying the deepening dusk a prolific hatch of duns, or a heavy fall of spinners renders the angler's artificial fly but a speck among a myriad of naturals. What makes the evening rise stand out is that during the summer months this may be the only time when fish are moved to feed on the surface becoming a target for the dry fly addict.

Living in the Borders it is only natural that most attempts to catch trout of an evening take place on the Tweed or one of its tributaries. Mostly it is the main river where the rewards are usually the greatest and disappointments the deepest.

Where to fish? Well the majority of the Tweed is open to trout anglers who are willing to purchase a permit from one of the many clubs and associations who control this branch of angling in the Scottish Borders. With permit purchased what type of water is the best? Invariably the places where access is not easy, where casting is restricted by overhanging trees and wading a matter of underwater boulder hopping on slippery ledges.

On much of the lower Tweed the physical feature of the river's immediate environs is one of haugh, a level riverside field, on one bank. This is often overlooked by a heugh, a steep bank on the other side, frequently wooded. Most likely the haugh side river bed is of smooth sloping gravel. While the heugh features a combination of rock ledges stones and boulders and deep water close to the bank. Pools may be almost a mile in length, known in salmon angling terms as dubs, which is but a Scots term for pool.

Seek out the heugh side - despite the difficulties this is the place where the cream of evening trout fishing may be enjoyed. Here savour the maximum elation when a strategy or new fly pattern has been successful, or the depths of gloom when all have failed as dusk falls upon yet another empty basket.

When normal summer water levels prevail, arrival at the riverside is best timed for between 7 and 8pm, much too early for an evening rise but no better place exists to while away an hour or two on a warm summer evening. Usually there are occasional trout rising to surface insects at this time. Cautious, cunning and crafty leviathans, sipping leisurely at some tiny insect always in the spots where wading is impossible and casting a fly over their position beyond ordinary mortals. Usually they do appear to be nearer the far bank on the haugh side, yet a long detour by foot or a longer one by car to the far bank reveals these fish are still rising nearer the far bank, on the recently vacated heugh side.

Besides these untouchables of indeterminate but usually over estimated length and weight, a few ordinary trout may be dimpling the surface here and there on the pool. At this time of the evening they could be feeding upon just about anything. Mostly it is either small, or spent or heaven forbid a combination of the two in the shape of the caenis spinner, the cause of indepth fisherman's cursing, which is of course the anglers term for the little blighter.

Another possibility is that a hatch of caenis is actually taking place with the resulting swarms of the insects, which change from dun to imago almost immediately after hatching, appear like smoke or mist in a column reaching from the river surface to the tree tops. Frantic rises to the hatching dun sometimes take place of an early evening. With a million flies on the surface the anglers artificial has little chance on these occasions. Or could they have been rising to a species of chironomid? A few seasons ago while sitting by the bank a mass of tiny flashing silver objects in a small silty backwater drew my attention. These turned out to be minute midge pupae ascending through a few inches of water, the 'silver' in fact, tiny air or gas bubbles attached to each insect.

A much preferred state of affairs is to arrive at the river bank to find one or two trout feeding steadily, rather than a frantic rise taking place. Usually my selection of an artificial for this time of day is something nondescript such as Badger and Yellow or Tups Indispensable, the former sometimes tied parachute style or as is the case with the latter tied on hooks down to size 20. Another useful thing, in size 18 and 20, is a sort of Greenwell Spider in a selection of hackle and body shades.

Anyway, for the sake of argument, let us imagine that we are by the riverside of a pleasant July evening following a hot summer's day, we are on the north bank where the tree clad heugh is already casting shade over part of the pool. A ring here and there denotes a trout or two feeding on the surface. With shaking hands, the leader and line are threaded through the rod rings and

after many attempts the three pound breaking strain nylon is poked through the eye of the size 18 Badger and Yellow. Large strides are taken to the rock ledge which leads to a position from which the fly can be placed over the fish's nose, it appears to be at least a 2½ pounder; but stop; the fly has yet to be anointed with a potion to make it float and more important the leader with another potion to make it sink. All set, well remember that your thigh boots are still rolled down and will allow entry of water over their tops at below knee depth. Now at last but caution is the watchword, these casually rising fish of an early evening are easily put down, a splashy cast and they are gone.

So ever so carefully entrance is made into the water, sliding the feet along the slippery rock, stepping across unseen underwater chasms until the desired spot is reached. Line is stripped from the reel and a few trial casts are made to get the distance, there he is again must be 2¾ pounds, another two feet of line should do the trick. Cockily the little speck drifts downstream over the spot where the trout just rose, a giant neb breaks the surface but it is obvious that the fish turned away at the last moment and did not in fact take the fly.

Don't cast over it again, rather reel in and change to a size smaller fly. Smaller, its a size 18 which is on? Yes but try a 20, its a paltry ragamuffin looking thing even when viewed through a pair of x 4 fly tying glasses. How on earth will this be seen ten yards distant, never mind the trout. He is still rising all three pounds of him. Drop the fly just upstream of his last known position. Again, the neb breaks the surface instinct says strike, the line tightens and there is the zig zig of a hooked fish. Take it easy it is only a 3lb point. Apply more pressure to keep it away from the weed bed, and hope the hook holds. Curse that rock ledge if it gets under that, all is lost.

What a relief it runs into clear water, every revolution of the singing reel means that this fish is tiring itself out in safe water. At last after a couple of false attempts a golden flanked pink spotted trout comes to the net. Later it is all of 1¼ pounds on the scales but it appeared to be a three pounder in the water.

During normal summer water levels when fortune smiles the basket on these small flies in early evening may be two or even three trout. As first shadow engulfs the entire length of the pool then the light begins to fade and the itch in anticipation of the evening rise begins to scratch. Now is the time to become ensconced on a favourite ledge with an appropriate artificial on the point. In high summer an appropriate artificial usually means something which represents the blue winged olive in dun or spinner form.

It's a personal matter this boiling down to the artificial fly in which the angler has the greatest confidence. For me this means something tied parachute style, with a ribbed hare's ear body to represent the hatching insect, silk or tying thread for the dun and pheasant tail herl when spinners are on the water. Or a Paradox pattern as discussed in the 1994 edition of Scotland for Fishing, especially if fish are seen to be feeding just below the surface.

Grey dusk is falling and the water remains dead, the few trout rising earlier appear to have completely lost interest in surface feeding. Then upon the calm surface of the pool little black dots appear, soon the length and breadth of the pool is ringed with feeding fish. There is only one way to find out if the selected artificial is also the version in favour with the finny inhabitants on this occasion.

Keyed up to fever pitch the first cast lands with the delicacy of a hawser, two hours ago when the trout were selective this disturbance would have ensured that this particular fish would have fled into the safety of the depths. Not now in the orgy of feeding such matters are of little concern, the next cast is a little more delicate and he is there.

Sometimes the rise may be a brief affair lasting only ten minutes or so, at others it continues into darkness until not only the artificial but even the rings of feeding fish are no longer discernible. Happy is the angler who can take three or four trout during the evening rise - in between there are snags. The artificial chosen is snubbed by steadily rising fish, embarking the fisher on a journey of fly changing, trying to thread the nylon through the tiny hook eye in dim light.

Sometimes despite a magnificent hatch of flies and a stupendous rise of trout it is possible to leave the riverside without a fish in the creel. A strange thing about the hatch of blue winged olives is that what was a deadly artificial fly one evening is totally useless the next. In fact showing the fish every previously deadly artificial can be futile, but then it is not the fish we catch that makes us keen, rather it is those which we want to catch by a chosen method as some entries from my diary reveal.

TURN TO PAGE 58 FOR GAME FISHING GAZETTEER

CLOSE SEASON

The following are the statutory close season dates for trout and salmon fishing in Scotland.

TROUT

The close season for trout in Scotland is from 7 October to 14 March, both days inclusive, but many clubs extend this close season still further to allow the fish to reach better condition.

Fresh trout may not be sold between the end of August and the beginning of April, and not at any time if less than eight inches long.

SALMON

Net Fishing	Rod Fishing	River District
1 Sept-15 Feb	1 Nov-15 Feb	Add
27 Aug-10 Feb	1 Nov-10 Feb	Ailort
27 Aug-10 Feb	1 Nov-10 Feb	Aline
27 Aug-10 Feb	1 Nov-10 Feb	Alness
27 Aug-10 Feb	1 Nov-10 Feb	Applecross
27 Aug-10 Feb	1 Nov-10 Feb	Arnisdale (Loch Hourn)
27 Aug-10 Feb	16 Oct-10 Feb	Awe
27 Aug-10 Feb	1 Nov-10 Feb	Ayr
27 Aug-10 Feb	1 Nov-10 Feb	Baa & Goladoir
27 Aug-10 Feb	1 Nov-10 Feb	Badachro & Kerry (Gairloch)
27 Aug-10 Feb	1 Nov-10 Feb	Balgay & Shieldaig
27 Aug-10 Feb	16 Oct-10 Feb	Beauly
27 Aug-10 Feb	1 Nov-10 Feb	Berriedale
10 Sept-24 Feb	1 Nov-24 Feb	Bervie
27 Aug-10 Feb	1 Nov-10 Feb	Bladenoch
27 Aug-10 Feb	1 Nov-10 Feb	Broom
27 Aug-10 Feb	16 Oct-31 Jan	Brora
10 Sept-24 Feb	1 Nov-24 Feb	Carradale
27 Aug-10 Feb	1 Nov-10 Feb	Carron (W. Ross)
10 Sept-24 Feb	1 Nov-24 Feb	Clayburn (Isle of Harris (East))
27 Aug-10 Feb	1 Nov-10 Feb	Clyde & Leven
27 Aug-10 Feb	1 Oct-25 Jan	Conon
14 Sept-28 Feb	15 Oct-28 Feb	Cree
27 Aug-10 Feb	17 Oct-10 Feb	Creed or Stornoway and Laxay (Isle of Lewis)
27 Aug-10 Feb	1 Nov-10 Feb	Creran (Loch Creran)
27 Aug-10 Feb	1 Nov-10 Feb	Croe & Shiel
27 Aug-10 Feb	1 Oct-31 Jan	Dee (Aberdeenshire)
27 Aug-10 Feb	1 Nov-10 Feb	Dee (Kirkcudbrightshire)
27 Aug-10 Feb	1 Nov-10 Feb	Deveron
27 Aug-10 Feb	1 Nov-10 Feb	Don
27 Aug-10 Feb	1 Nov-10 Feb	Doon
1 Sept-15 Feb	16 Oct-15 Feb	Drummachloy or Glenmore (Isle of Bute)
27 Aug-10 Feb	16 Oct-10 Feb	Dunbeath
21 Aug- 4 Feb	1 Nov-31 Jan	Earn
1 Sept-15 Feb	1 Nov-15 Feb	Echaig
1 Sept-15 Feb	1 Nov-15 Feb	Esk, North
1 Sept-15 Feb	1 Nov-15 Feb	Esk, South
27 Aug-10 Feb	1 Nov-10 Feb	Ewe (Isle of Harris (West))
27 Aug-10 Feb	6 Oct-10 Feb	Findhorn
10 Sept-24 Feb	1 Nov-24 Feb	Fleet (Kirkcudbright)
10 Sept-24 Feb	1 Nov-24 Feb	Fleet (Sutherland)
27 Aug-10 Feb	1 Nov-10 Feb	Forss
27 Aug-10 Feb	1 Nov-31 Jan	Forth
1 Sept-15 Feb	1 Nov-15 Feb	Fyne, Shira & Aray (Loch Fyne)
10 Sept-24 Feb	1 Nov-24 Feb	Girvan
27 Aug-10 Feb	1 Nov-10 Feb	Glenelg
27 Aug-10 Feb	1 Nov-10 Feb	Gour
27 Aug-10 Feb	1 Nov-10 Feb	Greiss, Laxdale or Thunga
27 Aug-10 Feb	1 Nov-10 Feb	Grudie or Dionard
27 Aug-10 Feb	1 Nov-10 Feb	Gruinard and Little Gruinard
27 Aug-10 Feb	1 Oct-11 Jan	Halladale, Strathy, Naver & Borgie
27 Aug-10 Feb	1 Oct-10 Jan	Helmsdale
27 Aug-10 Feb	1 Oct-11 Jan	Hope and Polla or Strathbeg
10 Sept-24 Feb	1 Nov-24 Feb	Howmore
27 Aug-10 Feb	1 Nov-10 Feb	Inchard
10 Sept-24 Feb	1 Nov-24 Feb	Inner (on Jura)
27 Aug-10 Feb	1 Nov-10 Feb	Inver
10 Sept-24 Feb	1 Nov-24 Feb	Iora (on Arran)
10 Sept-24 Feb	1 Nov-24 Feb	Irvine & Garnock
27 Aug-10 Feb	1 Nov-10 Feb	Kannaird
27 Aug-10 Feb	1 Nov-10 Feb	Kilchoan
27 Aug-10 Feb	1 Nov-10 Feb	Kinloch (Kyle of Tongue)
27 Aug-10 Feb	1 Nov-10 Feb	Kirkaig
27 Aug-10 Feb	1 Nov-10 Feb	Kishorn
27 Aug-10 Feb	1 Oct-10 Jan	Kyle of Sutherland
10 Sept-24 Feb	1 Nov-10 Feb	Laggan & Sorn (Isle of Islay)
27 Aug-10 Feb	1 Nov-10 Feb	Laxford

Net Fishing	Rod Fishing	River District	Net Fishing	Rod Fishing	River District
27 Aug-10 Feb	1 Nov-10 Feb	Little Loch Broom	27 Aug-10 Feb	1 Nov-10 Feb	Pennygowan or Glenforsa & Aros
27 Aug-10 Feb	1 Nov-10 Feb	Loch Duich			
27 Aug-10 Feb	1 Nov-10 Feb	Loch Luing			
27 Aug-10 Feb	17 Oct-10 Feb	Loch Roag	27 Aug-10 Feb	1 Nov-10 Feb	Resort
27 Aug-10 Feb	1 Nov-10 Feb	Lochy	1 Sept-15 Feb	1 Nov-15 Feb	Ruel
27 Aug-10 Feb	16 Oct-10 Feb	Lossie			
10 Sept-24 Feb	1 Nov-24 Feb	Luce	27 Aug-10 Feb	1 Nov-10 Feb	Sanda
27 Aug-10 Feb	1 Nov-10 Feb	Lussa (Isle of Mull)	27 Aug-10 Feb	1 Nov-10 Feb	Scaddle
			10 Sept-24 Feb	1 Nov-24 Feb	Shetland Isles
			27 Aug-10 Feb	1 Nov-10 Feb	Shiel
27 Aug-10 Feb	1 Nov-10 Feb	Moidart	27 Aug-10 Feb	1 Nov-10 Feb	Sligachan
27 Aug-10 Feb	1 Nov-10 Feb	Morar	27 Aug-10 Feb	1 Nov-10 Feb	Snizort
20 Sept-24 Feb	1 Nov-24 Feb	Mullangaren, Horasary and Lochnaciste (Isle of North Uist)	27 Aug-10 Feb	1 Oct-10 Feb	Spey
			10 Sept-24 Feb	1 Nov-24 Feb	Stinchar
			27 Aug-10 Feb	1 Nov-10 Feb	Sunart (except Earn)
			21 Aug- 4 Feb	16 Oct-14 Jan	Tay
27 Aug-10 Feb	1 Oct-10 Feb	Nairn	27 Aug-10 Feb	6 Oct-10 Jan	Thurso
27 Aug-10 Feb	1 Nov-10 Feb	Nell, Feochan and Euchar	27 Aug-10 Feb	1 Nov-10 Feb	Torridon
27 Aug-10 Feb	16 Oct-14 Jan	Ness	15 Sept-14 Feb	1 Dec-31 Jan	Tweed
10 Sept-24 Feb	1 Dec-24 Feb	Nith	10 Sept-24 Feb	1 Nov- 9 Feb	Ugie
			27 Aug-10 Feb	1 Nov-10 Feb	Ullapool
10 Sept-24 Feb	1 Nov-24 Feb	Orkney Isles	10 Sept-24 Feb	1 Dec-24 Feb	Urr
27 Aug-10 Feb	1 Nov-10 Feb	Ormsary (Loch Killisport), Loch Head & Stornoway	27 Aug-10 Feb	1 Nov-10 Feb	Wick
			10 Sept-24 Feb	1 Nov-10 Feb	Ythan

There is no close season for coarse fishing.

THE FORTH FISHERY CONSERVATION TRUST

The Trust was formed in August 1987, with the aim of improving all the fisheries within the Forth catchment area which extends from Fifeness to Balquidder in the north, and Loch Katrine to Torness in the south. The initial aim was to purchase a boat to assist the Forth District Salmon Fishery Board stop illegal netting of salmon on the Estuary.

Within twelve weeks two 18ft high speed launches were acquired for use by the new Superintendent Water Bailiff, Ian Baird, and the impact on the illegal netting operations has been dramatic. The River Teith and its tributaries experienced a good run of spring salmon and sea trout are running through almost unhindered.

The Trust has also stimulated discussions on salmon poaching and fish conservation at the hghest legal and government levels and will continue that dialogue.

Although a number of enthusiastic clubs have worked hard to open up fisheries, to restock and protect them, the Forth catchment area remains a virtually untapped fishery. These could be developed to provide leisure, tourism and employment for the region.

There are three major tasks the Trust wishes to undertake.

1. To increase efforts to eliminate all illegal fishing both on the estuary and throughout the whole river system.
2. To identify ownership of all stretches of water and fisheries in the area so that more effective supervision may be introduced.
3. To review the existing population and habitat of all fish species and assess the potential for increasing their numbers throughout the area.

This information will help all clubs, landowners and local inhabitants to make the best possible use of available resources and improve the quality of salmon, sea trout and coarse fishing throughout the Forth catchment area.

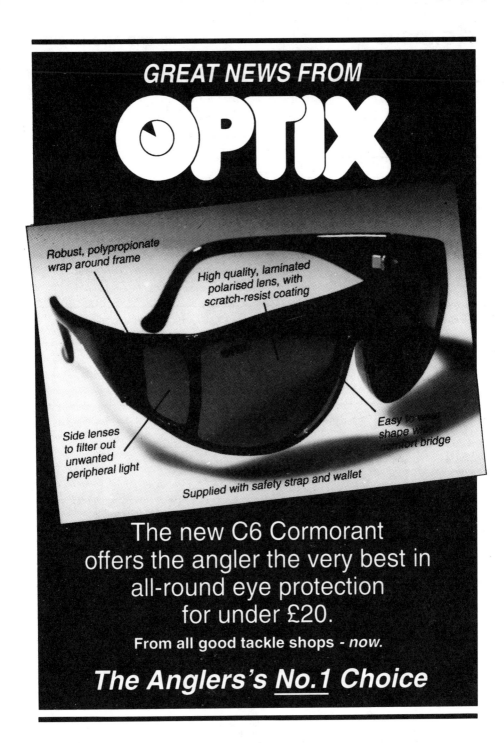

GREAT NEWS FROM

OPTIX

Robust, polypropionate wrap around frame

High quality, laminated polarised lens, with scratch-resist coating

Side lenses to filter out unwanted peripheral light

Easy to wear shape with comfort bridge

Supplied with safety strap and wallet

The new C6 Cormorant offers the angler the very best in all-round eye protection for under £20.

From all good tackle shops - *now*.

The Anglers's <u>No.1</u> Choice

Area Tourist Board
Scottish Borders Tourist Board

Director of Tourism
Scottish Borders Tourist Board
70 High Street
Selkirk TD7 4DD.

Tel: (01750) 20555

RIVER PURIFICATION BOARD
TWEED RIVER PURIFICATION BOARD

Burnbrae
Mossilee Road
Galashiels.

Tel: (01896) 2425

RIVERS

Water	Location	Species	Season	Permit available from	Other information
Blackadder	Greenlaw	Brown Trout	1 Apr. to 6 Oct.	Greenlaw Angling Club J. Purves, 9 Wester Row, Greenlaw. All hotels.	No bait fishing till 1st May. Sunday fishing. No spinning. No Sunday competitions.
Bowmont Water	Morebattle	Trout Grayling	15 Mar. to 6 Oct.	D.Y. Gray, 17 Mainsfield Avenue, Morebattle. Tel: (01573) 440528.	No ground baiting, No Sunday fishing from Primeside Mill up.
Eden Water	Kelso	Brown Trout	1 Apr. to 30 Sept.	Forrest & Sons, 35 The Square, Kelso. Tel: (01573) 224687. Intersport, 43 The Square, Kelso. Tel: (01573) 223381. Border Hotel, Woodmarket, Kelso TD5 7AX. Tel: (01573) 224791.	Fly only. No spinning. Restricted to 3 rods.
	Gordon	Brown Trout	15 Mar. to 6 Oct.	J.H. Fairgrieve, Burnbrae, Gordon. Tel: (01573) 410357.	No Spinning. No Sunday fishing.
Ettrick & Yarrow	Bowhill	Salmon Trout	1 Feb.-30 Nov. 15 Mar.-30 Sep.	Buccleuch Estates Ltd., Estate Office, Bowhill, Selkirk. Tel: (01750) 20753.	Fly only.
	Selkirk	Brown Trout	1 Apr. to 30 Sept.	P. & E. Scott (Newsagents), 6 High Street, Selkirk. Tel: (01750) 20749.	Night fishing 15 May-14 Sept. Week ticket only. No minnows or spinning. No Sundays.
Ettrick	Ettrick Bridge	Brown Trout Salmon	1 Apr.-30 Sep. 1 Feb.-30 Nov.	Ettrickshaws Hotel, Tel: (01750) 52229.	Packed Lunches and flask for residents. Permits also available for other waters.
Kale Water	Eckford	Trout Grayling	1 Apr. to 30 Sept.	Mr. Graham, Eckford Cottage, Eckford, Kelso. Tel: (0183-55) 255.	No Sundays.
	Morebattle	Trout Grayling	15 Mar. to 6 Oct.	D.Y. Gray, 17 Mainsfield Avenue, Morebattle. Tel: (01573) 440528. Templehall Hotel, Morebattle. Tel: (01573) 440249.	No ground baiting. No Sunday fishing.

Water	Location	Species	Season	Permit available from	Other information
Leader Water	Lauderdale	Trout	15 Mar. to 6 Oct.	M. & I. Rattray Newsagent, Lauder. J.S. Main, Saddler, 87 High Street, Haddington. Tel: (0162 082) 2148. Lauder Post Office. Tower Hotel, Oxton, By Lauder. Tel: (01578) 750235. Anglers Choice, 23 Market Square, Melrose TD6 9PL. Tel: (0189 682) 3070.	No Spinning. Sunday fishing. No Grayling fishing.
Leader Water/ Tweed	Earlston	Trout	15 Mar. to 30 Sept.	Earlston Angling Association C.T. Austin, 23 Summerfield, Earlston. Tel: 548. E. & M. Browne, Newsagent, Earlston. '.. & M. Pollard Newsagents, The Square, Earlston. Tel: (01896) 84330. Anglers Choice, 23 Market Square, Melrose. Tel: (0189 682) 3070. Hotels & pubs.	No Sunday fishing. Other restrictions as per permit.
Liddle Water	Newcastleton	Sea Trout	1 May to 30 Sept.	J.D. Ewart, Fishing Tackle Shop, Newcastleton. Tel: (013873) 75257.	Day & weekly tickets available.
	South Roxburgh shire	Salmon Sea Trout Herling Brown Trout	1 Feb.- 31 Oct. 1 May to 30 Sept. 15 Apr. to 30 Sept.	Esk & Liddle Fisheries, R.J.B. Hill, Bank of Scotland Buildings, Langholm. Tel: (013873) 80428. George Graham, Hagg-on-Esk, Old School, Canonbie. Tel: (013873) 71416.	Spinning allowed until 14 Apr. and otherwise only when water is above markers at Newcastleton, Kershopefoot and Penton Bridges. No Sunday fishing.
Lyne Water	Tweed Junction to Flemington Bridge	Trout Grayling	1 Apr. to 30 Sept.	Peeblesshire Trout Fishing Association D.G. Fyfe, 39 High Street, Peebles. Tel: (01721) 720131. Tweeddale Tackle Centre, 1 Bridgegate, Peebles EH45 8RZ. Tel: (01721) 720979. Sonny's Sports Shop, Innerleithen. Tel: (01896) 830806. Tweed Valley Hotel, Walkerburn. Tel: (0189 687) 636. J. Dickson & Son, 21 Frederick Street, Edinburgh. Tel: 0131-225 4218. Crook Inn, Tweedsmuir. Tel: (0189 97) 272.	No Sundays. No spinning. No bait fishing April & Sept. Tickets also cover Tweed.
Oxnam Water	Morebattle	Trout Grayling	15 Mar. to 6 Oct.	D.Y. Gray, 17 Mainsfield Avenue, Morebattle. Tel: (01573) 440528.	No ground baiting, no Sunday fishing from Bloodylaws up.

Water	Location	Species	Season	Permit available from	Other information
Teviot	Above Chesters	Salmon Sea Trout	1 Feb. to 30 Nov.	The Pet Store, Union Street, Hawick. Tel: (01450) 73543.	All rules and regulations on ticket. Limited to 9 rods on 3 beats per day. (9 day tickets Mon-Fri. 6 visitor season tickets only on application to:) Mr. R. Kohler, Hawick Angling Club, 8 Twirlees Terrace, Hawick. Tel: (01450) 73903.
	Eckford	Salmon Sea Trout Brown Trout	1 Feb.- 30 Nov. 15 Mar. to 30 Sep.	Mr. Graham Eckford Cottage, Eckford, Kelso. Tel: (0183-55) 255.	No Sundays. Limited to 4 day permits. Bait and spinning 15 Feb.-15 Sept., only. Spinning for Trout and Grayling prohibited.
	Jedforest	Salmon	1 Feb. to 30 Nov.	Jedforest Angling Association J.T. Renilson, 72 Howdenburn Court, Jedburgh TD8 6PX. Tel: (01835) 862681.	No Sundays. Salmon: 6 rods per day. Spinning 15 Feb.-14 Sept. Fly only 15 Sept.-30 Nov.
		Trout	1 Apr. to 30 Sept.	Shaws (Newsagent), 10 Canongate, Jedburgh. Tel: (01835) 863245.	No Sundays, No spinning. Fly only until 1st May.
	Kelso	Brown Trout Grayling	1 Apr. to 30 Sept.	Forrest & Sons, 35, The Square, Kelso. Tel: (01573) 224687. Intersport, 43, The Square, Kelso. Tel: (01573) 223381. Border Hotel, Woodmarket, Kelso TD5 7AX. Tel: (01573) 224791.	No Sundays. Restrictions on spinning. No maggots or ground bait. Size limit 10".
Teviot (and Ale Slitrig Borthwick Rule)	Hawick	Brown Trout	15 Mar. to 30 Sept.	The Pet Store, 1 Union Street, Hawick. Tel: (01450) 73543.	All rules and regulations on ticket.
		Salmon	1 Feb. to 30 Nov.	The Pet Store, Union Street, Hawick. Tel: (01450) 73543.	
Tweed (and Teviot)	Kelso	Brown Trout Coarse Fish	1 Apr. to 30 Sept.	Forrest & Sons, 35, The Square, Kelso. Tel: (01573) 224687.	

Water	Location	Species	Season	Permit available from	Other information
Tweed	Peeblesshire (substantial stretch of river)	Trout Grayling	1 Apr. to 30 Sept.	Peebleshire Trout Fishing Association Blackwood & Smith w.s, 39 High Street, Peebles EH45. Tel: (01721) 720131. Tweeddale Tackle Centre, 1 Bridgegate, Peebles EH45 8RZ. Tel: (01721) 720979. Tweed Valley Hotel, Walkerburn. Tel: (0189 687) 636. F. & D. Simpson, 28/30 West Preston Street, Edinburgh EH8 9PZ. Tel: 0131-667 3058. J. Dickson & Son, 21 Frederick Street, Edinburgh. Tel: 0131-225 4218.	No spinning. No bait fishing, Apr. & Sept. No Sunday fishing. Tickets also cover Lyne Water. Waders desirable. Fly only on Tweed from Lynefoot upstream.
	Clovenfords (Peel Water)	Salmon Sea Trout	1 Feb- 30 Nov	J.H. Leeming ARICS, Salmon Fishing Agent, Stichill House, Kelso TD5 7TB. 24hr Information Service FREEPHONE: 0800 387 675 Office: (01573) 470280 Fax: (01573) 470259 See also advert on page 10	Half mile single bank. 2 rods. Spinning or fly 15th Feb to 14th Sept. Fly only 15th Sept to 30th Nov.
	Coldstream (West Learmouth Beat)	Salmon Grilse Sea Trout	1 Feb to 30 Nov	J.H. Leeming ARICS, Salmon Fishing Agent, Stichill House, Kelso TD5 7TB. 24hr Information Service FREEPHONE 0800 387 675 Office: (01573) 470280. Fax: (01573) 470259. See also advert on page 10	2/3 miles of south bank. Average catch 201 fish. No spinning before 15th Feb or after 15th Sept.
	Coldstream (The Lees Beat)	Salmon Grilse Sea Trout	1 Feb to 30 Nov	J.H. Leeming ARICS, Salmon Fishing Agent, Stichill House, Kelso TD5 7TB. 24hr Information Service. FREEPHONE: 0800 387 675. Office: (01573) 470280. Fax: (01573) 470259. See also advert on page 10	2 miles including half mile double bank and well known Temple pool. Average catch 434 salmon. No spinning before 15th Feb or after 15th Sept.
	Cornhill	Salmon Sea Trout Brown Trout	Salmon 1 Feb. to 30 Nov.	Tillmouth Park Hotel, Cornhill-on-Tweed, Northumberland TD12 4UU. Tel: (01890) 882255.	No Sundays. Boats and ghillies available. Special terms for residents.
	Galashiels (Fairnilee Beat)	Salmon Sea Trout	1 Feb to 30 Nov	J.H. Leeming ARICS Salmon Fishing Agent, Stichill House, Kelso TD5 7TB. 24hr Information Service FREEPHONE: 0800 387 675 Office: (01573) 470280 Fax: (01573) 470259 See also advert on page 10	3.5 miles single bank 20 named pools. Ghillie, rod room, hut, boat and full facilities. Average catch 93 salmon and sea trout. No spinning before 15th Feb or after 15th Sept.
		Trout	1 Apr. to 30 Sept.	Messrs. J. & A. Turnbull, 30 Bank Street, Galashiels. Tel: (01896) 3191. Anglers Choice, 23 Market Square, Melrose TD6 9PL. Tel: (01896) 823070.	No Sundays. Day tickets available on Saturdays. No spinning.

Water	Location	Species	Season	Permit available from	Other information
Tweed cont.	Horncliffe (Tweedhill Beat)	Salmon Sea Trout	1 Feb to 30 Nov	J.H. Leeming ARICS, Salmon Fishing Agent, Stichill House, Kelso TD5 7TB. 24hr Information Service FREEPHONE: 0800 387 675. Office: (01573) 470280. Fax: (01573) 470259. See also advert on page 10	3 miles of single beat. Some tidal water. Average catch 128 fish.
	Innerleithen (Traquair Beat)	Salmon Sea Trout	1 Feb to 30 Nov	J.H. Leeming ARICS, Salmon Fishing Agent, Stichill House, Kelso TD5 7TB. 24hr Information Service FREEPHONE 0800 387 675 Office: (01573) 470280 Fax: (01573) 470259 See also advert on page 10	2 miles above and 1 mile below Innerleithen Bridge, Ghillie, fishing hut and good access to both banks. Average catch Oct/Nov 40 Salmon and Sea Trout. No spinning before 15 Feb or after 15 Sept.
	nr Kelso (Hendersyde Beat)	Salmon Sea Trout	1 Feb to 30 Nov	J.H. Leeming ARICS, Salmon Fishing Agent, Stichill House, Kelso TD5 7TB. 24hr Information Service FREEPHONE: 0800 387 675 Office: (01573) 470280 Fax: (01573) 470259. See also advert on page 10	3 miles of single bank fishing for 2 rods. Average catch of 273 fish.
	Ladykirk	Brown Trout	19 Mar. to 8 Oct.	Victoria Hotel, Norham, Tel: (01289) 382237.	No spinning. No ground baiting. Fly only above Norham Bridge to West Ford. No Sundays.
	Melrose	Trout Grayling	1 Apr. to 6 Oct.	Melrose & District Angling Association Anglers Choice, 23 Market Square, Melrose. Tel: (01896) 823070.	No spinning. No ground baiting. No Sundays. Minnow fishing not permitted. Spinning reels of all types prohibited.
	Melrose (Ravenswood Tweedswood)	Brown Trout	1 Apr. to 30 Sept.	Anglers Choice, 23 Market Square, Melrose. Tel: (01896) 823070.	Fly fishing only
	Melrose (Pavilion)	Salmon Sea Trout	1 Feb. to 30 Nov.	Anglers Choice, 23 Market Square, Melrose. Tel: 3070.	Fly only - 1 to 15 Feb. and 15 Sept. to 30 Nov. Feb. 16 to Sept. 14 fly and spinning.
	Nest	Salmon Sea Trout Trout	1 Feb.to 30 Nov. 1 Apr.- 30 Sep.	Tweed Valley Hotel, Walkerburn. Tel: (0189 687) 636.	Private salmon/sea trout beat approx. 1.75 miles, 4 rods. Fly only 15 Sept. to 30 Nov. Trout and grayling permits available to all. Week or day lets Spring/Summer. Week lets only October and November. Angling Course September.

Water	Location	Species	Season	Permit available from	Other information
Tweed cont.	Norham (Ladykirk Beat)	Salmon Grilse Sea Trout	1 Feb to 30 Nov	J.H. Leeming ARICS, Salmon Fishing Agent, Stichill House, Kelso TD5 7TB. 24hr Information Service FREEPHONE: 0800 387 675 Office: (01573) 470280 Fax: (01573) 470259 See also advert on page 10	3.5 miles of the north bank. Boats and Ghillies provided. Average catch 188 fish. No spinning before 15th Feb or after 15th Sept.
	Norham (Pedwell Beat)	Salmon Grilse Sea Trout	1 Feb to 30 Nov	J.H. Leeming ARICS, Salmon Fishing Agent, Stichill House, Kelso TD5 7TB. 24hr Information Service FREEPHONE: 0800 387 675 Office: (01573) 470280 Fax: (01573) 470259 See also advert on page 10	1.5 miles single bank. Average catch of 70 fish. No spinning before 15th Feb or after 15th Sept.
	Peel	Salmon Sea Trout	1 Feb. to 30 Nov.	Tweed Valley Hotel, Walkerburn. Tel: (0189 687) 636.	Private 2-rod salmon beat on south bank. Week or day lets Spring/Summer. Week lets only October and November. Angling Course September.
	Peebles (Wire Bridge Pool to Nutwood Pool - excluding Kailzie)	Salmon	21 Feb. to 30 Nov.	Peeblesshire Salmon Fishing Association Seasons: Blackwood & Smith, W.S., 39 High Street, Peebles. Tel: (01721) 720131. Day permits: Tweeddale Tackle Centre, 1 Bridgegate, Peebles EH45 8RZ. Tel: (01721) 720979.	Strictly fly fishing only. No Sunday fishing. Other regulations on tickets.
	St. Boswells (Bemersyde Beat)	Salmon Grilse Sea Trout	1 Feb to 30 Nov	J.H. Leeming ARICS Salmon Fishing Agent, Stichill House, Kelso TD5 7TB. 24hr Information Service FREEPHONE: 0800 387 675 Office: (01573) 470280. Fax: (01573) 470259. See also advert on page 10	1 mile of excellent water. Average catch 208 fish.
		Brown Trout Trout	1 Apr. to 30 Sept.	Dryburgh Abbey Hotel, St. Boswells. Tel: (01835) 822261. Anglers Choice, 23 Market Square, Melrose. Mr. Stuart Robb, Newsagent, St. Boswells.	Fly only 1 Apr. to 1 May. No ground baiting. No bait fishing until May 1. No Sundays. No spinning tackle. No coarse fishing allowed outside season. Access to restricted beats by special permits only. Full details shown on permits.
	Tweedsmuir	Brown Trout Grayling	1 Apr. to 30 Sept.	Crook Inn, Tweedsmuir. Tel: (018997) 272.	All rules and regulations on permits.

Please mention this Pastime Publications guide

Water	Location	Species	Season	Permit available from	Other information
Tweed cont.	Walkerburn	Salmon/ Sea Trout Trout	1 Feb.to 30 Nov. 1 Apr.- 30 Sep.	Tweed Valley Hotel, Walkerburn. Tel: (0189 687) 636.	Salmon tickets for hotel guests only after 14 Sept. Special salmon and trout weeks, tuition. Trout and grayling permits available to all.
	Haystoun (Beat 1.5 miles)	Salmon Sea Trout	15 Feb. to 30 Nov.	Fraser's Salmon Fishing & Hire Ltd., 16 Kingsmuir Crescent, Peebles. Tel: (01721) 722362.	No spinning in autumn - fly only. No Sunday fishing. Rods limited to 6 per day. Part-time ghillie included in permit price. 8 named salmon pools.
	Kingsmeadow (Beat [3/4] mile)	Salmon Sea Trout	15 Feb. to 30 Nov.	Fraser's Salmon Fishing & Hire Ltd., 16 Kingsmuir Crescent, Peebles. Tel: (01721) 722362.	Spinning allowed 15 Feb to 14 Sept. Rods limited to 2 per day. Easy car access to beat. Part-time ghillie included in permit price. 5 named salmon pools.
Whiteadder & Dye & Tributaries	30 miles	Brown/ Rainbow Trout	15 Mar. to 30 Sept.	Whiteadder Angling Association Mr. Cowan, Crumstane, Duns. (Bailiff). Tel: (01361) 83235. J.S. Main, Saddlers, 87 High Street, Haddington. Tel: (0162 082) 2148.	No Sundays. Fly only before 15 Apr. Worm from 15 Apr. only. Minnow from 1 May only. Tickets in advance. Size limit 8 inches. River stocked annually.
Whiteadder	Allanton	Trout	15 Mar to 30 Sept.	Berwick & District Angling Association. Mr. D. Cowan, 3 Church Street, Berwick. Tel: (01289) 330145.	Fly only before May. No spinning. No threadline. No maggot fishing. No ground baiting. 9 inch min. Max bag of 12 brown trout per day. No Sundays.

LOCHS & RESERVOIRS

Water	Location	Species	Season	Permit available from	Other information
Acréknowe Reservoir	Hawick	Brown Trout	15 Mar. to end Sept.	The Pet Shop, 1 Union Street, Hawick. Tel: (01450) 73543. Mr. R. Kohler, 8 Twirlees Terrace, Hawick. Tel: (01450) 73903.	Ticket covers all other trout waters managed by Hawick Angling Club. Boat available from Pet Shop. Fly fishing only.
Alemoor Loch	Hawick	Brown Trout Perch Pike		As Acréknowe	Bank fishing only.
Clearburn Loch	nr. Hawick	Trout		Tushielaw Inn, Ettrick Valley, Selkirkshire. Tel: (01750) 62205.	Boat supplied free.
Clerklands Loch	nr. Selkirk	Rainbow/ Brown Trout	15 Mar to 30 Sept	Lilliesleaf Post Office. Tel: (018357) 201 or (01835) 22216.	Sunday fishing. Fly only. 2 boats. Max. 4 rods. Bag limit 3/rod/session. Stocked throughout season.

Water	Location	Species	Season	Permit available from	Other information
Coldingham Loch	Reston	Brown/ Rainbow Trout	15 Mar to 6 Oct	Dr. E.J. Wise, West Loch House, Coldingham. Tel: (018907) 71270.	Fly only. 4 boats (max 8 rods). 4 bank rods. Sunday fishing. Frequent stocking throughout season. Advance booking essential.
Eildon Hall Loch	Melrose	Brown/ Rainbow Trout	15 Mar to 30 Oct	Langlands Service Station, Newtown, St. Boswells. Tel: St. Boswells 23310.	2 sessions: 9am to 4pm. 4pm to dusk. Sunday fishing. Bag limit 3 trout per session.
Fruid Reservoir	Tweedsmuir	Brown Trout	1 Apr. to 30 Sept.	Crook Inn, Tweedsmuir, Tel: (018997) 272 (8am to 8pm).	Fly fishing. Spinning and worm fishing. Sunday fishing. Bank fishing.
Hass Loch	nr. Letham	Rainbow Trout	1 Apr. to 31 Oct.	Jedforest Filling Station, Cleathaugh, Camptown. Tel: (018354) 330.	Loch is regularly stocked. Bank fishing for 7 rods per session. Sessions, Day: 9am-5pm Evening: 5pm-11pm. Fishing 7 days per week.
Heatherhope Reservoir	Hownam	Trout	15 Mar to 6 Oct	Mr. D.Y. Gray, 17 Mainsfield Avenue, Morebattle. The Garage, Morebattle. Templehall Hotel.	No ground baiting No Sunday fishing
Hellmoor Loch	Hawick	Brown Trout		As Acréknowe	No Boat. No competitions. Limit 6 trout.
Knowesdean Reservoir	Selkirk	Brown/ Rainbow Trout	15 Mar to 31 Oct	J. & A. Turnbull, 30 Bank Street, Galashiels. Tel: (01896) 3191.	Bag limit 3 fish. 2 sessions per day. Advance booking advisable.
Loch Lindean	Selkirk	Brown Trout	Apr. to Oct.	P. & E. Scott (Newsagent), 6 High Street, Selkirk TD7 4DA. Tel: (01750) 20749.	2 boats available.
Loch of the Lowes and St. Mary's Loch	Selkirk	Brown Trout Pike Perch Eels	1 Apr-30 Sept 1 May to 30 Sept	St. Mary's A.C. per Sec. J. Miller, 25 Abbotsford Court, Colinton Road, Edinburgh. Gordon Arms Hotel, Yarrow. Countrylife, 229 Balgreen Road, Edinburgh. F. & D. Simpson, 28/30 West Preston Street, Edinburgh. Tel: 0131-667 3058. Hook, Line & Sinker, 20 Morningside Road, Edinburgh. Sonny's Tackle Shop, Innerleithen. Tibbie Shiels Inn, St. Mary's Loch, Yarrow, Selkirk. Tel: (01750) 42231. Anglers Choice, 23 Market Square, Melrose. Glen Cafe (Loch side). Tweeddale Tackle Centre, 1 Bridgegate, Peebles. Tel: (01721) 720979.	Fly fishing only, until 30th April thereafter spinning and bait allowed. Club fishing apply Secretary or keeper. Sunday fishing. Weekly permits & rowing boats. from keeper, Mr. Brown (01750) 42243. Outboard engines of upto 5H.P. may be used, but none available for hire. No float fishing. Loch of the Lowes is bank fishing only. River Tweed Protection Order applies. Club memberships available.

Please mention this Pastime Publications guide

Water	Location	Species	Season	Permit available from	Other information
Megget Reservoir	Megget Valley	Trout	1 Apr. to 30 Sept.	Tibbie Shiels Inn, St. Mary's Loch, Yarrow, Selkirk. Tel: (01750) 42231	No bait fishing. 6 boats available. Max. bag limit 10 fish.
Peeblesshire Lochs	Tweed Valley	Brown/Rainbow Trout	Apr. to Oct.	Tweed Valley Hotel, Walkerburn. Tel: (0189 687) 636.	Stocked private lochans. Wild brown trout loch.
Portmore Game Fisheries	Peebles-Eddleston	Wild Brown Trout Rainbow Trout	1 Apr. to 31 Oct.	Portmore Game Fisheries at the Loch. Tel: (01968) 675684.	Average weight of fish caught: 2lbs. Popular flies: Lures at beginning; from May - dry & wet. Boats are available - contact: Steve McGeachie at above number.
Sunlaws Trout Pond	Morebattle	Rainbow Trout	All year	Sunlaws House Hotel, Kelso. Tel: (015735) 331.	2 sessions: 10am-4pm, 5pm-dusk. Bag limit 4 per day, 3 per evening. From end Oct. to start Apr. 1 day session only 10am-3.30pm.
Synton Loch	Hawick	Brown Trout		As Acréknowe Reservoir.	Boats available From Pet Store, 1 Union Street, Hawick. Fly only.
Talla Reservoir	Tweedsmuir	Brown Trout	1 Apr. to 30 Sept.	Crook Inn, Tweedsmuir. Tel: (018997) 272. (8am to 8pm).	Fly fishing only. 2 Boats.
Upper Loch	Bowhill	Brown/Rainbow Trout	1 Apr. to 28 Sept.	Buccleuch Estate Ltd., Estate Office, Bowhill, Selkirk. Tel: (01750) 20753.	Fly only. 2 rods per boat and limit of 8 fish per boat. Boat available on: Tues & Thurs all season; Mondays during June, July & Aug.
Watch Reservoir	Longformacus	Brown/Rainbow Trout	15 Mar.-30 Sept. All year	W.F. Renton, The Watch Fly Reservoir. Tel: (013617) 890331 & (01289) 306028.	Sunday fishing. Fly only. Strictly no use of bait/maggots etc.
West Water Reservoir	nr. Peebles	Brown Trout	1 May to 31 Aug	Boat fishing only. Permits from: Pentland Hills Regional Park Headquarters, Boghall Farm, Biggar Road, Edinburgh. Tel: 0131-445 5969.	2 boats. Fly fishing only.
Whiteadder Reservoir	nr. Gifford	Brown Trout	1 Apr to 30 Sept.	Waterkeeper, Hungry Snout, Whiteadder Reservoir. Tel: (013617) 890362 (8am to 8pm).	Bank fishing 1 June to 30 Sept. Sunday fishing. Fly fishing only. 4 boats are available.
Williestruther Loch	Hawick	Brown/Rainbow Trout		As Acréknowe Reservoir.	Any legal method.

Water	Location	Species	Season	Permit available from	Other information
Wooden Loch	Eckford	Rainbow Trout	1 Apr.-31 Oct.	Mr. Graham Eckford Cottage, Eckford, Kelso. Tel: (0183-55) 255.	1 boat. No bank fishing. Only rainbow trout after 30 Sept. Only 2 rods at any time. Advance booking necessary. No Sundays.

Alan Spence with trout caught early in evening.

Area Tourist Board
Scottish Borders Tourist Board

Director of Tourism
Scottish Borders Tourist Board
70 High Street
Selkirk TD7 4DD.

Tel: (01750) 20555

RIVER PURIFICATION BOARD
TWEED RIVER PURIFICATION BOARD

Burnbrae
Mossilee Road
Galashiels.

Tel: (01896) 2425

RIVERS

Water	Location	Species	Season	Permit available from	Other information
Annan	Hoddom & Kinmount Estates Ecclefechan	Salmon Sea Trout Brown Trout	25 Feb. to 15 Nov.	Miss Marsh, 1 Bridge End Cottage, Hoddom, Lockerbie DG11 1BE. Tel: (015763) 488.	No Sunday fishing. Fly water unless the spinning mark is covered.
	Halleaths Estate Lockerbie	Salmon Sea Trout	25 Feb. to 15 Nov.	Messrs. McJerrow & Stevenson, Solicitors, 55 High Street, Lockerbie, Dumfriesshire. Tel: (015762) 2123.	Limited number of tickets.
	Kirkwood & Jardine Hall Beats	Salmon Sea Trout Brown Trout	25 Feb to 15 Nov.	Mr. Anthony Steel, Kirkwood, Lockerbie. Tel: (0157 65) 212/200	Kirkwood is mainly fly fishing (spinning and worming only in spate conditions). Jardine Hall - spinning and worming allowed.
	Royal Four Towns Water Lockerbie	Salmon Sea Trout Brown Trout	25 Feb. to 15 Nov.	Clerk to the Commissioners, of Royal Four Towns Fishing Mrs. K. Ratcliffe, Clerk, Jay-Ar', Preston House Road, Hightae, Lockerbie. Tel: (01387) 810220. Castle Milk Estates Office, Norwood, Lockerbie. Tel: (0157 65) 203.	Boats prohibited. No shrimps, prawns or maggots. No Sunday fishing.
	St. Mungo Parish	Salmon Sea Trout Brown Trout	25 Feb. to 15 Nov.	Castle Milk Estates Office, Norwood, Lockerbie. Tel: (0157 65) 203.	Fly fishing only. No Sunday fishing.
	Warmanbie Estate	Salmon Sea Trout Brown Trout	25 Feb. to 15 Nov.	Warmanbie Hotel & Restaurant, Annan DG12 5LL. Tel: (01461) 204015.	Fly, spinning, worm all season. Access to many other stretches. For residents only.
Bladnoch	Newton Stewart	Salmon	1 Mar. to 31 Oct.	Newton Stewart Angling Association Galloway Guns & Tackle, 36 Arthur Street, Newton Stewart. Tel: (01671) 403404. Palakona Guest House, Queen Street, Newton Stewart DG8 6JL. Tel: (01671) 2323. (for Guests only)	

Water	Location	Species	Season	Permit available from	Other information
Cairn	Dumfries	Brown Trout Salmon Sea Trout	15 Mar.-6 Oct. 1 Apr.to end-Oct.	Dumfries & Galloway Angling Association, Secretary: D. Byers, 4 Bloomfield Edinburgh Road, Dumfries DG1 1SG. Tel: (01387) 53850.	Limited number of permits. No Sunday fishing. Restrictions depend on water level. Visitors Mon.-Fri. only.
Cree (and Pencill Burn)	Drumlamford Estate	Salmon Trout	April to October	The Keeper, The Kennels, Drumlamford Estate, Barrhill. Tel: (0146 582) 256.	No Sunday fishing.
	Newton Stewart	Salmon Sea Trout	1 Mar. to 14 Oct.	Newton Stewart Angling Association Galloway Guns & Tackle, 36 Arthur Street, Newton Stewart. Tel: (01671) 403404.	No Sunday fishing.
Cross Waters of Luce	New Luce	Salmon Sea Trout	1 May to 31 Oct.	Stranraer & District Angling Association. The Sports Shop, 90 George Street, Stranraer. Tel: (01776) 702705.	No Sunday fishing. Fly fishing only.
Black Water of Dee	Mossdale	Trout Pike Perch Salmon	15 Mar. to 30 Sept. 11 Feb. to 31 Oct.	Local Hotels & Shops.	
Esk	East Dumfriesshire	Salmon Sea Trout/ Herling Brown Trout	1 Feb.to 31 Oct. 1 May to 30 Sept. 15 Apr. to 30 Sept.	Esk & Liddle Fisheries R.J.B. Hill, Bank of Scotland Buildings, Langholm. Tel: (013873) 80428. George Graham, Hagg-on-Esk, Old School, Canonbie. Tel: (013873) 71416.	Spinning allowed until 14 April and otherwise only when water is above markers at Skippers Bridge, Canonbie Bridge & Willow Pool. No Sunday fishing.
Ken	New Galloway	Salmon Brown/ Rainbow Trout Perch Pike Roach	15 Mar. to 30 Sept.	Mr. Swain, Kenmure Arms Hotel, High Street, New Galloway. Tel: (016442) 240 or 360. John & Anne McNeil, Kenbridge Hotel, New Galloway. Tel: (016442) 211/744.	Boats available from hotel. Free fishing at hotel on River Ken.
Liddle	Newcastleton Ticket	Salmon Sea Trout Brown Trout	15 Apr.-31 Oct. 1 May-30 Sept. 15 Apr.-30 Sept.	J.D. Ewart, Tackle Agent, Newcastleton. Tel: (013873) 75257. R.J.B. Hill, Bank of Scotland Buildings, Langholm. Tel: (013873) 80428.	Spinning allowed when water is above markers at Newcastleton and Kershopefoot Bridges. No Sunday fishing. Day tickets available.
Milk	Scroggs Bridge	Sea Trout Brown Trout	1 Apr. to 30 Sept.	Mr. Anthony Steel, Kirkwood, Lockerbie. Tel: (0157 65) 212/200.	Mainly fly fishing. No Sunday fishing.
Minnoch	Newton Stewart	Salmon	1 Mar. to 30 Sept.	Galloway Guns & Tackle, 36 Arthur Street, Newton Stewart. Tel: (01671) 403404.	Fly, spin or worm.

Please mention this Pastime Publications guide

Water	Location	Species	Season	Permit available from	Other information
Nith	Dumfries	Salmon Sea Trout Brown Trout	25 Feb. to 30 Nov. 15 Mar. to 6 Oct.	Director of Finance, Nithsdale District Council, Municipal Chambers, Dumfries. Tel: (01387) 53166, ext. 230.	No Sunday fishing. Visitors fishing Mon. to Fri. only. Advance booking.
				Dumfries & Galloway Angling Association Secretary, D. Byers, 4 Bloomfield Edinburgh Road, Dumfries DG1 1SG. Tel: (01387) 53850	Limited number of permits. Weekly permits from Mon.- Fri. Advance booking possible. Spinning restrictions.
	Thornhill	Salmon Sea Trout Brown Trout	25 Feb. to 30 Nov. 1 Apr.- 31 Sept.	The Drumlanrig Castle Fishings, The Buccleuch Estates Ltd., Drumlanrig Mains, Thornhill DG3 4AG. Tel: (018486) 283.	Lower, Middle & Upper beats. Average weight of fish caught: Salmon - 9lbs 8oz, Grilse - 6lbs, Sea Trout - 2lbs, Brown Trout - 8oz, Grayling 8oz. Popular flies: Stoats Tail, General Practitioner, Silver Doctor, Flying C, Silver Toby. Spinning. Worming (until 31 Aug, in Yellow Spate) Weekly and daily lets up to 3 rods/beat.
		Salmon Sea Trout Brown Trout	25 Feb. to 30 Nov. 1 Apr.- 31 Sept.	The Drumlanrig Castle Fishings, The Buccleuch Estates Ltd., Drumlanrig Mains, Thornhill DG3 4AG. Tel: (018486) 283.	Nith Linns Average weight of fish caught: Salmon - 9lbs 8oz, Grilse - 6lbs, Sea Trout - 2lbs, Brown Trout - 8oz, Grayling - 8oz. Popular flies: Stoats Tail, General Practitioner, Silver Doctor, Flying C, Silver Toby. Spinning. Worming (until 31 Aug.) Weekly and daily lets up to 4 rods.
		Salmon Sea Trout Brown Trout	25 Feb.- 30 Nov. 1 Apr. to 30 Sept.	Mid Nithsdale Angling Assoc., Secretary, Mr. I.R. Milligan, 37 Drumlanrig Street, Thornhill DG3 5LS. Tel: (01848) 330555.	No day permits on Saturdays. Spinning & worming allowed, only in flood conditions. Advisable to book for autumn fishing.
Nith (and Tributaries Kello Crawick Euchan Mennock)	Sanquhar	Salmon Sea Trout Brown Trout Grayling	15 Mar. to 30 Nov. Jan., Feb.	Upper Nithsdale Angling Club. Pollock & McLean, Solicitors, 61 High Street, Sanquhar. Tel: (01659) 50241.	No Sunday fishing. Visitors and residents. Day tickets - (Mon-Fri) limit of 30 per day during months: Sept., Oct. & Nov. Week tickets - limit of 10 per week during season. 3-day tickets available.

Water	Location	Species	Season	Permit available from	Other information
Tarf	Kirkcowan	Sea Trout Brown Trout	Easter - 30 Sept.	A. Brown, Three Lochs Holiday Park, Kirkcowan, Newton Stewart. Tel: (01671) 830304.	
Upper Tarf	Nr. Newton Stewart	Salmon Trout	1 Mar.- 14 Oct. 15 Mar.- 6 Oct.	Palakona Guest House, Queen Street, Newton Stewart DG8 6JL. Tel: (01670) 2323 - guests only. Galloway Country Sports. Tel: (01988) 840695 - all day tickets.	Fly, spin or worm.
Urr	Castle Douglas	Salmon Sea Trout Brown Trout	25 Feb. to 30 Nov. 15 Mar. to 6 Oct.	Castle Douglas and District Angling Association Tommy's Sport Shop, King Street, Castle Douglas. Tel: (01556) 502851. Dalbeattie Angling Association Ticket Sec., M. McCowan & Son, 43 High Street, Dalbeattie. Tel: (01556) 610270.	
	Dalbeattie	Salmon Sea Trout Brown Trout	25 Feb.to 30 Nov. 15 Mar. to 6 Oct.	Dalbeattie Angling Assoc., Ticket Sec. M. McCowan & Son, 43 High Street, Dalbeattie. Tel: (01556) 610270.	
White Esk	Eskdalemuir	Salmon Sea Trout	15 Apr.-30 Oct 15 Apr.-30 Sept.	Hart Manor Hotel, Eskdalemuir, by Langholm. Tel: (013873) 73217.	Fly and spinner only.

LOCHS & RESERVOIRS

Water	Location	Species	Season	Permit available from	Other information
Barend Loch	Sandyhills	Rainbow Trout	No close season	Barend Properties, Reception, Sandyhills, Dalbeattie. Tel: (0138778) 663.	
Barscobe Loch	Balmaclellan	Brown Trout	15 Mar. to 6 Oct.	Lady Wontner, Barscobe, Balmaclellan, Castle Douglas. Tel: (0164 42) 245/294.	Fly fishing only. Obtain permit first.
Black Esk Reservoir	Eskdalemuir	Brown Trout	1 Apr. to 30 Sept.	Hart Manor Hotel, Eskdalemuir, by Langholm. Tel: (013873) 73217.	Fly and spinner only.
Black Loch	Newton Stewart	Stocked Brown Trout	15 Mar.- 30 Sept.	Forest Enterprise, Creebridge. Tel: (01671) 402420. Clatteringshaws Wildlife Visitors Centre, New Galloway. Tel: (0164 42) 285.	Fly only until 1 July. Sunday fishing.
Black Loch	Nr. Kirkcowan	(Stocked) Brown Trout Pike	15 Mar. to 6 Oct. No close season	Palakona Guest House, Queen Street, Newton Stewart. Tel: (01671) 402323 - guests only. Galloway Country Sports, Tel: (01988) 840695 - all day tickets.	Any legal method permitted.

Water	Location	Species	Season	Permit available from	Other information
Bruntis Loch	Newton Stewart	Brown/ Rainbow Trout	1 May to 30 Sept.	Newton Stewart Angling Association. Galloway Guns & Tackle, 36 Arthur Street, Newton Stewart. Tel: (01671) 403404.	Fly fishing only (fly & worm from June 1). Bank fishing only. Sunday fishing.
Clattering-shaws Loch	6 miles west of New Galloway	Brown Trout Pike Perch	Open all year for coarse fish	Clatteringshaws Wildlife Visitors Centre, New Galloway. Tel: (0164 42) 285. Galloway Guns & Tackle, 36 Arthur Street, Newton Stewart. Tel: (01671) 403404. Kenmure Arms Hotel, High Street, New Galloway. Tel: (016442) 240.	Fly fishing, spinning or worm fishing permitted.
Dalbeattie Reservoir	Dalbeattie	Brown/ Rainbow Trout	1 Apr. to 30 Sept.	Dalbeattie Angling Association M. McCowan & Son, 43 High Street, Dalbeattie. Tel: (01556) 610270.	Bank fishing. Fly only. Boats for hire.
Loch Dee	Castle Douglas	Brown Trout	15 Mar. to 30 Sept.	Forest Enterprise, Creebridge. Tel: (01671) 402420. Forest Enterprise, 21 King Street, Castle Douglas. Tel: (01556) 503626. Clatteringshaws Wildlife Visitors Centre, New Galloway. Tel: (0164 42) 285.	Fly fishing only, sunrise to sunset. Bank fishing only. Sunday fishing. Annual fly fishing competition in August.
Dindinnie Reservoir	Stranraer	Brown Trout	1 May to 30 Sept.	Stranraer & District Angling Association. The Sports Shop, 90 George Street, Stranraer. Tel: (01776) 702705. Local hotels.	Fly fishing only. Sunday fishing.
Loch Dornal	Drumlamford Estate,	Coarse Stocked Trout	Apr. to Oct.	The Keeper, The Kennels, Drumlamford Estate, Barrhill. Tel: (0146 582) 256.	Spinning allowed. Boats available. Fly fishing.
Loch Drumlamford	Drumlamford Estate	Stocked Trout	April to October	The Keeper, The Kennels, Drumlamford Estate, Barrhill. Tel: (0146 582) 256.	Fly fishing only. Boats available.
Loch Dunskey (lower)	Portpatrick	Brown Trout	1 Apr. to 15 Sept.	Keeper, Dunskey Estate, Portpatrick. Tel: (01776) 810364/810211.	Fly only. Boat available. Loch Dunskey (Upper) (11 acres)
	Portpatrick	Rainbow Trout	1 Apr. to 15 Sept.	Keeper, Dunskey Estate, Portpatrick. Tel: (01776) 810364/810211.	2 boats. Fly only. Maximum 4 rods.
Loch Ettrick	Closeburn	Rainbow Trout (stocked) Brown Trout	1 Apr. to 31 Oct	John Crofts, Blawbare, Ettrick, Thornhill DG3 5HL. Tel: (01848) 330154. Closeburn Post Office. Tel: (01848) 31230.	Average weight of fish: 1lb to 2lbs. Popular flies: Nymphs. Fly fishing only. 4 boats available.

Water	Location	Species	Season	Permit available from	Other information
Fynntalloch Loch	Newton Stewart	Brown/ Rainbow Trout	1 May to 6 Oct.	Newton Stewart Angling Assoc., Galloway Guns & Tackle, 36 Arthur Street, Newton Stewart. Tel: (01671) 403404.	Fly fishing only. Bank fishing only. Sunday fishing.
Glenkiln Reservoir	Dumfries	Brown Trout (stocked) Rainbow Trout	1 Apr. to 30 Sept.	Dumfries & Galloway Regional Council, Director of Water & Sewerage, Marchmount House, Dumfries DG1 1PW. Tel: (01387) 60756.	Enquiries to Mr. Ling at No. opposite.
Jericho Loch	Dumfries	Brown/ Rainbow Trout Brook Trout	1 Apr. to 31 Oct.	Mouswald Caravan Park, Mouswald, by Dumfries. Tel: (0138 783) 226. McMillan's Tackle Shop, Friars Vennel, Dumfries. Pattie's Tackle Shop, Queensberry Street, Dumfries. Thistle Stores, Locharbriggs, Dumfries. Club Bookings - contact: Jimmy Younger, Tel: (01387) 75247. Day tickets from:- Tourist Information Centre, Dumfries, Tel: (01387) 53862.	Bank fishing only. Fly fishing only. Popular flies: Lures, Nymphs, Traditionals. Sunday fishing.
Loch Ken	West Bank Lochside Aird's (Viaduct)	Salmon Trout and coarse fish	Open all year for coarse fish	Shops, hotels in New Galloway	Surcharged if permits bought from bailiffs.
	New Galloway	Brown Trout Salmon Pike Perch Roach	15 Mar. to 30 Sept. All year round	Kenmure Arms Hotel, High Street, New Galloway. Tel: (016442) 240. Local shops.	Sunday fishing allowed except for Salmon. Worm & spinning permitted. Boats available.
Kettleton Reservoir	by Thornhill	Brown/ Rainbow Trout	1 Apr. to 30 Sept.	I.R. Milligan, 37 Drumlanrig Street, Thornhill. Tel: (01848) 330555.	Fly fishing only. Popular flies: Muddler, Black Pennel
Kirriereoch Loch	Newton Stewart	Brown Trout (stocked)	1 May to 6 Oct.	Newton Stewart Angling Association. Galloway Guns & Tackle, 36 Arthur Street, Newton Stewart. Tel: (01671) 403404. Merrick Caravan Park, Glentrool. Tel: (01671) 84 280.	Fly fishing only (fly & worm after June 1). Bank fishing only. Sunday fishing.
Knockquassan Reservoir	Stranraer	Brown Trout	1 May to 30 Sept.	Stranraer & District Angling Association. The Sports Shop, 90 George Street, Stranraer. Tel: (01776) 702705. Local hotels.	Bank fishing only. Fly only. Sunday fishing.
Lairdmannoch Loch	Twynholm	Wild Brown Trout	1 Apr. to 30 Sept.	G.M. Thomson, & Co. Ltd., 27 King Street, Castle Douglas. Tel: (01556) 502701/502973.	Boat fishing only. Limited rods. Limited days. Self-catering Accom. Available.

Water	Location	Species	Season	Permit available from	Other information
Lillies Loch	Castle Douglas	Brown Trout	15 Mar. to 30 Sept.	Forest Enterprise, Creebridge. Tel: (01671) 402420. Forest Enterprise, 21 King Street, Castle Douglas. Tel: (01556) 503626.	Bank fishing only. Any legal method. Sunday fishing.
Lochenbreck Loch	Lauriston	Brown/ Rainbow Trout	1 Apr. to 30 Sept.	Watson McKinnel, 15 St. Cuthbert Street, Kirkcudbright. Tel: (01557) 330693. M. & E. Brown, 52 High Street, Gatehouse of Fleet. Tel: (01557) 814222. (shop hours: 6.30am-5pm).	8.30 am to 10 pm. Bank and fly fishing. Five boats. Sunday fishing.
Loch of the Lowes	Newton Stewart	Brown trout (stocked)	15 Mar. to 30 Sept.	Forest Enterprise, Creebridge. Tel: (01671) 402420. Clatteringshaws Wildlife Visitors Centre, New Galloway. Tel: (0164 42) 285.	Fly only. Sunday fishing.
Morton Castle Loch	Thornhill	Stocked Brown/ Rainbow Trout	1 Apr. to 30 Sept.	The Buccleuch Estates Ltd., Drumlanrig Mains, Thornhill DG3 4AG. Tel: (018486) 283.	Average weight of fish: 2.25lbs Popular flies: Montanna, Damsel, P/T Nymph, Aces of Spades, Coachman (dry). Fly fishing only. Bank and boat fishing. Let on a daily basis for up to 3 rods.
Mossdale Loch	Mossdale Nr. New Galloway	Stocked Rainbow Trout Wild Brown Trout	15 Mar. to 30 Sept.	Mossdale Post Office, Mossdale, Castle Douglas DG7 2NF. Tel: (016445) 281.	Fly fishing only from boat. Boats available from Post Office. Sunday fishing.
Loch Nahinie	Drumlamford Estate	Stocked Trout	April to October	The Keeper, The Kennels, Drumlamford Estate, Barrhill. Tel: (0146 582) 256.	Fly fishing only. Boats available.
Ochiltree Loch	Newton Stewart	Brown/ Rainbow Trout	1 May to 6 Oct.	Newton Stewart Angling Assoc., Galloway Guns & Tackle, 36 Arthur Street, Newton Stewart. Tel: (01671) 403404.	Fly fishing only. Bank fishing only. Sunday fishing.
Penwhirn Reservoir	Stranraer	Brown Trout	15 Mar. to 30 Sept.	Stranraer & District Angling Association. The Sports Shop, 90 George Street, Stranraer. Tel: (01776) 702705. Local hotels.	Fly fishing and spinning. Bank fishing. Sunday fishing.
Piltanton Burn	Dunragit	Brown/ Rainbow Trout Salmon	1 May to 31 Oct.	Mr. J. Duffy, 2 Orchard Road, Dunragit, Stranraer. The Sports Shop, 90 George Street, Stranraer. Tel: (01671) 403403.	Spinning & worming allowed. Fly Fishing.
Purdom Stone Reservoir	Hoddom & Kinmount Estates, Lockerbie	Brown Trout	1 Apr. to 15 Sept.	The Water Bailiff, 1 Bridge End Cottage, Hoddom, Lockerbie. Tel: Ecclefechan 488.	Fly fishing only.

Water	Location	Species	Season	Permit available from	Other information
Loch Roan	Castle Douglas	Brown/ Rainbow Trout	1 Apr. to 6 Oct.	Tommy's Sports Shop, King Street, Castle Douglas. Tel: (01556) 502851.	Fly fishing only. Four boats.
Soulseat Loch	Stranraer	Brown/ Rainbow Trout	15 Mar. to 30 Sept.	Stranraer & District Angling Association. The Sports Shop, 90 George Street, Stranraer. Tel: (01776) 702705. Local hotels.	Fly, spinning and bait. Bank fishing and two boats. Sunday fishing.
Spa-wood Loch	Nr. Newton Stewart	Wild Brown Trout	15 Mar. to 30 Sept.	Palakona Guest House, Queen Street, Newton Stewart DG8 6JL. Tel: (01671) 2323.	Average weight of fish: 1lb 8oz. Fly only - guests only.
Starburn Loch	Thornhill	Stocked Brown/ Rainbow Trout	1 Apr. to 31 Aug.	The Buccleuch Estates Ltd., Drumlanrig Mains, Thornhill DG3 4AG. Tel: (018486) 283.	Average weight of fish: 2.2lbs. Popular flies: Montanna, Damsel, P/T Nymph, Ace of Spades, Coachman (dry). Fly fishing only. Bank and boat fishing available. Let on a daily basis for up to 3 rods.
Stroan Loch	Mossdale	Brown Trout Pike Perch	1 Apr.to 30 Sept.	Forest Enterprise, 21 King Street, Castle Douglas. Tel: (01556) 503626. Kenmure Arms Hotel, High Street, New Galloway. Tel: (016442) 240.	On Raiders Road Forest Drive.
Loch Whinyeon	Gatehouse of Fleet	Brown Trout	1 Apr. to 30 Sept.	M. & E. Brown, 52 High Street, Gatehouse of Fleet. Tel: (01557) 814 222. Watson McKinnel, 15 St. Cuthbert Street, Kirkcudbright. Tel: (01557) 30693.	8 am to 10 pm. Bank & boat fishing (2 boats available). Fly fishing only.

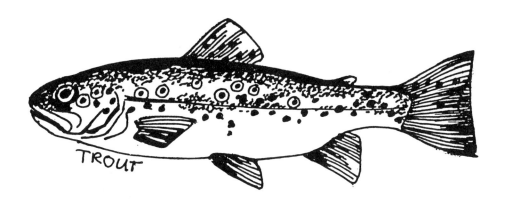

TROUT

STRATHCLYDE (SOUTH)

CLYDE AND AYRSHIRE RIVERS AND LOCHS

Constituent Area Tourist Boards

Ayrshire Tourist Board
Director of Tourism,
Tourist Information Centre,
Burns House,
Park House Street, Ayr.
Tel: (01292) 284196.

Clyde Valley Tourist Board
Tourism Officer,
Tourist Information Centre,
Horsemarket,
Ladyacre Road,
Lanark ML11 7LQ.
Tel: (01555) 661661

Tourist Information Centre
Tourist Officer,
Tourist Information Centre,
Promenade, Largs,
Ayrshire KA30 8BG.
Tel: (01475) 673765

Isle of Arran Tourist Board
Area Tourist Officer,
Information Centre, The Pier,
Brodick, Isle of Arran KA27 8AU.
Tel: (01770) 302140.

Greater Glasgow Tourist Board
Chief Executive,
Greater Glasgow Tourist Board,
39 St. Vincent Place,
Glasgow G1 2ER.
Tel: 0141-227 4885/4880.

RIVER PURIFICATION BOARD
CLYDE RIVER PURIFICATION BOARD
River House,
Murray Road,
East Kilbride,
Tel: (013552) 38181.

RIVERS

Water	Location	Species	Season	Permit available from	Other information
Annick	Irvine	Salmon Sea Trout Brown Trout	15 Mar. to 31 Oct. 15 Mar. to 6 Oct.	Mr. R.W. Gillespie, 16 Marble Avenue, Dreghorn.	
Annick (and Glazert)	Kilmaurs	Salmon Sea Trout Brown Trout	15 Mar.to 31 Oct. 15 Mar. to 6 Oct.	Kilmaurs Angling Club, T.C. McCabe, 8 East Park Crescent, Kilmaurs. Mr. D. Dunn, 22 Habbieauld Road, Kilmaurs. Tel: (01563) 23846. Pages etc. Main Street, Kilmaurs. Tel: (01563) 38570.	
Avon	Strathaven	Brown Trout Grayling	15 Mar.- 6 Oct. No Close Season	Country Lines, 29 Main Street, The Village, East Kilbride. Tel: (013552) 28952. Sportsman Emporium, Hamilton. Tel: (01698) 283903. P. & R. Torbet, 15 Strand Street, Kilmarnock. Tel: (01563) 41734.	Any legal method.
Ayr	Craigie Park	Salmon Sea Trout Trout	10 Feb. to 31 Oct.	Gamesport of Ayr, 60 Sandgate, Ayr. Tel: (01292) 263822.	No bait restriction. Fly, spin or worm.
	Failford	Salmon Sea Trout Trout	10 Feb. to 31 Oct.	Gamesport of Ayr, 60 Sandgate, Ayr. Tel: (01292) 263822.	No Saturday or Sunday visitor permits.
	Mauchline	Salmon Sea Trout Brown Trout	15 Mar. to 31 Oct. 15 Mar. to 15 Sept.	Linwood & Johnstone Newsagent, The Cross, Mauchline. Tel: (01290) 550219.	
Ayr (Cessnock Lugar)	Mauchline	Salmon Sea Trout Brown Trout	11 Feb. to 31 Oct. 15 May- 6 Oct.	Linwood & Johnstone Newsagents, The Cross, Mauchline. Tel: (01290) 550219.	

Water	Location	Species	Season	Permit available from	Other information
Ayr (Lugar)	Mauchline	Salmon Sea Trout Brown Trout	15 Mar. to 30 Oct. 15 Mar.- 15 Sept.	Linwood & Johnstone Newsagents, The Cross, Mauchline. Tel: (01290) 550219.	
Cart	Busby	Brown Trout	15 Mar to 6 Oct.	Tackle & Guns, 920 Pollokshaws Road, Glasgow G41 2ET. Tel: 0141-632 2005.	Average weight of fish caught: 8oz-10oz Popular flies: small spider flies. Bait fishing allowed, no spinning.
Cessnock	Mauchline	Brown Trout	15 Mar. to 15 Sept.	Linwood & Johnstone, Newsagents, The Cross, Mauchline. Tel: (01290) 550219.	
Clyde	Motherwell, Lanark, Carstairs, Roberton & Crawford	Brown Trout Grayling Coarse	15 Mar. to 30 Sept. All year.	Country Lines, 29 Main Street, The Village, East Kilbride. Tel: (013552) 28952. Lawrence Angling, 268 Dumbarton Road, Glasgow. Tel: 0141-339 1085.	
	Thankerton & Roberton	Brown Trout Grayling	15 Mar. to 6 Oct. 7 Oct.-14 Mar.	B.F. Dexter, Secretary, Lamington & District Angling Improvement Association, 18 Boghall Park, Biggar. Waterbailiffs: Mr. McMahon at Wolfclyde Bridge & Mr. J. Grierson at Symington. W.P. Bryden, Newsagent, 153 High Street, Biggar. Tel: (01899) 20069 - (open 6am-5pm. Mon-Sat)	Spinning with legal lures allowed from 1st May. Fly fishing at all times. Flies in normal use size 14. Ground baiting and keep nets are not allowed. No Sunday fishing.
Douglas (and Clyde)	Douglas Water	Brown Trout Grayling	15 Mar.-30 Sep. All year.		Permits widely available in tackle shops in Glasgow and Lanarkshire.
Garnock	Kilbirnie	Brown Trout Salmon Sea Trout	15 Mar. to 6 Oct. 15 Mar.-31 Oct.	Kilbirnie Angling Club I. Johnstone, 12 Grahamston Avenue, Glengarnock, KA14 3AF. Tel: (01505) 682154. R.T. Cycles, Glengarnock. Tel: (01505) 682191.	No Sunday fishing after July 1.
Garnock (and Lugton)	Kilwinning	Salmon Sea Trout Brown Trout	15 Mar. to 31 Oct. 15 Mar.-6 Oct.	Jamieson Hardware, 130 Main Street, Kilwinning. Tel: (01294) 551470.	Day permits.
Gryfe	Bridge of Weir	Brown Trout Salmon Sea Trout	15 Mar.-6 Oct. 15 Mar.-31 Oct.	M. Duncan, Newsagent, Main Street, Bridge of Weir. Tel: (01505) 612477.	No Saturday or Sunday fishing.
Iorsa	Isle of Arran	Salmon Sea Trout	June to Oct.	The Estate Office, Dougarie, Isle of Arran. Tel: (01770) 840259.	

Please mention this Pastime Publications guide

Water	Location	Species	Season	Permit available from	Other information
Irvine	Hurlford and Crookedholm	Salmon Sea Trout Brown Trout	15 Mar. to 31 Oct. 15 Mar. to 6 Oct.	P. & R. Torbet, 15 Strand Street, Kilmarnock. Tel: (01563) 41734.	
	Kilmarnock	Salmon Sea trout Brown Trout	15 Mar. to 31 Oct. 15 Mar.-6 Oct.	McCririck & Sons, 38 John Finnie Street, Kilmarnock. Tel: (01563) 25577.	No Sunday fishing after 31st July.
Irvine (and Annick)	Dreghorn	Salmon Sea Trout Brown Trout	15 Mar. to 31 Oct. 15 Mar.-6 Oct.	Mr. R.W. Gillespie, 16 Marble Avenue, Dreghorn.	River Irvine only, extension of season for salmon and sea trout - 1 to 15 November. Fly only.
Irvine (and Cessnock)	Galston	Salmon Sea Trout Brown Trout	15 Mar. to 30 Nov. 15 Mar.-6 Oct.	P. & R. Torbet, 15 Strand Street, Kilmarnock. Tel: (01563) 41734.	
Kelvin	Glasgow-Strathkelvin	Salmon Sea Trout	11 Feb. to 31 Oct.	Lawrence Angling, 268 Dumbarton Road, Glasgow G11 6TU. Tel: 0141-339 1085.	Any legal bait permitted.
Machrie	Arran	Salmon Sea Trout	June to Oct.	Margo M. Wilson, Boltachan House, Aberfeldy PH15 2LA. Tel: (01887) 820496.	No Sunday fishing. Booking: Nov.-Oct.
Rotten Calder	E. Kilbride	Brown Trout	15 Mar. to 6 Oct.	Country Lines, 29 Main Street, The Village, East Kilbride. Tel: (013552) 28952.	Any legal method.

LOCHS & RESERVOIRS

Water	Location	Species	Season	Permit available from	Other information
Loch Arklet	Stirling & Trossachs	Brown Trout	30 Mar. to 28 Sept.	Strathclyde Reg. Council, Water Department, 419 Balmore Road, Glasgow, Tel: 0141-355 5333. Or on location.	Fly fishing by rowing boat only. No live bait/spinning. Rowing boats supplied. 7 days fishing.
Loch Belston	Sinclairston	Brown Trout Rainbow Trout	15 Mar. to 15 Sept.	Bailiff at Loch	Boats available.
		Rainbow Trout	No close season	Gamesport of Ayr, 60 Sandgate, Ayr. Tel: (01292) 263822.	
Loch Bradan	Straiton	Brown Trout (Stocked)	15 Mar. to 30 Sept.	Forest Enterprise, Straiton. Tel: (0165 57) 637. Mr. R. Heaney, Tallaminnoch, Straiton. Tel: (0165 57) 617.	Five Boats. Sunday fishing.
Loch Brecbowie	Straiton	Brown Trout	15 Mar. to 30 Sept.	Forest Enterprise, Straiton. Tel: (0165 57) 637. Mr. R. Heaney, Tallaminnoch, Straiton. Tel: (0165 57) 617.	Fly fishing advised. Sunday fishing.

Water	Location	Species	Season	Permit available from	Other information
Burnfoot Reservoir	Nr. Fenwick	Brown/ Rainbow Trout	15 Mar. to 6 Oct.	Kilmaurs A.C., Mr. T.C. McCabe, 8 East Park Crescent, Kilmaurs. Mr. D. Dunn, 22 Habbieauld Road, Kilmaurs. Tel: (01563) 23846. Pages Etc., Main Street, Kilmaurs. Tel: (01563) 38570.	Average weight of fish caught: 1lb-5lbs Popular flies: Butcher, Montanna, Nymph, Viva, Soldier Palmer Any legal method - no swim feeders or floats.
Busbie Muir Reservoir	Ardrossan	Brown Trout	1 Apr. to 6 Oct.	Ardrossan Eglinton A.C., Alpine Stores, Dalry Road, Ardrossan. Tel: (01294) 467979.	Obtain permits before fishing. Average weight of fish caught: 8-12oz. Popular flies: Wickhams, Kate McLaren, Soldier Palmer, Grouse & Claret, Invicta, Blae & Black. Two boats, keys available from Alpine Store.
Camphill Reservoir	Kilbirnie	Brown Trout	1 Apr. to 6 Oct.	Kilbirnie A.C., I. Johnstone, 12 Grahamstone Avenue, Glengarnock KA14 3AF. Tel: (01505) 682154. R.T. Cycles, Glengarnock. Tel: (01505) 682191.	Fly only. Boat only.
Dhu Loch	Straiton	Brown Trout	15 Mar. to 30 Sept.	Mr. R. Heaney, Tallaminnoch, Straiton. Tel: (0165-57) 617.	Fly only.
Glen Finglas	Stirling & Trossachs	Brown Trout	30 Mar. to 28 Sept.	Strathclyde Reg. Council, Water Department, 419 Balmore Road, Glasgow, Tel: 0141-336 5333. Or on location.	Fly fishing by rowing boat only. No live bait/ spinning. Rowing boats supplied. 7 days fishing.
Loch Goin (between orange markers)	Nr. Eaglesham	Brown Trout	15 Mar. to 6 Oct.	Kilmaurs A.C., Mr. T.C. McCabe, 8 East Park Crescent, Kilmaurs. Mr. D. Dunn, 22 Habbieauld Road, Kilmaurs. Tel: (01563) 23846.	Average weight of fish caught: 8oz to 3lbs. Popular flies: traditional small flies. No other baits - fly only.
Craigendunton Reservoir	Nr. Kilmarnock	Rainbow/ Brown Trout	15 Mar. to 6 Oct.	Kilmarnock A.C., McCririck & Sons, 38 John Finnie Street, Kilmarnock. Tel: (01563) 25577.	Average weight of fish caught: Rainbow - 1lb 8oz, Brown - 12oz. Fly and spinning only; no live bait. Obtain permits before fishing.
Harelaw Dam	Neilston	Brown Trout	15 Mar. to 6 Oct.	Tackle & Guns, 920 Pollokshaws Road, Glasgow. Tel: 0141-632 2005. Lawrence Angling, 268 Dumbarton Road, Glasgow G11 6TU. Tel: 0141-339 1085.	Average weight of fish caught: 1lb 2oz. Popular flies: Black Pennel, Soldier Palmer, Sedges, and Dry Fly. For boats day or evening Contact: Dougie Brown, 10 Garrioch Drive, Glasgow. Tel: 0141 946 6060.

Water	Location	Species	Season	Permit available from	Other information
Loch Katrine	Stirling & Trossachs	Brown Trout	30 Mar. to 28 Sept.	Strathclyde Reg. Council, Water Department, 419 Balmore Road, Glasgow, Tel: 0141-336 5333. Or on location.	Fly fishing by rowing boat only. No live bait/spinning. Rowing boats supplied. 7 days fishing.
Kilbirnie Loch	Kilbirnie	Brown/Rainbow Trout	15 Mar. to 6 Oct.	Kilbirnie Angling Club, I. Johnstone, 12 Grahamston Avenue, Glengarnock KA14 3AF. Tel: (01505) 682154. R.T. Cycles, Glengarnock. Tel: (01505) 682191.	All legal methods. Boats available.
Mill Glen Reservoir	Ardrossan	Brown Trout	15 Mar. to 6 Oct.	Ardrossan Eglinton A.C., Alpine Stores, Dalry Road, Ardrossan. Tel: (01294) 467979.	Obtain permits before fishing. Average weight of fish caught: 8-12oz. Popular flies: Wickhams, Kate McLaren, Soldier Palmer, Grouse & Claret, Invicta, Blae & Black. Fly fishing only.
North Craig Reservoir	Kilmaurs	Rainbow Trout	Open all year	Kilmaurs A.C., T.C. McCabe, 8 East Park Crescent, Kilmaurs. Mr. D. Dunn, 22 Habbieauld Road, Kilmaurs. Tel: (01563) 23846. Pages Etc. Main Street, Kilmaurs. Tel: (01563) 38570.	Average weight of fish caught: 1-5lbs. Popular flies: Butcher, Soldier Palmer, Blue Zulu, Baby Doll, Viva. Any legal method
Penwhapple Reservoir	Nr. Girvan	Stocked Brown Trout	1 Apr. to 15 Sept.	Mrs. Stewart, Lanes Farm, Nr. Girvan. (¼ mile from reservoir).	Fly fishing only (Mon-Sat). No Sunday fishing. Average weight of fish caught: 1lb. Popular flies: Kate McLaren, Zulu, Invicta; traditional patterns. 4 boats available.
Prestwick Reservoir	Monkton	Rainbow Trout	15 Mar to 15 Nov.	Gamesport of Ayr. 60 Sandgate, Ayr. Tel: (01292) 263822. Newhall's Newsagent, Monkton. Wheatsheaf Inn, Monkton.	Average weight of fish caught: 1-4lbs. Popular flies: Butcher, Greenwell Glory. Worm fishing.
Raith Reservoir (Prestwick)	Monkton by Ayr	Rainbow Trout	15 Mar. to 15 Nov.	Gamesport of Ayr, 60 Sandgate, Ayr. Tel: (01292) 263822.	
Loch Skelloch	Straiton	Brown Trout (Stocked)	15 Mar. to 30 Sept.	Mr. R. Heaney, Tallaminnoch, Straiton. Tel: (0165 57) 617.	Fly fishing only. Boats available. Sunday fishing.
Strathclyde Country Park Loch (and adjacent River Clyde)	Motherwell	Grayling Trout	15 Mar. to 29 Sept.	Booking Office, Strathclyde Country Park, 366 Hamilton Road, Motherwell. Tel: Motherwell 266155.	

Constituent Area Tourist Boards

Bute and Cowal Tourist Board
Area Tourist Officer,
Information Centre,
7 Alexandra Parade,
Dunoon, Argyll PA23 8AB.
Tel: (01369) 3785.

Area Tourist Officer,
Tourist Information centre,
15 Victoria Street,
Rothesay,
Isle of Bute PA20 0AJ.
Tel: (01700) 502151.

West Highlands & Islands of Argyll Tourist Board,
Area Tourist Officer,
Tourist Information Centre,
Argyll Square, Oban,
Argyll PA34 4AR.
Tel: (01631) 63122.

RIVER PURIFICATION BOARD
CLYDE RIVER PURIFICATION BOARD
River House,
Murray Road,
East Kilbride, G75 0LA.
Tel: (013552) 38181.

RIVERS

Water	Location	Species	Season	Permit available from	Other information
Aros	Mull	Salmon Sea Trout	End June to Mid Oct.	Tackle and Books, Main Street, Tobermory, Isle of Mull. Tel: (01688) 2336.	No Sunday fishing.
Awe	Inverawe Taynuilt	Salmon Sea Trout	May to Oct	Inverawe Fisheries Taynuilt, Argyll. Tel: (018662) 446	Fly fishing only.
Bellart	Mull	Sea Trout Salmon	June to End Oct.	Tackle & Books, Main Street, Tobermory, Isle of Mull. Tel: (01688) 2336.	No Sunday fishing.
Cur	13 miles from Dunoon	Salmon Sea Trout Brown Trout	1 Apr. to 31 Oct.	Purdies of Argyll, 112 Argyll Street, Dunoon. Tel: (01369) 3232 Dunoon & District Angling Club.	Fishing all legal methods. Bookings, Hon. Sec., D. & D.A.C., Ashgrove'', 28 Royal Crescent, Dunoon PA23 7AH. Tel: (01369) 5732.
Douglas	Inveraray	Salmon Sea Trout	May to Mid-Oct.	Argyll Caravan Park, Inveraray, Argyll. Tel: (01499) 2285.	No Sunday fishing. Fly fishing only.
Euchar	Kilninver	Salmon Sea Trout Brown Trout	1 June to 15 Oct.	Mrs. Mary McCorkindale, Glenann' Kilninver, by Oban, Argyll. Tel: (0185 26) 282.	No Sunday fishing.
		Salmon Sea Trout	Mid-July to Mid-Oct.	J.T.P. Mellor, Barncromin Farm, Knipoch, by Oban, Argyll. Tel: (0185 26) 273.	(Tues, Wed & Thurs.)
	Kilninver (Lagganmore)	Salmon Sea Trout Brown Trout	June to 14 Oct.	Lt. Col. P.S. Sandilands, Lagganmore, Kilninver, by Oban. Tel: (0185 26) 200.	Not more than 3 rods per day. Fly fishing only. No Sunday fishing.

Water	Location	Species	Season	Permit available from	Other information
Finnart	12 miles from Dunoon	Salmon Sea Trout Brown Trout	1 Apr. to 15 Oct.	Dunoon & District Angling Club. Purdie's of Argyll, 112 Argyll Street, Dunoon. Tel: (01369) 3232.	Fishing all legal methods. Advanced bookings Hon. Sec., D.& D.A.C., Ashgrove", 28 Royal Crescent, Dunoon PA23 7AH. Tel: (01369) 5732.
Forsa	Mull	Salmon Sea Trout	Mid-June to End Oct.	Tackle and Books, Main Street, Tobermory. Tel: (01688) 2336.	No Sunday fishing.
Goil	Lochgoil head	Salmon Sea Trout	May to end-Oct.	River Goil Angling Club J. Lamont, Shore House Inn, Lochgoilhead. Tel: (0130 13) 340.	Fly and worm. No spinning. No sea baits. No Sundays.
Grey	Islay	Salmon Sea Trout	July to October	Brian Wiles, Head Gamekeeper's House, Islay House Square, Bridgend. Tel: (01496) 810293.	Fly only. No night fishing.
Laggan	Islay	Salmon Sea Trout	July to October	Brian Wiles, Head Gamekeeper's House, Isle House Square, Bridgend. Tel: (01496) 810293.	Fly fishing only. No night fishing.
Massan	6 miles from Dunoon	Salmon Sea Trout Brown Trout	1 Apr. to 31 Oct.	Dunoon & District Angling Club. Purdies of Argyll, 112 Argyll Street, Dunoon. Tel: (01369) 3232.	All legal methods. Advanced booking Hon. Sec., D. & D.A.C., Ashgrove", 28 Royal Crescent, Dunoon PA23 7AH. Tel: (01369) 5732.
Orchy	Dalmally	Salmon	11 Feb. to 15 Oct.	W.A. Church, Croggan Crafts, Dalmally, Argyll. Tel: (01838) 200201.	
Ruel	Glendaruel	Salmon Sea Trout	16 Feb. to 31 Oct.	Glendaruel Hotel, Clachan of Glendaruel, Argyll PA22 3AA. Tel: (0136982) 274.	No Sunday fishing.
Sorn	Islay	Salmon Sea Trout	October	Brian Wiles, Head Gamekeeper's House, Islay House Square, Bridgend. Tel: (01496) 810293.	Fly fishing only. No night fishing.

LOCHS & RESERVOIRS

Water	Location	Species	Season	Permit available from	Other information
Loch A'Bharrain	Nr. Oban	Brown Trout	15 Mar. to 6 Oct.	D. Graham, Combie Street, Oban. Sports Centre, Oban. Anglers' Corner, 2 John Street, Oban. Tel: (01631) 66374. Post Office, Kilmelford. Mr. Morrison, Ledaig Leisure, Benderloch.	Standard trout flies wet or dry (12 & 14). Peaty loch with small fish.
Loch a'Chaorainn	Nr. Kilmelford	Brown Trout	15 Mar. to 6 Oct.	D. Graham, Combie Street, Oban. Sports Centre, Oban. Anglers' Corner, 2 John Street, Oban. Tel: (01631) 66374. Post Office, Kilmelford. Mr. Morrison, Ledaig Leisure, Benderloch.	Popular flies: imitations of natural flies. The loch contains trout up to 2lbs.

Water	Location	Species	Season	Permit available from	Other information
Loch a'Cheigin	Nr. Kilmelford	Brown Trout	15 Mar. to 6 Oct.	D. Graham, Combie Street, Oban. Sports Centre, Oban. Anglers' Corner, 2 John Street, Oban. Tel: (01631) 66374. Post Office, Kilmelford. Mr. Morrison, Ledaig Leisure, Benderloch.	Popular flies: standard trout patterns, size 14.
Loch a'Chlachain	Nr. Kilmelford	Brown Trout	15 Mar. to 6 Oct.	D. Graham, Combie Street, Oban. Sports Centre, Oban. Anglers' Corner, 2 John Street, Oban. Tel: (01631) 66374. Post Office, Kilmelford. Mr. Morrison, Ledaig Leisure, Benderloch.	Popular flies: standard trout flies, wet or dry (12 & 14).
Loch a'Chreachain	Nr. Kilmelford	Brown Trout	15 Mar. to 6 Oct.	D. Graham, Combie Street, Oban. Sports Centre, Oban. Anglers' Corner, 2 John Street, Oban. Tel: (01631) 66374. Post Office, Kilmelford. Mr. Morrison, Ledaig Leisure, Benderloch.	Popular flies: standard pattern trout flies sizes 12 & 14 also big lure type flies for the bigger trout.
Loch a'Cruaiche	Nr. Kilmelford	Brown Trout	15 Mar. to 6 Oct.	D. Graham, Combie Street, Oban. Sports Centre, Oban. Anglers' Corner, 2 John Street, Oban. Tel: (01631) 66374. Post Office, Kilmelford. Mr. Morrison, Ledaig Leisure, Benderloch.	Small weedy loch with small trout.
Loch a'Mhinn	Nr. Kilmelford	Brown Trout	15 Mar. to 6 Oct.	D. Graham, Combie Street, Oban. Sports Centre, Oban. Anglers' Corner, 2 John Street, Oban. Tel: (01631) 66374. Post Office, Kilmelford. Mr. Morrison, Ledaig Leisure, Benderloch.	Popular flies: standard trout flies, wet or dry (12 & 14). The loch contains small fat trout, frequently difficult to catch.
Loch a'Phearsain	Nr. Kilmelford	Brown Trout	15 Mar. to 6 Oct.	D. Graham, Combie Street, Oban. Sports Centre, Oban. Anglers' Corner, 2 John Street, Oban. Tel: (01631) 66374. Post Office, Kilmelford. Mr. Morrison, Ledaig Leisure, Benderloch.	Average weight of fish: 8oz to 1lb. Popular flies: standard patterns, sizes 12 & 14.
Loch an Daimh	Nr. Kilmelford	Brown Trout	15 Mar. to 6 Oct.	D. Graham, Combie Street, Oban. Sports Centre, Oban. Anglers' Corner, 2 John Street, Oban. Tel: (01631) 66374. Post Office, Kilmelford. Mr. Morrison, Ledaig Leisure, Benderloch.	The loch contains trout up to 6oz, but they are difficult to catch. Popular flies: standard trout flies, wet or dry (10 &14).

Water	Location	Species	Season	Permit available from	Other information
Loch an Losgainn Beag	Nr. Kilmelford	Brown Trout	15 Mar. to 6 Oct.	D. Graham, Combie Street, Oban. Sports Centre, Oban. Anglers' Corner, 2 John Street, Oban. Tel: (01631) 66374. Post Office, Kilmelford. Mr. Morrison, Ledaig Leisure, Benderloch.	Popular flies: standard trout flies, wet or dry (10 to 14). The loch contains very large trout that are difficult to catch. Reputed to fish best in the evening during June.
Loch an Losgainn Mor	Nr. Kilmelford	Brown Trout	15 Mar. to 6 Oct.	D. Graham, Combie Street, Oban. Sports Centre, Oban. Anglers' Corner, 2 John Street, Oban Tel: (01631) 66374. Post Office, Kilmelford. Mr. Morrison, Ledaig Leisure, Benderloch.	Popular flies: standard trout flies, wet or dry (10 to 14). The loch contains trout of 6oz. but they are difficult to catch.
Loch Airigh-Shamhraidh	Musdale	Brown Trout	15 Mar. to 6 Oct.	D. Graham, Combie Street, Oban. Sports Centre, Oban. Anglers' Corner, 2 John Street, Oban. Tel: (01631) 66374. Post Office, Kilmelford. Mr. Morrison, Ledaig Leisure, Benderloch.	Popular flies: standard trout flies wet or dry (12 & 14). Loch is full of easily caught trout.
Aros Lake	Aros	Rainbow Trout	1 Apr. to 30 Nov.	Brown's Shop, Tobermory. Tel: (01688) 2020.	Popular flies: Butcher, Teal & Green, Soldier Palmer, Grouse & Claret (size 10 & 12). Bank fishing only. No spinning.
Loch Ascog	Argyll	Brown/ Rainbow Trout	15 Mar. to 5 Oct.	Kyles of Bute Angling Club. Several shops in Kames and Tighnabruaich.	Fly only.
Loch Assopol	Mull	Salmon Sea Trout Brown Trout	April to beg. Oct.	Argyll Arms Hotel, Bunessan, Isle of Mull. Tel: (016817) 240.	Fly and spinner only. No Sunday fishing.
Glen Astil Lochs (2)	Isle of Islay	Brown Trout	15 Mar to 30 Sept.	I.G. Laurie, Newsagent, 19 Charlotte Street, Port Ellen, Isle of Islay. Tel: (01496) 302264.	Fly only. No Sunday fishing. No catch limit. Permit covers all 5 lochs of Port Ellen Angling Club (see Loch Kinnabus). Boat available.
Loch Avich	Taynuilt	Brown Trout Rainbow Trout	15 Mar. to 6 Oct.	Mr. N.D. Clark, 11, Dalavich, By Taynuilt, Argyll PA35 1HN. Tel: Lochavich 209. W.A. Church, Croggan Crafts, Dalmally, Argyll. Tel: (01838) 200201.	5 boats available.
	Nr. Kilmelford	Brown Trout	15 Mar. to 6 Oct.	D. Graham, Combie Street, Oban. Sports Centre, Oban. Anglers' Corner, 2 John Street, Oban. Tel: (01631) 66374. Post Office, Kilmelford. Mr. Morrison, Ledaig Leisure, Benderloch.	Popular flies: standard patterns, sizes 12 & 14.

Water	Location	Species	Season	Permit available from	Other information
Loch Awe	South Lochaweside by Dalmally	Salmon Sea Trout Brown Trout Rainbow Trout Perch Char Pike	11 Feb. to 15 Oct. 15 Mar. to 6 Oct. All year	Ardbrecknish House, by Dalmally, Argyll. Tel: (018663) 223/256.	Boats, tackle and permits available. Clubs welcome.
		Salmon Sea Trout Brown Trout Rainbow Trout Perch Char Pike	15 Mar. to 15 Oct. 15 Mar. to 6 Oct. All year	The Portsonachan Hotel, Nr.Dalmally, Argyll PA33 1BL. Tel: (0186 63) 224.	
		Brown/ Rainbow Trout Salmon	15 Mar. 15 Oct.	Ford Hotel, Ford. Tel: (0154 681) 273.	
	Taynuilt	Salmon Sea Trout Brown Trout Rainbow Trout	12 Feb. to 15 Oct. 15 Mar. to 6 Oct.	Mr. N.D. Clark, 11, Dalavich, By Taynuilt, Argyll PA35 1HN. Tel: Lochavich 209. D. Graham, Combie Street, Oban. Sports Centre, Oban. Anglers' Corner, 2 John Street, Oban. Tel: (01631) 66374. Lawrence Angling, 268 Dumbarton Road, Glasgow G11 6TU. Tel: 0141-339 1085.	Boats available.
		Salmon Brown Trout Sea Trout Rainbow Trout Char Perch Pike	16 Mar. to 6 Oct. (No close season Pike)	Country Lines, 29 Main Street, The Village, East Kilbride. Tel: (013552) 28952.	Separate Pike permit available. Restrictions detailed on permit.
	Argyll	Brown/ Rainbow Trout	15 Mar. to 6 Oct.	Lochgilphead Tourist Office, Lochnell Street, Lochgilphead. Tel: (01546) 602344. Oban Tourist Office, Boswell House, Argyll Square, Oban. Tel: (01631) 63122. W.A. Church, Croggan Crafts, Dalmally, Argyll. Tel: (01838) 200201.	Permits also available for Pike fishing (no close season).
Ballygrant Loch	Ballygrant	Brown Trout	15 Mar. to 6 Oct.	Port Askaig Stores, Port Askaig, Isle of Islay. Tel: (01496) 840245.	Average weight of fish caught: 8-16oz. Boats are available.
Loch Bealach Ghearran	Nr. Minard Village	Brown Trout	15 Mar. to 6 Oct.	Mr. R. Hardie, No. 1, Nursery Cottages, Birdfield, Minard, Argyll. Mr. D. McNeil, Hydro Cottage, Lochgair. Forest District Office, Whitegates, Lochgilphead.	Average weight of fish caught: 8oz. Popular flies: most dark flies.

Water	Location	Species	Season	Permit available from	Other information
Big Feinn Loch	Nr. Kilmelford	Brown Trout	15 Mar. to 6 Oct.	D. Graham, Combie Street, Oban. Sports Centre, Oban. Anglers' Corner, 2 John Street, Oban. Tel: (01631) 66374. Post Office, Kilmelford. Mr. Morrison, Ledaig Leisure, Benderloch.	The loch contains ɪery large trout which are very difficult to catch. It fishes best at the beginning of the season in windy conditions. Popular flies: large salmon flies - Demons or Terrors.
Blackmill Loch	Nr. Minard Village	Brown Trout	15 Mar. to 6 Oct.	Mr. R. Hardie, No. 1, Nursery Cottages, Birdfield, Minard, Argyll. Mr. D. McNeil, Hyrdo Cottage, Lochgair. Forest District Office, Whitegates, Lochgilphead.	Average weight of fish caught:8oz. Popular flies: most dark flies.
Cam Loch	Nr. Ford	Brown Trout	15 Mar. to 6 Oct.	Ford Hotel, Ford. Tel: Ford 273.	Average weight of fish caught: 8oz. Popular flies: most dark flies.
Loch Crauch Maolachy	Nr. Kilmelford	Brown Trout	15 Mar. to 6 Oct.	D. Graham, Combie Street, Oban. Sports Centre, Oban. Anglers' Corner, 2 John Street, Oban. Tel: (01631) 66374. Post Office, Kilmelford. Mr. Morrison, Ledaig Leisure, Benderloch.	Stocked trout reach 2lbs or more. Standard patterns, sizes 12 & 14.
Dubh Loch	Kilninver	Loch Leven Trout Brown Trout	April to Mid-Oct.	J.T.P. Mellor, Barndromin Farm, Knipoch, by Oban. Tel: (0185 26) 273.	Boat on loch.
Loch Dubh-Bheag	Nr. Kilmelford	Brown Trout	15 Mar. to 6 Oct.	D. Graham, Combie Street, Oban. Sports Centre, Oban. Post Office, Kilmelford. Mr. Morrison, Ledaig Leisure, Benderloch.	Popular flies: standard trout patterns, sizes 12 & 14
Loch Dubh-Mor	Nr. Kilmelford	Brown Trout	15 Mar. to 6 Oct.	D. Graham, Combie Street, Oban. Sports Centre, Oban. Anglers' Corner, 2 John Street, Oban. Tel: (01631) 66374. Post Office, Kilmelford. Mr. Morrison, Ledaig Leisure, Benderloch.	Average weight of fish caught: 4oz. Popular flies: standard patterns, 10 & 12.
Dunoon Reservoir	Dunoon	Rainbow & Brook Trout	1 Mar. to 31 Nov.	Dunoon & District Angling Club. Purdies of Argyll, 112 Argyll Street, Dunoon. Tel: (01369) 3232.	Fly fishing only.
Ederline Lochs 18 hill lochs	Ford	Wild Brown Trout	May to 6 Oct.	The Keeper, Keepers Cottage, Ederline, Ford, Lochgilphead. Tel: (0154 681) 215.	Average weight of fish caught: 8oz. Fly only. Boats available on 5 lochs.
Loch Ederline (& 3 smaller lochs)	Ford	Pike Perch	No close season	The Keeper, Keepers Cottage, Ederline, Ford, Lochgilphead. Tel: (0154 681) 215.	All baits allowed. 3 boats available.

Water	Location	Species	Season	Permit available from	Other information
Loch Fad	Bute	Brown Trout Rainbow Trout	15 Mar. to 6 Oct.	Bailiff at Loch. Tel: (01700) 504871. Isle of Bute Trout Co. Ltd., Ardmaleish, Isle of Bute PA20 0QJ. Tel: (01700) 502451.	23 Boats available. Bank fishing. Whole day and evening tickets. No night fishing.
		Rainbow Trout Brown Trout	March to October	Carleol Enterprises Angling Holidays, 3 Alma Terrace, Rothesay. Tel: (01700) 503716.	Accommodation and permits are available.
Loch Fada	Isle of Colonsay	Brown Trout	15 Mar. to 30 Sept.	The Hotel, Isle of Colonsay, Argyll PA61 7YP. Tel: (019512) 316.	Fly fishing only. Boats are available.
Loch Finlaggan	Islay	Brown Trout	15 Mar. to 30 Sept.	Brian Wiles, Islay House Square, Bridgend, Isle of Islay, Argyll PA44 7NZ. Tel: (01496) 810293.	Two boats.
Forestry Hill Lochs	Ford	Brown Trout	15 Mar. to 6 Oct.	Ford Hotel, Ford, Argyll. Tel: (0154-681) 273.	
Loch Frisa	North end of Mull	Brown Trout Sea Trout	Apr. to Oct.	Tackle and Books, Main Street, Tobermory, Mull. Tel: (01688) 2336.	1 Boat by arrangement.
Loch Glashan	Nr. Lochgair Village	Brown Trout	15 Mar. to 6 Oct.	Mr. R. Hardie, No. 1, Nursery Cottages, Birdfield, Minard, Argyll. Mr. D. McNeil, Hydro Cottage, Lochgair. Forest District Office, Whitegates, Lochgilphead.	Average weight of fish caught: 12oz. Popular flies: most dark flies. One boat is available.
Loch Gleann A'Bhearraidh	Lerags by Oban	Brown Trout	15 Mar. to 6 Oct.	Cologin Homes Ltd., Lerags, by Oban, Argyll. Tel: (01631) 64501. The Barn Inn, Cologin, Lerags, by Oban.	One boat available.
Loch Gully	Nr. Kilmelford	Brown Trout	15 Mar. to 6 Oct.	D. Graham, Combie Street, Oban. Sports Centre, Oban. Anglers' Corner, 2 John Street, Oban. Tel: (01631) 66374. Post Office, Kilmelford. Mr. Morrison, Ledaig Leisure, Benderloch.	The loch contains some good fat trout. Popular flies: standard patterns, 12 & 14.
Iasg Loch	Nr. Kilmelford	Brown Trout	15 Mar. to 6 Oct.	D. Graham, Combie Street, Oban. Sports Centre, Oban. Anglers' Corner, 2 John Street, Oban. Tel: (01631) 66374. Post Office, Kilmelford. Mr. Morrison, Ledaig Leisure, Benderloch.	Popular flies: standard patterns, 10 & 12.
Inverawe	Taynuilt	Rainbow Trout	Mar. to Dec.	Inverawe Fisheries, Taynuilt, Argyll. Tel: (018662) 446.	3 lochs. Fly fishing only. Fishing lessons available.

Water	Location	Species	Season	Permit available from	Other information
Kinnabus Lochs (3)	Islay	Brown Trout Arctic Char	15 Mar. to 30 Sept.	I.G. Laurie, Newsagent, 19 Charlotte Street, Port Ellen, Isle of Islay. Tel: (01496) 302264.	Boat available. Fly only. No Sunday fishing. No catch limit. Ticket covers all five lochs (see Glen Astil).
Lochgilphead Lochs	Lochgilphead	Brown Trout	15 Mar. to 6 Oct.	Lochgilphead and District A.C. c/o The Sports Shop, 31 Lochnell Street, Lochgilphead PA31 8JL. Tel: (01546) 602390.	10 lochs. Fly only. No Sunday fishing.
Loch Loskin	1 mile from Dunoon	Brown/Sea Trout	1 Apr. to 30 Sept.	Dunoon & District Angling Club. Purdies of Argyll, 112 Argyll Street, Dunoon. Tel: (01369) 3232.	Fly only. Boat only.
Loch Lossit	Ballygrant	Brown Trout	15 Mar. to 6 Oct.	Port Askaig Stores, Port Askaig, Isle of Islay. Tel: (01496) 840245.	Average weight of fish caught: 8-16oz. Boats are available.
Loch Lussa	Campbeltown	Brown Trout	15 Mar. to 6 Oct.	A.P. MacGrory & Co., 16/20 Main Street, Campbeltown. Tel: (01586) 552132.	
Mishnish & Aros Lochs	Mull	Brown Trout	15 Mar. to 30 Sept. (Aros all year)	Tobermory A.A., c/o Brown's Shop, Tobermory. Tel: (01688) 2020.	Average weight of fish caught: 12oz. Popular flies: Soldier Palmer, Teal & Green. Spinners on Aros only. 3 boats available. No Sunday fishing.
Loch na Curraigh	Nr. Kilmelford	Brown Trout	15 Mar. to 6 Oct.	D. Graham, Combie Street, Oban. Sports Centre, Oban. Anglers' Corner, 2 John Street, Oban. Tel: (01631) 66374. Post Office, Kilmelford. Mr. Morrison, Ledaig Leisure, Benderloch.	The loch has some fat 8oz-1lb trout that sometimes rise freely. The south-end is floating bog and fishing from this bank is not advised. Popular flies: standard trout flies, wet or dry (12 & 14).
Loch nam Ban	Nr. Kilmelford	Brown Trout	15 Mar. to 6 Oct.	D. Graham, Combie Street, Oban. Sports Centre, Oban. Anglers' Corner, 2 John Street, Oban. Tel: (01631) 66374. Post Office, Kilmelford. Mr. Morrison, Ledaig Leisure, Benderloch.	Fish upto 2lbs have been caught on occasion. Popular flies: standard trout flies, wet or dry (12 & 14).
Loch na Sailm	Nr. Kilmelford	Brown Trout	15 Mar. to 6 Oct.	D. Graham, Combie Street, Oban. Sports Centre, Oban. Anglers' Corner, 2 John Street, Oban. Tel: (01631) 66374. Post Office, Kilmelford. Mr. Morrison, Ledaig Leisure, Benderloch.	The loch has been damned to improve fishing. Popular flies: Standard trout pattern, sizes 12 & 14.

Water	Location	Species	Season	Permit available from	Other information
Loch Nell	Nr. Oban	Salmon, Sea Trout Brown Trout Char	15 Mar. to 6 Oct. (Brown Trout)	D. Graham, Combie Street, Oban. Sports Centre, Oban. Anglers' Corner, 2 John Street, Oban. Tel: (01631) 66374. Post Office, Kilmelford. Mr. Morrison, Ledaig Leisure, Benderloch.	Popular flies: standard patterns Salmon and Sea Trout flies (8 &10). Fly, spinning and Bubble & fly are permitted. Boat available.
Oude Reservoir	14 miles from Oban	Brown Trout	15 Mar. to 6 Oct.	D. Graham, Combie Street, Oban. Sports Centre, Oban. Anglers' Corner, 2 John Street, Oban. Tel: (01631) 66374. Post Office, Kilmelford. Mr. Morrison, Ledaig Leisure, Benderloch.	Bank fishing can be difficult because of the fluctuating water level. Popular flies: standard trout flies, wet or dry (12 & 14). A boat is often located on this loch for periods.
Powderworks Dam	Argyll	Brown/ Rainbow Trout	15 Mar. to 5 Oct.	Kyles of Bute A.C., c/o Kames Hotel. Tel: (01700) 811489. Several shops in Kames and Tighnabruaich.	Fly and bait only, no spinning.
Loch Quien	Bute	Brown Trout	15 Mar. to 6 Oct.	Bute Estate Office, Rothesay, Isle of Bute. Tel: (01700) 502627.	Fly only. Salmon and trout fishing in sea around Bute.
Loch Scammadale	Kilninver	Salmon Sea Trout Brown Trout	1 June to 15 Oct. 15 Mar.- 6 Oct.	Mrs. McCorkindale Glenann', Kilninver, by Oban, Argyll. Tel: (0185 26) 282.	No Sunday fishing.
Loch Seil	Kilninver	Sea Trout Brown Trout	Apr. to Mid- Oct.	J.T.P. Mellor, Barndromin Farm, Knipoch, by Oban, Argyll. Tel: (0185 26) 273.	Boat on Loch.
Sior Lochs	Nr. Oban	Brown Trout	15 Mar. to 6 Oct.	D. Graham, Combie Street, Oban. Sports Centre, Oban. Anglers' Corner, 2 John Street, Oban. Tel: (01631) 66374. Post Office, Kilmelford. Mr. Morrison, Ledaig Leisure, Benderloch.	Popular flies: standard trout flies, wet or dry (12 & 14). The lochs fish best in April & May.
Loch Squabain	Mull	Salmon Sea Trout Brown Trout		Tackle & Books, Main Street, Tobermory, Mull. Tel: (01688) 2336.	Boat fishing only.
Loch Tarsan	8 miles from Dunoon	Brown Trout	1 Apr. to 30 Sept.	Dunoon & District Angling Club. Purdies of Argyll, 112 Argyll Street, Dunoon. Tel: (01369) 3232.	Fly only
Tighna- bruaich Reservoir (2 other lochs)	Tighna- bruaich	Brown/ Rainbow Trout	15 Mar. to 5 Oct.	Kyles of Bute Angling Club. Several shops in Kames and Tighnabruaich, Argyll. Kames Hotel. Tel: (01700) 811489.	Motor boat available for sea fishing.
Torr Loch	North end of Mull	Wild Brown Trout Sea Trout	April to Oct.	Tackle and Books, Main Street, Tobermory, Mull. Tel: (01688) 2336.	No Sunday fishing. 2 boats. Banks clear.

Water	Location	Species	Season	Permit available from	Other information
Loch Tralaig	Nr. Kilmelford	Brown Trout	15 Mar. to 30 Sept.	Mrs. E. Mellor, Barndromin Farm, Knipoch, by Oban. Tel: (0185 26) 273.	Fishing from bank only.
Loch Turamin	Isle of Colonsey	Brown Trout	15 Mar. to 30 Sept.	The Hotel, Isle of Colonsey, Argyll.	Fly fishing only. Boats are available.
Wee Feinn Loch	Nr. Kilmelford	Brown Trout	15 Mar. to 6 Oct.	D. Graham, Combie Street, Oban Sports Centre, Oban. Anglers' Corner, 2 John Street, Oban. Tel: (01631) 66374. Post Office, Kilmelford. Mr. Morrison, Ledaig Leisure, Benderloch.	A small loch that contains trout up to 2lbs. Popular flies: standard trout patterns, sizes 10 & 12.

Constituent Area Tourist Boards

Edinburgh Marketing
Waverley Market,
3 Princes Street,
Edinburgh EH2 2QP.
Tel: 0131-557 2727.

Forth Valley Tourist Board
Tourist Officer,
Tourist Information Centre,
Burgh Hall,
The Cross, Linlithgow,
West Lothian EH49 7AH.
Tel: (01506) 844600.

Loch Lomond, Stirling and Trossachs Tourist Board
Tourism Manager,
Loch Lomond,
Stirling and Trossachs Tourist Board,
41 Dumbarton Road,
Stirling FK8 2LQ.
Tel: (01786) 475019.

St. Andrews and North East Fife Tourist Board
Tourism Manager,
St. Andrews and North East Fife Tourist Board,
70 Market Street,
St. Andrews,
Fife KY16 9NU.
Tel: (01334) 74609.

Kirkcaldy District Council
Tourist Officer,
Kirkcaldy District Council,
Information Centre,
Durie Street,
Leven, Fife.
Tel: (01333) 429464.

East Lothian Tourist Board
Tourism Director,
East Lothian Tourist Board,
Brunton Hall,
Musselburgh, EH21 6AE.
Tel: 0131-665 3711.

Other Tourist Organisations
MIDLOTHIAN

RIVER PURIFICATION BOARD
FORTH RIVER PURIFICATION BOARD
Clearwater House,
Herriot Watt Research Park,
Avenue North,
Edinburgh EH14 4AP.
Tel: 0131-449 7296.

RIVERS

Water	Location	Species	Season	Permit available from	Other information
Allan	Bridge of Allan	Salmon Sea Trout Brown Trout	15 Mar. to 31 Oct. 15 Mar. to 6 Oct.	Country Pursuits, 46 Henderson Street, Bridge of Allan. Tel: (01786) 834495.	
Almond	Cramond	Salmon Sea Trout Brown Trout	1 Feb. to 31 Oct. 15 Mar. to 6 Oct.	Country Life, Balgreen Road, Edinburgh. Tel: 0131-337 6230. Post Office, Davidsons Mains, Edinburgh.	Mouth to Old Cramond Brig. East bank only.
	West Lothian	Salmon Sea Trout Brown Trout	1 Feb. to 31 Oct. 15 Mar. to 6 Oct.	City Sports, 18 Almondvale South, Livingston. Tel: (01506) 34822. Country Life, Balgreen Road, Edinburgh. Tel: 0131-337 6230.	20 miles of river.
Devon	Dollar	Salmon Sea Trout Brown Trout	15 Mar. to 30 Oct. 15 Mar. to 5 Oct.	Devon Angling Association, R. Breingan, 33 Redwell Pl., Alloa. Tel: (01259) 215185. Scobbie Sports, 2/4 Primrose Street, Alloa. Tel: (01259) 722661. D.W. Black, The Hobby & Model Shop, 10-12 New Row, Dunfermline. Tel: (01383) 722582. D. Crockart & Son, 47 King Street, Stirling. Tel: (01786) 734433.	No Sunday fishing. Devonside Bridge upstream with excluded stretches. Fly fishing only from 15 Mar.-12 Apr.

Water	Location	Species	Season	Permit available from	Other information
Devon cont.	Hillfoots	Salmon Sea Trout Brown Trout	15 Mar. to 31 Oct. 15 Mar. to 6 Oct.	Country Pursuits, 46 Henderson Street, Bridge of Allan. Tel: (01786) 834495.	No Sunday fishing.
Eden	Cupar Area	Brown Trout Sea Trout Salmon	15 Mar.to 5 Oct. 15 Feb. to 31 Oct.	J.&R. Caldwell, Foodstore & Fishing Tackle, Main Street, Methilhill, Fife. Tel: (01592) 712215.	All legal methods permitted.
Endrick	Drymen	Salmon Sea Trout Brown Trout	11 Feb. to 31 Oct. 15 Mar. to 6 Oct.	Loch Lomond Angling Improvement Association. Clements Chartered Accountants, 29 St. Vincent Place, Glasgow G1 2DT. Tel: 0141-221-0068.	Members only. No Sunday fishing. No worm fishing. Spinning restricted.
		Dace Chub Roach Eels	Open all year	The Bridge House, Drymen G63 0EY. Tel: (01360) 60355.	Fishes Spring to Autumn. Good dace shoals.
Esk	Musselburgh (Estuary to Buccleuch Estate both banks)	Salmon Sea Trout Brown Trout	15 Mar.to 31 Oct. 15 Mar. to 6 Oct.	Givan's Newsagent, 67 Eskside West, Musselburgh. Tel: 0131-665 3371. Country Life, Balgreen Road, Edinburgh. Tel: 0131-337 6230.	No Sunday fishing. A max. of 6 fish per day. Spinning reels are prohibited. Further regulations on permit.
Esk (North and South)	Midlothian	Brown/ Rainbow Trout Grayling	15 Mar to 6 Oct. 7 Oct.-14 Mar. special winter permit.	Esk Valley Angling Improvement Association. Kevin Burns, 53 Fernieside Crescent, Edinburgh. Tel: 0131-664 4685. F. & D. Simpson, 28/30 West Preston Street, Edinburgh EH8 9PZ. Tel: 0131-667 3058. Country Life, Balgreen Road, Edinburgh. Tel: 0131-337 6230. Laird & Dog Hotel, High Street, Lasswade. Bailiffs at water.	Fly rod and reel only to be used. Stocked at beginning of every month. Reductions for disabled, children and OAP's. Platform at Lasswade for disabled. Regulations on permit. Sunday fishing.
Forth	Stirling	Salmon Sea Trout Brown Trout	1 Feb.to 31 Oct. 15 Mar. to 6 Oct.	D. Crockart & Son, 47 King Street, Stirling. Tel: (01786) 73443. Mitchell's Tackle, 13 Bannockburn Road, Stirling. Tel: (01786) 445587. Country Pursuits, 45 Henderson Street, Bridge of Allan. Tel: (01786) 834495.	Information leaflet, maps, prices, rules, permits - Tel: (01786) 50403. No bait fishing before 1 Apr. or after 1 Sept.
	Gartmore Bridge-Buchlyvie (6[1/2]m beat)	Salmon Sea Trout Brown Trout	1 Feb.- 31 Oct.	Lawrence Angling, 268 Dumbarton Road, Glasgow G11 6TU. Tel: 0141-339 1085.	Fishing by any legal method permitted.
Fruin	Helensburgh	Salmon Sea Trout Brown Trout	11 Feb. to 31 Oct. 1 Mar. to 6 Oct.	Loch Lomond Angling Improvement Association. Clements Chartered Accountants, 29 St. Vincent Place, Glasgow. Tel: 0141-221-0068.	Members only. Fly fishing only.

Water	Location	Species	Season	Permit available from	Other information
Water of Leith	Edinburgh	Brown Trout	1 Apr. to 30 Sept.	Lothian Regional Council, Reception, George IV Bridge, Edinburgh. Tel: 0131-229 9292, ext. 3286. Post Office, 36 Main Street, Balerno. Post Office, Bridge Road, Colinton, Edinburgh. Tel: 0131-441 1003. Country Life, Balgreen Road, Edinburgh. Tel: 0131-337 6230.	Fly fishing above Slateford Road Bridge. No spinning. Regulations on permit.
Leven	Dumbarton	Salmon Sea Trout Brown Trout	11 Feb. to 31 Oct. 15 Mar. to 6 Oct.	Loch Lomond Angling Improvement Association. Clements Chartered Accountants, 29 St. Vincent Place, Glasgow. Tel: 0141-221-0068. Tackle & Guns, 920 Pollokshaws Road, Glasgow. Tel: 0141-632 2005. Country Lines, 29 Main Street, The Village, East Kilbride. Tel: (013552) 28952. Lawrence Angling, 268 Dumbarton Road, Glasgow. Tel: 0141-339 1085.	Members may fish all Association waters. No Sunday fishing. Day tickets available.
Leven (Fife)	Markinch to Leven	Brown Trout Salmon Sea Trout	15 Mar.-30 Sept. 11 Feb. to 15 Oct.	J. Caldwell, Newsagent & Fishing Tackle, Main Street, Methilhill, Fife. Tel: (01592) 712215.	All legal methods. No shrimp or prawn.
Teith	Callander	Salmon Sea trout Brown Trout	1 Feb. to 31 Oct.	J. Bayne, Main Street, Callander. Tel: (01877) 330218.	Information leaflet, maps, prices, rules, permits: Tel: (01786) 50403. No Sunday fishing.
				Country Pursuits, 46 Henderson Street, Bridge of Allan. Tel: (01786) 834495.	Season permits only.
	Stirling (Blue Banks)	Salmon Sea Trout	1 Feb. to 31 Oct.	D. Crockart & Son, 47 King Street, Stirling, Tel: (01786) 73443.	
	Gart Farm by Callander	Salmon Sea Trout	1 Feb. to 31 Oct.	Country Pursuits, 46 Henderson Street, Bridge of Allan. Tel: (01786) 834495.	Season permits only.
Tyne	Haddington	Brown Trout Rainbow Trout Sea Trout	15 Mar. to 6 Oct.	East Lothian Angling Association. J.S. Main, Saddlers, 87 High Street, Haddington. Tel: (0162 082) 2148. John Dickson & Son Ltd., 21 Frederick Street, Edinburgh EH2 2NE. Tel: 0131-225 4218. Country Life, Balgreen Road, Edinburgh. Tel: 0131-337 6230.	Twenty miles of river. No Sunday fishing. No threadlines. No spinning.

Please mention this Pastime Publications guide

Water	Location	Species	Season	Permit available from	Other information

LOCHS & RESERVOIRS

Water	Location	Species	Season	Permit available from	Other information
Loch Achray	By Callander	Brown Trout Perch Pike	15 Mar. to 6 Oct.	Forestry Commission, Queen Elizabeth Forest Park Visitor Centre, Aberfoyle. Tel: (01877) 382383. Loch Achray Hotel, Trossachs. Tel: (01877) 376229/376240. Bayne's Fishing Tackle Shop, Callander.	Bank fishing only.
Loch Ard	Kinlochard	Brown Trout	15 Mar. to 6 Oct.	Altskeith Hotel, Kinlochard FK8 3TL. Tel: (01877) 387266.	Average weight of fish caught: 12oz. Popular flies: Silver Butcher, Kate McLaren, Alexandra. Fly fishing only. Boats are available.
Loch Arklet	By Inversnaid	Brown Trout	15 Mar. to 27 Sept.	Strathclyde Water, 419 Balmore Road, Glasgow G22 6NU or at Loch Arklet.	Average weight of fish caught: 8 to 12oz. Popular flies: Silver Butcher, Grouse & Claret, Black Pennel, Greenwell's Glory. No live bait allowed. Rowing boats only are available.
Beecraigs Loch	Linlithgow	Brown Trout Rainbow Trout Brook Trout	1 Mar. to 31 Oct.	Beecraigs Country Park. The Park Centre, nr. Linlithgow. Tel: (01506) 844516.	Fly fishing only. Boat fishing only. Night fishing 11pm to 7am, May to August. Advance booking essential.
Bonaly Reservoir	Edinburgh	Brown/Rainbow Trout	1 Apr. to 30 Sept.	None Required.	
Bowden Springs	Linlithgow	Rainbow/Brown Trout	3 Jan. to 23 Dec.	W.R. Martin, Bowden Springs Fishery, Carribber, Linlithgow. Tel: (01506) 847269.	Bank and boat fishing. Fly fishing only. Minimum size 1 lb. Corporate days.
Cameron Reservoir	St. Andrews	Brown Trout	Mid-Apr. to End-Sept.	St. Andrews Angling Club, Secretary, Mr. P. Malcolm, 54 St. Nicholas Street, St. Andrews. Tel: (01334) 76347. The bailiff at the fishing hut on Cameron Reservoir. During season Tel: (01334) 84236.	Average weight of fish caught: 1lb. Fly fishing only. 6 boats are available. Sunday fishing available.
Upper Carriston Reservoir	Nr. Markinch	Brown Trout	1 Apr. to 30 Sept.	J. & R. Caldwell Foodstore & Fishing Tackle, Main Street, Methilhill, Fife. Tel: (01592) 712215.	Average weight of fish caught: 1lb to 1lb 8oz. Fly fishing only. Bank fishing only - maximum 20 anglers. Day session: 10am-5pm. Evening session: 6pm-11pm
Carron Valley Reservoir	Denny	Brown Trout	13 Apr. to 19 Sept.	Director of Finance, Central Regional Council, Viewforth, Stirling. Tel: (01786) 443000.	Boat fishing only.

94

Water	Location	Species	Season	Permit available from	Other information
Clubbiedean Reservoir	Edinburgh	Brown/ Rainbow Trout	1 Apr. to 30 Sept.	Lothian Regional Council, Pentland Hills Regional Park H.Q., Boghall Farm, Biggar Road, Edinburgh. Tel: 0131-445 5969.	Three boats. Bag limit 6 trout. Fly fishing only. Sessions: May to August.
Cocksburn Loch	Bridge of Allan	Brown Trout	1 Apr. to 6 Oct.	Country Pursuits, 46 Henderson Street, Bridge of Allan. Tel: (01786) 834495.	Average weight of fish caught: 8-12oz. Boat fishing only. Popular flies: small dark flies.
Crosswood Reservoir	West Calder	Brown Trout Brook Trout Rainbow Trout	1 Apr. to 30 Sept.	Lothian Regional Council, Pentland Hills Regional Park H.Q., Boghall Farm, Biggar Road, Edinburgh. Tel: 0131-445 5969. Dept. of Water & Drainage, Lomond House, Beveridge Square, Livingston. Tel: (01506) 414004.	Three boats available. 1 boat available - Boghall Farm. 2 boats available - Livingston. Fly fishing only.
Loch Drunkie	Aberfoyle	Brown Trout	15 Mar. to 6 Oct.	Forestry Commission Queen Elizabeth Forest Park Visitor Centre, Aberfoyle.	Bank fishing only.
Loch Fitty	Kingseat, Dunfermline	Salmon Brown/ Rainbow Trout	1 Mar. to Xmas	The Fishing Lodge, Loch Fitty, Dunfermline, Fife. Tel: (01383) 620666.	Boat and Bank fly fishing. Day - 10am-5pm. Evenings - 5.30pm-dark. Reductions for single anglers, and Father & schoolboy Son'. Boats.
Gartmorn Dam Fishery	Nr. Alloa	Brown Trout	1 Apr. to 30 Sept.	Sept to April: Speirs Centre, 29 Primrose Street, Alloa FK10 1JJ. Tel: (01259) 213131. April to Sept: Visitor Centre, Gartmorn Dam Country Park, by Sauchie FK10 3AZ. Tel: (01259) 214319.	Average weight of fish caught: 1lb 4oz. Popular flies: Nymphs, Buzzers, Olives, Wickhams. 9 boats available. Disabled anglers' wheelyboat. 2 sessions: 9am-5pm & 5pm-Dusk.
Gladhouse Reservoir	Midlothian	Brown Trout	1 Apr. to 30 Sept.	Lothian Regional Council, Pentland Hills Regional Park H.Q., Boghall Farm, Biggar Road, Edinburgh. Tel: 0131-445 5969.	Average weight of fish caught: 1lb to 2lbs. Local Nature Reserve. Double-sessions: May-August Day: 8am-4.30pm. Evening: 5pm-Sunset, plus 1 hour. Sunday fishing. Fly fishing only.
Glencorse Reservoir	Penicuik	Brown Trout Brook Trout Rainbow Trout	1 Apr. to 30 Sept.	Lothian Regional Council, Pentland Hills Regional Park H.Q., Boghall Farm, Biggar Road, Edinburgh. Tel: 0131-445 5969.	Fly fishing only. 4 boats. Sessions: May to Aug.
Glen Finglas Reservoir	By Callander	Brown Trout	15 Mar. to 27 Sept.	Strathclyde Water, 419 Balmore Road, Glasgow G22 6NU or at Glen Finglas.	Average weight of fish caught: 8 to 12oz. Popular flies: Silver Butcher, Grouse & Claret, Black Pennel, Greenwell's Glory. No live bait allowed. Rowing boat only, are available.

Water	Location	Species	Season	Permit available from	Other information
Loch Glow	Cleish Hills, Nr. Kelty	Brown Trout	15 Mar. to 6 Oct.	Tackle shops in Dunfermline, Cowdenbeath, Kelty & Kinross.	Fly, bait & spinning. Regularly stocked with brown trout; some tagged fish. Further information Mr. J.W. Mill, Tel: (01383) 722128.
Harlaw Reservoir	Balerno	Brown/ Rainbow Trout	1 Apr. to 30 Sept.	Day tickets: Fleming's Grocery Shop, 42 Main Street, Balerno. Tel: 0131-449 3833. Season Permits: Dalmeny Estate Office, South Queensferry, West Lothian.	Average weight of fish caught: 1-2lbs. Fly fishing only. Bank fishing only. Season tickets issued by ballot - applications must be in by 1st March.
Harperrig Reservoir	West Calder	Brown Trout	1 Apr. to 30 Sept.	Dept. of Water & Drainage, Lomond House, Beveridge Square, Livingston. Tel: (01506) 414004. Bank fishing permits from machine at reservoir.	Correct coins required for machine, 50p 10p 5p denominations. Four boats and bank fishing. No Sunday fishing. Fly fishing only.
Hopes Reservoir	Gifford	Brown Trout	1 Apr. to 30 Sept.	Lothian Regional Council, Dept. of Water & Drainage, Alderston House, Haddington. Tel: (0162 082) 4131, ext. 217.	2 boats.
Loch Katrine	Stronach-lachar	Brown Trout	15 Mar. to 27 Sept.	Strathclyde Water, 419 Balmore Road, Glasgow G22 6NU or at Stronachlachar.	Average weight of fish caught: 8 to 12oz. Popular flies: Silver Butcher, Grouse & Claret, Black Pennel, Greenwell's Glory. No live bait allowed. Rowing boats only are available.
Lake of Menteith	Port of Menteith	Rainbow Trout	2 Apr. to 29 Oct.	Lake of Menteith Fisheries Ltd., Port of Menteith, Perthshire. Tel: (01877) 385664.	28 boats are available. No bank fishing.
Lindores Loch	Newburgh	Brown/ Rainbow Trout	Mar. to 30 Nov.	F.G.A. Hamilton, The Byre, Kindrochet, St. Fillans PH6 2JZ. Tel: (01764) 685337.	Two sessions. 9 am - 5 pm 5 pm - 10 pm
Linlithgow Loch	Linlithgow	Brown/ Rainbow Trout	15 Mar. to 6 Oct.	Tel: (01831) 288921.	Average weight of fish caught: 1lb 8oz. Popular flies: black lures, Green Peter, Grouse & Claret, Buzzers. Fly fishing only. 12 boats are available.
Lochore	Ballingry	Brown/ Rainbow Trout	1 Mar. to 30 Nov.	Lochore Meadows Country Park, Crosshill, Lochgelly, Fife. Tel: (01592) 860086.	Sessions: any 8 hours till dusk, bank. Boats: Day, 9am-4.30pm, Evening - 5 pm-dusk. Fly fishing. Spinning and Bait fishing from bank from 1 June.

Water	Location	Species	Season	Permit available from	Other information
Loch Lomond	Balloch to Ardlui	Salmon Sea Trout Brown Trout Pike Roach Perch	11 Feb. to 31 Oct. 15 Mar.-6 Oct. No close season	Loch Lomond Angling Improvement Association Clements Chartered Accountants, 29 St. Vincent Place, Glasgow. Tel: 0141-221-0068. Country Lines, 29 Main Street, The Village, East Kilbride. Tel: (013552) 28952. Lawrence Angling, 268 Dumbarton Road, Glasgow. Tel: 0141-339 1085.	Boats for hire locally. No Sunday fishing. Day permits available.
	Ardlui	Salmon Sea Trout Brown Trout Pike	11 Feb. to 31 Oct. 15 Mar. to 6 Oct.	Ardlui Hotel, Loch Lomond. Tel: (0130 14) 243.	Popular flies: Silver Victor, Mallard, Claret. Other baits: Toby, Rapala, Sprat. Boats are available.
	Balmaha	Salmon Sea Trout Pike	Mar to Oct. All year.	MacFarlane & Son, The Boatyard, Balmaha. Tel: (0136 087) 214.	Boats and outboard motors are available. Rods available. Permits sold.
	Rowardennan by Drymen	Salmon Sea Trout Brown Trout Pike	11 Feb. to 31 Oct. 15 Mar. to 6 Oct. All year.	Rowardennan Hotel, Rowardennan. Tel: (01360) 870273.	Average weight of fish caught: Salmon - 9lbs, Sea Trout - 3 lbs, Brown Trout - 1lb 12oz. Other baits: Toby for trawling.
	Inverbeg	Salmon Sea Trout Brown Trout Pike Perch	11 Feb. to 31 Oct. 15 Mar. to 6 Oct. All Year.	Inverbeg Caravan Park, Inverbeg. Tel: (01436) 860267	Popular flies: March Brown, Peter Ross. Live bait allowed.
Maltings Fishery	West Barns, Dunbar EH42 1RG.	Brown/ Rainbow Trout	All year for Rainbow.	Dunbar Trout Farm, Tel: (01368) 863244. (Or at the fishery).	Fly only. Maximum fly size no. 10 long shank.
Morton Fishery	Mid Calder	Rainbow Trout	11 Mar. to 29 Oct.	Morton Fishery, Morton Reservoir, Mid Calder, W. Lothian. Tel: (01506) 882293.	Fly fishing only. Advance bookings. Double sessions May-Aug, 9 am-5 pm, 5 pm-dusk. Bag limits 3-6 fish per rod.
North Third	By Cambus-barron	Rainbow/ Brown Trout	15 Mar. to 31 Oct.	North Third Trout Fishery, "Greathill", Cambusbarron, Stirling. Tel: (01786) 471967.	Fly fishing only. Boat and bank. Day permits only. Advance bookings advisable. Fishery record for rainbow trout 19lbs 2oz. Loch stocked in 1992 with American brook trout.
Lochan Reoidhe	Aberfoyle	Brown Trout	15 Mar. to 6 Oct.	Forestry Commission Queen Elizabeth Forest Park Visitor Centre, Aberfoyle.	Fly fishing only. Limited rods. Advance bookings accepted.

Water	Location	Species	Season	Permit available from	Other information
Selm Muir Loch	Nr. Livingston	Rainbow Trout	All year	Selm Muir Loch.	Average weight of fish caught: 1lb 4oz. Popular flies: Montana Nymph, small black lures. Other baits: maggots, sweetcorn, no spinning.
Swanswater Fishery	Stirling	Rainbow/ Brown Trout	All year for Rainbow	Swanswater Fishery.	Average weight of fish caught: 1lb 12oz. Popular flies: Viva, Black Pennel. Fly fishing only. 3 boats are available. Smokehouse & farmshop.
Threipmuir Reservoir	Balerno	Brown/ Rainbow Trout	1 Apr. to 30 Sept.	Day tickets: Flemings, Grocer, 42 Main Street, Balerno. Tel: 0131-449 3833. Season permits: Dalmeny Estate Office, South Queensferry, West Lothian.	Average weight of fish caught: 1-2lbs. Fly fishing only. Bank fishing only. Season tickets issued by ballot - applications must be in by 1st March.
Loch Venachar	Callander	Brown Trout	15 Mar. to 6 Oct.	J. Bayne, Main Street, Callander. Tel: (01877) 330218.	Boats for hire.
Loch Voil	Balquhidder	Brown Trout Salmon Sea Trout Char	15 Mar. to 6 Oct.	Stronvar Country House Hotel, Balquhidder FK19 8PB. Tel: (01877) 384688. C.M. Oldham & I.T. Emslie, Muirlaggan, Balquidder, Lochearnhead FK19 8PB. Tel: (01877) 384219.	Hotel Guests only. Advanced bookings necessary. Popular flies: Blae & Black, Kate McLaren, Grouse & Claret, Black Spider, Greenwell's Glory, Butcher, Professor (size 12). Other baits: spinners, rapala, toby, kynoch killer for salmon. 5 boats are available.

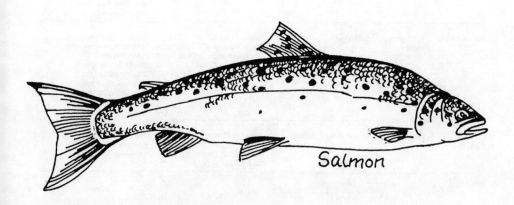

Salmon

Constituent Area Tourist Boards

City of Dundee Tourist Board
Director,
City of Dundee Tourist Board,
Tourism Information Department,
4 City Square,
Dundee DD1 3BA.
Tel: (01382) 23141, ext. 4384

Perthshire Tourist Board
Director of Tourism,
Tourist Information Centre,
45 High Street,
Perth PH1 5TJ.
Tel: (01738) 627958.

Angus Tourist Board
Tourist Manager,
Tourist Information Centre,
Market Place, Arbroath,
Angus DD11 1HR.
Tel: (01241) 876680.

RIVER PURIFICATION BOARD
TAY RIVER PURIFICATION BOARD
1 South Street,
Perth PH2 8NJ.
Tel: (01738) 627989.

RIVERS

Water	Location	Species	Season	Permit available from	Other information
Braan	Amulree	Brown Trout	15 Mar. to 6 Oct.	Bunnie's Tearooom. Post Office, Amulree. Tel: (01350) 725200.	Fly fishing only.
	Cochill Burn	Brown Trout	15 Mar to 6 Oct.	Kettles of Dunkeld, Atholl Street, Dunkeld. Tel: (01350) 727556.	Fly fishing only.
Dean	Strathmore	Brown Trout	15 Mar. to 6 Oct.	Strathmore Angling Improvement Association, Mrs. M.C. Milne, 1 West Park Gardens, Dundee. Tel: (01382) 67711.	
Devon	Hillfoots, Tillicoultry to Crook of Devon	Salmon Sea Trout Brown Trout	15 Mar. to 31 Oct. 15 Mar.- 6 Oct.	Country Pursuits, 46 Henderson Street, Bridge of Allan. Tel: (01786) 834495.	Fly fishing only from: 15 March to 12 April.
Dochart	Killin	Brown Trout	15 Mar. to 6 Oct.	J.H. Rough, J.R. News, Main Street, Killin. Tel: (01567) 820362. Clachaig Hotel, Killin. Tel: (01567) 820270.	All legal lures permitted. Fly only on lower beat.
Earn	Crieff	Salmon Sea Trout Brown Trout	1 Feb. to 15 Oct. 15 Mar.- 6 Oct.	Crieff Angling Club. Adam Boyd Newsagents, 39 King Street, Crieff. Tel: (01764) 653871.	No shrimp, prawn, diving minnow or floats. No bait before 1st May.
Earn	By Crieff	Salmon Sea Trout Brown Trout	1 Feb. to 31 Oct. 15 Mar.- 6 Oct.	Country Pursuits, 46 Henderson Street, Bridge of Allan. Tel: (01786) 834495.	(Lower Strowan Beat) Permit available for season only (day per week throughout season).
Ericht	Glenericht	Salmon Brown Trout	1 Apr.-15 Oct. 15 Mar. to 6 Oct.	Bridge of Cally Hotel, Blairgowrie, Perthshire. Tel: (01250) 886231.	Fly fishing only.
	Craighall (upper)	Salmon Brown Trout	15 Jan.-15 Oct. 15 Mar to 6 Oct.	A.L. Rattray, Craighall, Blairgowrie PH10 7JB. Tel: (01250) 874749 or (01738) 30926.	Subject to availability.

Water	Location	Species	Season	Permit available from	Other information
Garry	Blair Atholl	Brown Trout	15 Mar. to 6 Oct.	Highland Shop, Blair Atholl. Tel: (01796) 481303.	Any legal method permitted.
Isla	Strathmore	Brown Trout	15 Mar. to 6 Oct.	Strathmore Angling Improvement Association, Mrs. M.C. Milne, 1 West Park Gardens, Dundee. Tel: (01382) 67711.	
Lochay	Killin	Brown Trout Pike Perch	15 Mar. to 6 Oct.	J.R. Rough, J.R. News, Main Street, Killin. Tel: (01567) 820362.	Fly only on upper beat.
Lunan	Arbroath	Sea/ Brown Trout	15 Mar. to 6 Oct.	Arbroath Cycle and Tackle Centre, 274 High Street, Arbroath. Tel: (01241) 73467.	Fly, bait or spinning.
Lyon	Aberfeldy	Salmon	15 Jan. to 15 Oct.	Fortingall Hotel, Fortingall, by Aberfeldy. Tel: (01887) 830367.	No Sunday fishing. Max. 5 rods on each of 2 beats. Maps, tackle etc. available. (6 miles single bank).
	Tirinie Fishings	Salmon Brown Trout	15 Jan.-15 Oct. 15 Mar.- 6 Oct.	Coshieville Hotel, By Aberfeldy PH15 2NE.	Max. 4 rods. No bait fishing. No Sunday fishing. Boat & ghillie available for hire.
South Esk	Kirriemuir	Salmon Sea Trout	16 Feb. to 31 Oct.	H. Burness, Kirriemuir Angling Club, 13 Clova Road, Kirriemuir. Tel: (01575) 573456.	No permits on Saturdays. No Sunday fishing. Fly only in parts in low water. Booking advisable. Map available.
Tay	Aberfeldy	Brown Trout	15 Mar. to 6 Oct.	Jamiesons Sports Shop, 41 Dunkeld Street, Aberfeldy. Tel: (01887) 20385.	Fly only until 1st May.
		Salmon Brown Trout	15 Jan.-15 Oct. 15 Mar. to 6 Oct.	Weem Hotel, Weem, by Aberfeldy. Tel: (01887) 820381.	Salmon - any legal means. Trout - fly or small mepps only.
		Salmon Sea Trout	15 Jan. to 15 Oct.	Country Pursuits, 46 Henderson Street, Bridge of Allan. Tel: (01786) 834495.	(Killiechassie Beat) 4 rods maximum. Ghillie available. No prawns/shrimps after 1 Sept.
		Salmon Sea Trout	15 Jan. to 15 Oct.	Country Pursuits, 46 Henderson Street, Bridge of Allan. Tel: (01786) 834495.	(Derculich Beat) Maximum 3 rods. Ghillie available. No bait.
		Salmon Sea Trout	15 Jan. to 15 Oct.	Country Pursuits, 46 Henderson Street, Bridge of Allan. Tel: (01786) 834495.	(Lower Farleyer) 4 rods maximum. Ghillie Available. No Prawns/shrimps after 1 Sept.
		Salmon Sea Trout	15 Jan. to 15 Oct.	Country Pursuits, 46 Henderson Street, Bridge of Allan. Tel: (01786) 834495.	(Moness Beat) Maximum 3 rods. Boat & ghillie available. No prawns/shrimps after 1 Sept.

Water	Location	Species	Season	Permit available from	Other information
Tay cont.		Salmon Sea Trout	15 Jan. to 15 Oct.	Country Pursuits, 46 Henderson Street, Bridge of Allan. Tel: (01786) 834495.	(Lower Bolrocks Beat) 4 rods maximum. Boat & ghillie available. No prawns/shrimps after 1 Sept.
	Grandtully	Salmon Brown Trout Grayling	15 Jan.-15 Oct. 15 Mar. to 6 Oct.	Country Pursuits, 46 Henderson Street, Bridge of Allan. Tel: (01786) 834495.	Fly or spinning. Boat & ghillie available. Booking advisable. Rod hire and tackle. 5-rod beat.
		Salmon Sea Trout	15 Jan. to 15 Oct.	Country Pursuits, 46 Henderson Street, Bridge of Allan. Tel: (01786) 834495.	(Findyate Beat) Maximum 3 rods. Boat & ghillie available. No prawns/shrimps after 1 Sept. Good Spring beat.
		Salmon Sea Trout	15 Jan. to 15 Oct.	Country Pursuits, 46 Henderson Street, Bridge of Allan. Tel: (01786) 834495.	(Clochfoldich Beat) Maximum 3 rods. Boat & ghillie available. No prawns/shrimps after 1 Sept. Good Spring beat.
	Dalguise	Salmon	15 Jan. to 15 Oct.	Country Pursuits, 46 Henderson Street, Bridge of Allan. Tel: (01786) 834495. Finlayson Hughes, 29 Barossa Place, Perth. Tel: (01738) 30926.	1¼ miles both banks. Boats & ghillies available.
	Dunkeld	Salmon Brown Trout	15 Jan.-15 Oct. 15 Mar.-6 Oct.	Stakis Hotels Ltd., Dunkeld House Hotel, Dunkeld. Tel: (01350) 727771.	Two boats with two rods. Experienced ghillies. 8 bank rods. Tuition. No salmon fishing on Sundays. Booking advisable.
		Brown Trout Grayling	15 Mar. to 6 Oct.	Kettles of Dunkeld, Atholl Street, Dunkeld. Tel: (01350) 727556.	Fly fishing only. Tackle hire.
		Salmon Sea Trout	15 Jan. to 15 Oct.	Country Pursuits, 46 Henderson Street, Bridge of Allan. Tel: (01786) 834495.	(Upper Newtyle Beat) Maximum 5 rods. Boat and ghillie available. No prawns/shrimps after 1 Sept.
		Salmon Sea Trout	15 Jan. to 15 Oct.	Country Pursuits, 46 Henderson Street, Bridge of Allan. Tel: (01786) 834495.	(Lower Newtyle Beat) Maximum 5 rods. Boat & ghillie available. No prawns/shrimps after 1 Sept.
	Stanley	Salmon Sea Trout Brown Trout	15 Jan.- 13 Oct. 12 Mar.- 6 Oct.	Tayside Hotel, Stanley, Nr. Perth. Tel: (01738) 828249. Tackle & Guns, 920 Pollokshaws Road, Glasgow. Tel: 0141-632 2005 (Jan-May Spring Salmon)	Day permits available May-July. Ghillies by arrangement. Advisable to book in advance.

Water	Location	Species	Season	Permit available from	Other information
Tay cont.	Perth	Salmon Sea Trout Flounder Roach	15 Jan. to 15 Oct.	Director of Leisure & Recreation, Perth & Kinross District Council, 3 High Street, Perth. Tel: (01738) 39911, ext. 3603, (Monday to Friday). Tourist Information Centre, 45 High Street, Perth PH1 5TJ. Tel: (01738) 638353 Weekends & public holidays.	Advisable to book in advance. Only 20 permits per day. Only 2 permits in advance by any one person. No weekly permits.
Tilt	Blair Atholl	Salmon	End-May to 15 Oct.	The Highland Shop, Blair Atholl. Tel: (01796) 481303.	(Private Beat, 3 miles) Booking advised. Fly or spinning only.
Tummel	Pitlochry	Salmon Sea Trout	15 Jan. to 15 Oct.	Pitlochry Angling Club c/o Tourist Information Centre, Pitlochry. Tel: Mr. Gardiner, (01796) 472157 (eve./weekends).	Permits available Monday to Saturday. Booking in advance is advisable.
	Pitlochry to Ballinluig	Brown Trout Grayling	15 Mar. to 6 Oct.	Tourist Information Centre, Pitlochry. Atholl Sports, Atholl Road, Pitlochry. Mitchells of Pitlochry, 23 Atholl Road, Pitlochry. Tel: (01796) 472613. Season tickets and club enquiries to: Pitlochry Angling Club Secretary, Mr. Harriman, Sunnyknowe, Nursing Home Brae, Pitlochry. Tel: (01796) 472484 (eve./weekends).	Pitlochry Angling water. Five miles of river, both banks. Map and rules on permits. Grayling permits available in the winter.
	Moulinearn to Ballinluig	Salmon Sea Trout	15 Jan. to 15 Oct.	Pitlochry Angling Club c/o Tourist Information Centre, Pitlochry. Tel: Mr. Gardiner (01796) 472157 (eve./weekends).	Only available July & August.
Tummel (Upper)	Kinloch Rannoch	Brown Trout	15 Mar. to 6 Oct.	E.M. Beattie (Sec.), 2 Schiehallion Place, Kinloch Rannoch. Tel: (01882) 632261. Local shops & hotels.	Average weight of fish caught: 12oz. Other baits: spinning and live.

LOCHS & RESERVOIRS

Water	Location	Species	Season	Permit available from	Other information
Loch Bainnie	Spittal of Glenshee	Brown Trout	18 Mar. to 11 Aug.	Invercauld Estates Office, Braemar AB35 5XQ. Tel: Braemar 41224.	Boat available from: Mr. G. Kerr, Gamekeeper, Wester Binzean, Glenshee. Tel: Glenshee 206. No spinning or use of live bait.
Ben Vrackie Loch	By Pitlochry	Brown Trout	15 Mar. to 30 Sept.	Mr. Seaton, Gamekeeper's House, Baledmund Estate, Pitlochry.	Average weight of fish caught: 8oz. Any legal method permitted.
Blair Walker Pond	Blair Atholl	(Stocked) Brown/ Rainbow Trout	15 Mar. to 6 Oct.	The Highland Shop, Blair Atholl. Tel: (01796) 481303.	Fly only.

Water	Location	Species	Season	Permit available from	Other information
Butterstone Loch	Dunkeld	Rainbow/ Brown Trout	20 Mar. to 22 Oct.	The Bailiff, Lochend Cottage, Butterstone, by Dunkeld. Tel: (01350) 724238.	Fly fishing only. 15 Boats. Day Session: 9 am-5 pm. Evening: 5.30 pm-dusk.
Castlehill Reservoir	Glendevon	Brown Trout	1 Apr. to 30 Sept.	Fife Reg. Council, Craig Mitchell House. Flemington Road, Glenrothes. Tel: (01592) 754411). Glendevon Treatment Works. Tel: (01259) 781453.	Fly fishing only. Boat £10 inc. 2 rods. Bank £3.
Loch Dochart	by Crianlarich	Salmon Brown Trout	1 Feb. to 6 Oct.	Portnellan House, by Crianlarich FK20 8QS. Tel: (01838) 300284.	Popular flies: Black Pennel, Black & Peacock, Mullard, Claret. Any legal method permitted. Boats available.
Dunalastair Reservoir	Kinloch Rannoch	Brown Trout Pike	15 Mar. to 6 Oct.	Lassintullich Fisheries. Tel: (01882) 632206. Lochgarry Cottage (Isla Blair), Tel: (01882) 632354. Dunalastair Hotel, Tel: (01882) 632323.	Five boats. No bank fishing. Fly fishing only for trout - average weight: 1lb 9oz.
Loch Earn	Lochearn-head	Brown Trout	15 Mar. to 6 Oct.	Clachan Cottage Hotel, Lochside, Lochearnhead. Tel: (01567) 830247.	Fishing Mon. to Sun. Fly rod, Fly reel and any legal method, max. B.S. 4lbs. Min. taking size 8″. Prohibited baits: diving minnow.
		Brown/ Rainbow Trout	Mar. to Oct.	St. Fillans Post Office, St. Fillans.	Average weight of fish caught: 12oz-2lbs. The loch is regularly stocked.
Loch Eigheach	Moor of Rannoch	Brown Trout	15 Mar. to 6 Oct.	Rannoch & District Angling Club, John Brown, The Square, Kinloch Rannoch. Tel: (01882) 632268.	Bank fishing only.
Errochty Dam	Nr. Blair Atholl	Brown Trout Pike	15 Mar. to 6 Oct. No close season	The Highland Shop, Blair Atholl. Tel: (01796) 481303.	Any legal method permitted.
Loch Faskally	Pitlochry	Salmon Brown Trout Pike Perch	May to 15 Oct. Mar. to Sept.	Mr. D. McLaren, Pitlochry Boating Station, Loch Faskally, Pitlochry. Tel: (01796) 472919/472759	Any legal lure for salmon and trout. Boats available. Cafe facilities. Fishing tackle bait when available. Car park.
Loch Freuchie	Amulree	Brown Trout Pike	15 Mar. to 6 Oct.	Bunnies Tearoom. Post Office, Amulree. Tel: (01350) 725200.	Fly fishing only. Coarse fishing.
Glendevon (Upper & Lower Reservoir)	Glendevon	Brown Trout	1 Apr. to 30 Sept.	Fife Regional Council, Craig Mitchell House. Flemington Road, Glenrothes. Tel: (01592) 754411. Glendevon Treatment Works. Tel: (0125981) 453.	Fly fishing only. No Sunday fishing. Bank fishing allowed on Lower Glendevon. Boat £10 incl. 2 rods. Bank £3.

Water	Location	Species	Season	Permit available from	Other information
Glenfarg	Glenfarg	Brown Trout	1 Apr. to 30 Sept.	Fife Regional Council, Craig Mitchell House, Flemington Road, Glenrothes. Tel: (01592) 754411. Glenfarg Treatment Works. Tel: (015773) 561.	Fly fishing only. No Sunday fishing. Boat available.
Heathery-ford	Just off Junction 6 on M90 at Kinross	Brown/ Rainbow Trout	Mid-March to Dec.	Kinross Trout Fishery, office on site. Tel: (01577) 864212	All bank fishing, top quality trout. Trout master water. Fly fishing only.
Holl	Lomond Hills	Brown Trout	1 Apr. to 30 Sept.	Fife Regional Council, Craig Mitchell House, Flemington Road, Glenrothes. Tel: (01592) 754411.	Fly fishing only. No Sunday fishing. Boat available.
Loch Iubhair	Nr. Crianlarich	Salmon Brown Trout	1 Feb. to 6 Oct.	Portnellan House, by Crianlarich FK20 8QS. Tel: (01838) 300284.	Popular flies: Black Pennel, Black & Peacock, Mullard, Claret. Any legal method permitted. Boats are available.
Loch Kinardochy	Tummel bridge	Brown Trout	15 Mar. to 6 Oct.	Mitchells of Pitlochry, 23 Atholl Road, Pitlochry PH16 5BX. Tel: (01796) 472613.	Fly fishing from boat only. Advance booking recommended.
Lochan- na- Laraig	Killin	Trout	15 Mar. to 6 Oct.	J.H. Rough, J.R. News, Main Street, Killin. Tel: (01567) 820362.	All legal lures.
Loch Lee	Glen Esk	Brown Trout Arctic Char	1 May to 12 Aug.	Head Keeper, Invermark, Glenesk, by Brechin DD9 7YZ. Tel: (01356) 670208.	Average weight of fish caught: 8oz to 12oz. Popular flies: any small dark flies. 3 boats - 3 rods per boat. No Sunday fishing. No bank fishing.
Loch Leven	Kinross	Brown Trout (Loch Leven strain)	2nd Apr. to 6th Oct.	Lochleven Fisheries, The Pier, Kinross. Tel: (01577) 863407.	Fly and boat fishing only.
Lintrathen Reservoir	Kirriemuir	Brown Trout	1 Apr. to 6 Oct.	Lintrathen Angling Club Jack Yule, 61 Hillrise, Kirriemuir, Angus DD8 4JS. Tel: Loch (01575) 560327. Tel: Home (01575) 573816. Club bookings: Dr. Parratt, 91 Strathearn Road, Broughty Ferry, Dundee. Tel: (01382) 77305. (Not after start of season).	20 boats & 2 disabled boats. Sunday fishing. Max. catch 15 fish per boat. Tel. for details of sessions and backwater dam. Bank fishing only.
Monikie	Monikie	Brown Trout	Beg. Apr. to 6 Oct.	Tel: Newbigging 300.	Average weight of fish caught: 1lb 4oz. Popular flies: Bibio, Kate McLaren, Ace of Spades. Boats: (10) Island Pond, (4) North Pond, (4) Crombie. Fly only. Boat only.

Water	Location	Species	Season	Permit available from	Other information
Loch Nan Ean	Dalmunzie	Brown Trout	18 Mar. to 11 Aug.	Invercauld Estates Office, Braemar AB35 5XQ. Tel: Braemar 41224.	No spinning or use of live bait permitted.
Loch Rannoch	Kinloch Rannoch	Brown Trout	15 Mar. to 6 Oct.	Loch Rannoch Conservation Association, Cuilmore Cottage, Kinloch Rannoch. Loch Rannoch Hotel. Tel: (01882) 632201. Bunrannoch Hotel, Tel: (01882) 632367.	Fly fishing only. 6 am - 10 pm. 15 foot open boats. No live bait. Ghillie service. Rod hire. Small tackle shop.
		Brown Trout Pike Perch	15 Mar. to 6 Oct.	E.M. Beattie (Sec.), 2 Schiehallion Place, Kinloch Rannoch. Tel: (01882) 632261. Local shops and hotels.	Average weight of fish caught: 8oz to 1lb. No live bait allowed. Boats are available from: Dunalastair or Loch Rannoch hotels.
Rescobie Loch	Forfar	Brown/ Rainbow Trout	15 Mar. to 31 Oct.	Bailiff, Rescobie Loch, South Lodge, Reswallie, By Forfar DD8 2SA. Tel: (01307) 818384.	Fly fishing only. Bank & Boat.
Sandy- knowes Fishery	Bridge of Earn	Rainbow Trout	1 Mar. to 30 Nov.	E. Christie, The Fishery Office, Sandyknowe Fishery, Bridge of Earn. Tel: (01738) 813033.	Bank fly fishing only. Session times 10 am-2 pm, 2 pm-6 pm, 6 pm-10 pm. Bag limit - 4 trout per session. Open 7 days. No Sunday evenings.
Loch Tay	Killin	Brown Trout	15 Mar. to 5 Oct.	J.H. Rough, J.R. News, Main Street, Killin. Tel: (01567) 820362.	All legal lures permitted.
		Salmon	15 Jan.- 15 Oct.	Clachaig Hotel, Killin. Tel: (01567) 820270.	3 boats available with outboards.
	Milton Morenish	Salmon Trout	15 Jan.-15 Oct. 15 Mar.-6 Oct.	Loch Tay Highland Lodges, Milton Morenish, by Killin. Tel: (01567) 820323.	Sixteen boats available. Ghillie and rod hire. Special offers for mid-week fishing.
Loch Tummel	West of Pitlochry	Trout Pike Perch	Apr. to Oct.	Queen's View Visitor Centre, Strathtummel, by Pitlochry PH16 5NR.	
Loch Turret	Crieff	Brown Trout	1 Apr. to 30 Sept.	The Director, Central Scotland Water Development Board, Balmore, Torrance, Glasgow G64 4AJ. Tel: (01360) 620511. Adam Boyd Newsagents, 39 King Street, Crieff. Tel: (01764) 653871.	Four boats with outboards. Fly only.

Constituent Area Tourist Boards

Aviemore and Spey Valley Tourist Board
Area Tourist Officer,
Tourist Information Centre,
Grampian Road, Aviemore,
Inverness-shire PH22 1PP.
Tel: (01479) 810363.

Banff and Buchan Tourist Board
Tourism Manager,
Tourist Information Centre,
Collie Lodge,
Banff AB4 1AU.
Tel: (01261) 812419.

Kincardine and Deeside Tourist Board
Tourist Officer,
Tourist Information Centre,
Bridge Street, Banchory,
Kincardineshire AB31 2SX.
Tel: (01330) 822000.

City of Aberdeen Tourist Board
Director,
City of Aberdeen Tourist Board,
St. Nicholas House, Broad Street,
Aberdeen AB9 1DE.
Tel: (01224) 632727.

Gordon District Tourist Board
Director,
Gordon District Tourist Board,
St. Nicholas House, Broad Street,
Aberdeen AB9 1DE.
Tel: (01224) 632727.

Moray Tourist Board,
Chief Tourist Officer,
Tourist Information Centre,
17 High Street, Elgin,
Morayshire IV30 1EG.
Tel: (01343) 542666.

RIVER PURIFICATION BOARD
NORTH EAST RIVER PURIFICATION BOARD
Greyhope House,
Greyhope Road, Torry,
Aberdeen AB1 3RD.
Tel: (01224) 248338.

RIVERS

Water	Location	Species	Season	Permit available from	Other information
Avon	Ballindalloch	Salmon Sea Trout	11 Feb. to 30 Sept.	Delnashaugh Inn, Ballindalloch, Banffshire AB37 9AS. Tel: (01807) 500255.	No prawn. Fly fishing Sept. No lead attached to fly.
	Tomintoul	Salmon Sea Trout	Feb. to end Sept.	Gordon Hotel, Tomintoul, Banffshire AB37 9ET. Tel: (01807) 580206.	No prawn. Fly fishing Sept. No lead attached to fly.
Bogie	Huntly	Salmon Sea Trout Brown Trout	11 Feb. to 31 Oct. 1 Apr. to 6 Oct.	Clerk of Fishings, Huntly Fishings Committee, Murdoch, McMath & Mitchell, 27/29 Duke Street, Huntly. Tel: (01466) 792291.	Permit covers Bogie, Deveron and Isla.
Carron	Stonehaven	Brown Trout Sea Trout Salmon	1 May to 31 Aug.	Davids Sports Shop, 31 Market Square, Stonehaven. Tel: (01569) 762239.	Visitors permits for Sea pool to railway viaduct. For further information: Mr. A.G. Kellas, 44 Farburn Drive, Stonehaven AB3ʼ 2BZ. Tel: (01569) 764227.
Clunie	Braemar	Brown Trout	15 Mar. to 20 Sept.	Invercauld Estates Office, Braemar AB35 5XQ. Tel: Braemar 41224. Tourist Information Centre, Braemar.	Fly fishing only.

Water	Location	Species	Season	Permit available from	Other information
Cowie	Stonehaven	Salmon Sea Trout Brown Trout	1 May to 31 Aug.	Davids Sports Shop, 31 Market Square, Stonehaven. Tel: (01569) 762239.	Visitors permits for Sea pool to railway viaduct. For further information: Mr. A.G. Kellas, 44 Farburn Drive, Stonehaven AB3 2BZ. Tel: (01569) 764227.
Dee	Aboyne	Salmon Sea Trout	1 Feb. to 30 Sept.	Glen Tanar Estate, Glen Tanar, Aboyne. Tel: (013398) 86451.	No Sunday fishing. Day permits available.
Deveron	Huntly	Salmon Sea Trout Brown Trout	11 Feb. to 31 Oct. 1 Apr. to 6 Oct.	Clerk of Fishings, Huntly Fishings Committee, Murdoch, McMath & Mitchell, 27/29 Duke Street, Huntly. Tel: (01466) 792291.	Permits cover Deveron, Bogie and Isla.
		Salmon Sea Trout Brown Trout	11 Feb. to 31 Oct.	Castle Hotel, Huntly AB54 4SH. Tel: (01466) 792696.	2 rods on hotel's own beat. Other private beats also available. Fly & spinning only.
	Turriff	Salmon Sea Trout Brown Trout	11 Feb. to 31 Oct.	Turriff Ang. Assoc., I. Masson, The Cross, 6 Castle Street, Turriff. Tel: (01888) 62428.	No day tickets. Six weekly available to visitors. Restrictions on spinning.
Don	Manar Fishings	Salmon Sea Trout Brown Trout	11 Feb. to 31 Oct. 1 Apr.- 30 Sept.	J.J. Watson 44 Market Place, Inverurie. Tel: (01467) 620321.	No worm, shrimp or prawn. Limit of 4 rods per day.
	Strathdon	Salmon Brown Trout	11 Feb. to 31 Oct.	Colquhonnie Hotel, Strathdon. Tel: (019756) 51210.	Fly & spinning only.
	Kintore	Salmon Sea Trout Brown Trout	11 Feb. to 31 Oct.	Kintore Arms Inn, Kintore. Tel: (01467) 632216. J.A. Copland, Newsagent, 2 Northern Road, Kintore. Tel: (01467) 632210.	No worm till 1 Apr. No natural minnow. No shrimp or prawn. Reductions for school children and OAP's.
	Inverurie	Salmon Sea Trout Brown Trout	11 Feb. to 31 Oct. 1 Apr.- 30 Sept.	J.J. Watson, 44 Market Place, Inverurie. Tel: (01467) 620321.	No worm till 1 Apr. No natural minnow. No shrimp or prawn. Reductions for school children and OAP's. Booking advised.
	Inverurie (Keithhall & Ardmurdo Beats)	Salmon Sea Trout Brown Trout	11 Feb to. 31 Oct. 1 Apr.- 30 Sept.	J.J. Watson, 44 Market Place, Inverurie. Tel: (01467) 620321.	No worm till 1 Apr. No natural minnow. No shrimp or prawn. Booking advised.
Dulnain	Grantown- on-Spey	Salmon Sea Trout Brown Trout	11 Feb. to 30 Sept. 15 Mar.- 30 Sept.	Strathspey Angling Assoc., Mortimer's, 3 High Street, Grantown-on-Spey. Tel: (01479) 872684.	Visitors resident in Grantown, Cromdale, Duthill, Carrbridge, Dulnain Bridge and Nethy Bridge areas. 12 miles of river.

Please mention this Pastime Publications guide

Water	Location	Species	Season	Permit available from	Other information
Findhorn (Broom of Moy Beat)	Forres	Salmon Sea Trout	11 Feb. to 30 Sept.	J. Mitchell, Springbank, Findhorn, Forres. Tel: (01309) 690406.	Popular flies: all shrimp, Stoats Tail, Dunkeld, Munro Killer. Spinning or worming allowed. Let by the week. Some day rods in early part of season.
Gairn	Nr. Ballater	Brown Trout	15 Mar. to 20 Sept.	Invercauld Estates Office, Braemar AB35 5XQ. Tel: Braemar 41224. Countrywear, Bridge Street, Ballater.	Fly fishing only.
Isla	Huntly	Salmon Sea Trout Brown Trout	11 Feb. to 31 Oct. 1 Apr. to 6 Oct.	Clerk of Fishings, Huntly Fishings Committee, Murdoch, McMath & Mitchell, 27/29 Duke Street, Huntly. Tel: (01466) 792291.	Permit covers Isla, . Deveron and Bogie.
Muckle burn	By Forres	Salmon Sea Trout	11 Feb. to 30 Sept.	I. Grant, Tackle Shop, 97D High Street, Forres. Tel: (01309) 672936.	Reductions for juniors
Spey	Aberlour	Salmon Sea Trout Brown Trout	11 Feb. to 30 Sept.	J.A.J. Munro, 93-95 High Street, Aberlour. Tel: Aberlour 871428.	3 tickets per hotel, (Aberlour, Lour & Dowans or 6 day tickets, first come first served.) One fish above bridge (9 am-5 pm), one fish below bridge (9 am-midnight), other fish sold for club funds. No day tickets on Saturday or local holidays.
	Grantown on-Spey	Salmon Sea Trout Brown Trout	11 Feb. to 30 Sept. 15 Mar.-30 Sept.	Strathspey Angling Assoc., Mortimer's 3 High Street, Grantown-on-Spey. Tel: (01479) 872684.	7 miles both banks. No Sunday fishing. Visitors must reside in Grantown, Cromdale, Duthil, Carrbridge, Dulnain Bridge and Nethy Bridge.
	Nethy Bridge Boat of Garten	Salmon Sea Trout Brown Trout	11 Feb. to 30 Sept.	Abernethy Angling Improvement Assoc. Boat of Garten. Allen's, Deshar Road, Boat of Garten. Tel: (01479) 834372.	6.25 miles both banks. No Sunday fishing. Visitors should reside in Boat of Garten, Nethy Bridge, Carrbridge or Dulnain Bridge. No shrimp or prawn allowed.
	Boat of Garten	Salmon Sea Trout Brown Trout	11 Feb. to 30 Sept. 15 Mar.-30 Sept.	Allen's, Deshar Road, Boat of Garten. Tel: (01479) 831372.	

Water	Location	Species	Season	Permit available from	Other information
Spey cont.	Aviemore	Salmon Sea Trout Brown Trout	11 Feb. to 30 Sept.	Rothiemurchus Estate, Inverdruie, Aviemore PH22 1QH. Tel: (01479) 810703. Major Campbell, Kinrara Estate Office, Aviemore. Tel: (01479) 811292. The Rowan Tree Restaurant & Guesthouse. Tel: (01479) 810207.	Beats on River Spey.
		Salmon Sea Trout Brown Trout	11 Feb. to 30 Sept.	Abernethy Angling Improvement Assoc., Speyside Sports, 64 Grampian Road, Aviemore. Tel: (01479) 810656.	Day tickets & weekly tickets available. No Sunday fishing.
	Kincraig	Brown Trout Salmon Sea Trout	11 Feb. to 30 Sept.	Alvie Estate Office, Kincraig, by Kingussie. Tel: (01540) 651255/651249. Dalraddy Caravan Park, Aviemore. Tel: (01479) 810330.	Fly fishing or spinning.
Ugie	Peterhead	Salmon Sea Trout Brown Trout	11 Feb. to 31 Oct.	Dicks Sports, 54 Broad Street, Fraserburgh. Tel: (01346) 514120. Robertson Sports, 1-3 Kirk Street, Peterhead AB4 6RT. Tel: (01779) 472584.	Bag limit - 8 fish per day. Fly, spinning or worm entire season. No shrimps, prawns or illegal baits.
Ury	Inverurie	Salmon Sea Trout Brown Trout	11 Feb. to 31 Oct. 1 Apr.- 30 Sept.	J.J. Watson, 44 Market Place, Inverurie AB5 3XN. Tel: (01467) 620321.	No worm till 1 Apr. No natural minnow. No shrimp or prawn. Reductions for school children and OAP's. Sunday fishing - trout only.
Ythan	(Estuary) Newburgh	Salmon Sea Trout	11 Feb. to 31 Oct.	The Ythan Fishery, Mrs. Forbes, 3 Lea Cottages, Newburgh, Ellon, Aberdeenshire AB41 0BN. Tel: (01358) 789297.	Limited fishing available. Details from Mrs. Forbes.
	Fyvie	Salmon Sea Trout	11 Feb. to 31 Oct.	Fyvie Angling Assoc., Local shop, hotel, cafe, bank.	No shrimps or prawns. No worming May to August.

LOCHS & RESERVOIRS

Water	Location	Species	Season	Permit available from	Other information
Aboyne Loch	Aboyne	Pike Perch		The Warden, Aboyne Loch, Holiday Park. Tel: (013398) 86244.	Fishing parties restricted on Sat. and Sun.
Loch Alvie	Aviemore	Brown Trout Pike	15 Mar. to 6 Oct.	Alvie Estate Office, Kincraig, by Kingussie. Tel: (01540) 651255/651249. Dalraddy Caravan Park, Aviemore. Tel: (01479) 810330.	1 Boat. Fly fishing or spinning only.
Avielochan	Aviemore	Rainbow/ Brown Trout	1 Apr. to 30 Sept.	Mrs. MacDonald, Avielochan, Aviemore. Tel: (01479) 810847.	Boat available. Fly fishing only. Sunday fishing 9am-5pm. 5pm-10pm.

Water	Location	Species	Season	Permit available from	Other information
Avielochan cont.		Wild Brown Trout Stocked Rainbow Trout		Allen's, Deshar Road, Boat of Garten. Tel: (01479) 831372 Speyside Sports, Aviemore. Tel: (01479) 810656.	Fly fishing only. Stocked rainbow trout up to 7lbs
Loch of Blairs	Forres	Brown/ Rainbow Trout	30 Mar. to 30 Sept.	I. Grant, Tackle Shop, 97D High Street, Forres. Tel: (01309) 672936.	Average weight of fish caught: 1lb 8oz. Popular flies: lures, conventional wet flies, dry flies. Two sessions. Boat fishing. Fly only. Sunday fishing. 3 boats available.
Loch Dallas	Boat of Garten	Brown/ Rainbow Trout	1 Apr. to 30 Sept.	Mortimer's 3 High Street, Grantown-on-Spey. Tel: (01479) 872684. Allan's Store, Boat of Garten. Tel: (01479) 831372.	Fly fishing only (10am-6pm). Boat fishing. No Sunday fishing. 1 boat (2 rods).
Loch Ericht	Dalwhinnie	Brown Trout	15 Mar. to 6 Oct.	Badenoch Angling Association, Loch Ericht Hotel, Dalwhinnie. Tel: (01528) 522257.	Bank fishing.
Glenlatterach Reservoir	By Elgin	Stocked Brown Trout	1 May to 30 Sept.	The Warden, Millbuies Lochs, Longmorn, Elgin. Tel: (0134 386) 234.	Fly fishing only. 3 boats available. Bank fishing.
Loch Insh	Kincraig	Salmon Sea Trout Brown Trout Char Pike	11 Feb. to 30 Sept. 15 Mar. to 6 Oct. All year.	Alvie Estate Office, Kincraig, by Kingussie. Tel: (01540) 651255/651249. Dalraddy Caravan Park, Aviemore. Tel: (01479) 810330.	One boat. Boat fishing only. Fly fishing or spinning.
		Salmon Sea Trout Brown Trout Arctic Char Pike	May to Sept.	Loch Insh Watersports, Boat House, Kincraig. Tel: (01540) 651272.	Boat are available.
Loch Laggan	Laggan	Brown Trout	15 Mar. to 6 Oct.	Loch Ericht Hotel, Dalwhinnie. Tel: (01528) 522257.	Bank fishing.
Loch Lochindorb	by Forres	Brown Trout	15 Mar. to 6 Oct.	The Lodge, Lochindorb.	Average weight of fish caught: 4oz to 1lb. Popular flies: black flies. Spinning and worming allowed. Boat and bank fishing.
Loch McLeod	Nr. Grantown on Spey	Brown/ Rainbow Trout	1 Apr. to 30 Sept.	Strathspey Estate Office, Heathfield, Grantown-on-Spey. Tel: (01479) 872529.	Bank fishing only. No fishing on Sundays. 2 rods per day. Fly fishing only (10am-6pm).
Millbuies Loch	By Elgin	Brown/ Rainbow Trout	Late Mar to Mid-Oct.	Moray District Council, Dept. of Leisure & Libraries, High Street, Elgin. The Warden, Millbuies Lochs, Longmorn, Elgin. Tel: (0134 386) 234.	Boat fishing. Fly fishing only. Four boats available.

Water	Location	Species	Season	Permit available from	Other information
Loch Mor	Dulnain Bridge	Brown/ Rainbow Trout	Apr. to Sept.	Mortimer's 3 High Street, Grantown-on-Spey. Tel: (01479) 872684.	Fly fishing only.
Loch Na Bo	Lhanbryde	Brown Trout	1 Apr. to 30 Sept.	D. Kinloch, Gardener's Cottage, Loch-na-Bo, Lhanbryde, Elgin. Tel: (01343 84) 2214.	Fly fishing only.
Rothie- murchus Estate (Fish farm lochs)	Aviemore	Rainbow Trout Brown Trout Pike	Check with manager, Aviemore.	Rothiemurchus Fish Farm, by Aviemore PH22 1QH. Tel: (01479) 810703.	Stocked rainbow trout loch. Open all year except when frozen. Additional private lochs available.
Loch Saugh	Fettercairn/ Drumtochty Glen	Brown Trout	15 Mar. to 6 Oct.	Brechin Angling Club, W.G. Balfour, S Cookston Crescent, Brechin DD9 6BP. Tel: (01356) 622753. Ramsay Arms Hotel, Fettercairn. Tel: (015614) 334. Drumtochty Arms Hotel, Auchenblae AB30 1XR. Tel: (01561) 320210. David Rollston-Smith Fishing Tackle, Guns & Sport, 180 High Street, Montrose. Tel: (01674) 672692. G. Carroll Angling Supplies, Brechin.	Fly fishing only from bank.
Glen Tanar Loch	Glen Tanar	Rainbow Trout	Mar. to Dec.	Glen Tanar Estate, Glen Tanar, Aboyne. Tel: (013398) 86451.	3 boats. Boat fishing by day or evening.
Loch Vaa	Aviemore	Brown/ Rainbow Trout	1 Apr. to 30 Sept.	Mortimer's 3 High Street, Grantown-on-Spey. Tel: (01479) 872684.	Boat fishing only. 2 boats - 2 rods per boat. Fly fishing only. No Sunday fishing. Fishing 10am-6pm only.
Loch Vrotichan	Cairnwell	Brown Trout	18 Mar. to 11 Aug.	Invercauld Estates Office, Braemar AB35 5XQ. Tel: Braemar 41224. Tourist Information Centre, Braemar. Tourist Information Centre, Ballater.	Fly fishing only.

Constituent Area Tourist Boards

Fort William and Lochaber Tourism Ltd.
Area Tourist Officer,
Tourist Information Centre,
Cameron Centre, Cameron Square,
Fort William,
Inverness-shire PH33 6AJ.
Tel: (01397) 703781.

Isle of Skye and South West Ross Tourist Board
Area Tourist Officer,
Tourist Information Centre,
Meall House, Portree,
Isle of Skye IV51 9BZ.
Tel: (01478) 612137.

**Inverness, Loch Ness and Nairn
Tourist Board**
Area Tourist Officer,
Tourist Information Centre,
Castle Wynd, Inverness IV2 3BG.
Tel: (01463) 234353.

**RIVER PURIFICATION BOARD
HIGHLAND RIVER PURIFICATION BOARD**
Graesser House,
Fodderty Way,
Dingwall.
Tel: (01349) 62021.

RIVERS

Water	Location	Species	Season	Permit available from	Other information
Brogaig	North Skye	Sea Trout Brown Trout	1 Mar. to 31 Oct.	Jansport, Wentworth Street, Portree, Skye. Tel: (01478) 612559.	
Coe	Glencoe	Salmon Sea Trout	15 Apr. to 15 Oct.	National Trust for Scotland, Vistor Centre, Glencoe. Tel: (018552) 307.	No Sunday fishing.
Croe		Salmon Sea Trout	1 Mar. to 30 Sept.	National Trust for Scotland, Morvich Farm, Inverinate, By Kyle. Tel: (0159 981) 219.	Fly fishing only.
Farrar	Struy	Salmon Brown Trout	June-15 Oct. 15 Mar.- 30 Sept.	Culligran Estate, Glen Strathfarrar, Struy, nr. Beauly IV4 7JX. Tel/Fax: (01463) 761285.	Fly fishing only.
Garry (upper)	Garry Gualach to Poulary Bridge	Salmon Brown Trout	15 Mar.- 14 Oct. !5 Mar.- 6 Oct.	Mr. Isaacson, Garry Gualach Country Holidays, Invergarry. Tel: (01809) 511230.	Fly only 1 May to end of season.
Glass	Struy	Salmon Brown Trout	June-15 Oct. 15 Mar.- 30 Sept.	Culligran Estate, Glen Strathfarrar, Struy, nr. Beauly IV4 7JX. Tel/Fax: (01463) 761285.	Fly fishing only.
Lealt	North Skye	Salmon Sea Trout Brown Trout	1 Mar. to 31 Oct.	Jansport, Wentworth Street, Portree, Skye. Tel: (01478) 612559.	
Moriston	Glen- moriston Estuary beat	Salmon	15 Jan. to 15 Oct.	Vincent Tait, Head Gamekeeper. Tel: (01320) 351219.	Fly & spinning only.
	Dundreggan Beat	Salmon Brown Trout	1 May-end Sept. Mar. to Sept.	Vincent Tait, Head Keeper. Tel: (01320) 351219.	Fly and spinning only.

Water	Location	Species	Season	Permit available from	Other information
Nairn	Nairn/ Culloden Moor	Salmon Sea Trout	11 Feb. to 7 Oct.	Nairn Angling Association P. Fraser, High Street, Nairn. Tel: (01667) 453038. Clava Lodge Holiday Homes, Culloden Moor, Inverness IV1 2EJ. Tel: (01463) 790228,	
Nevis	Fort William	Salmon Sea Trout		Rod & Gun Shop 18 High Street, Fort William. Tel: (01397) 702656.	
Polloch	Strontian	Salmon Sea Trout Brown Trout	1 May to 31 Oct.	Post Office, Strontian.	Average weight of fish caught: Salmon - 6lbs, Sea Trout - 1lb, Brown Trout - 1lb. Popular flies: dark flies. Worm & spinning allowed. No prawn fishing.
Snizort	Skye	Salmon Sea Trout Brown Trout	1 Jul. to 15 Oct.	Skeabost House Hotel, Skeabost, Isle of Skye. Tel: (0147 032) 202.	Discounts for residents.
Staffin	North Skye	Salmon Sea Trout Brown Trout	1 Mar. to 31 Oct.	Jansport, Wentworth Street, Portree, Skye. Tel: (01478) 612559.	
Strontian	Strontian	Salmon Sea Trout Brown Trout	1 May to 31 Oct.	Post Office Strontian.	Average weight of fish caught: Salmon - 6 to 10lbs, Sea Trout - 1lb. Popular flies: Blue Charm, Hair Fly. Worm (if river in spate) & spinning. No prawns.

LOCHS & RESERVOIRS

Water	Location	Species	Season	Permit available from	Other information
Loch Abhana	by Cannich	Brown Trout	April to 6 Oct.	Glen Affric Hotel, Cannich. Tel: Cannich 214.	Fly fishing only. Boat or bank.
Ardtornish Estate Waters	Morvern	Salmon Sea Trout Brown Trout	Apr.-Oct.	Ardtornish Estate Office, Morvern, by Oban, Argyll. Tel: (01967) 421288.	Six boats for hire.
Loch Arkaig	Fort William	Sea Trout Brown Trout Salmon (occasional) Pike	Mar.-Oct.	Locheil Estate Fishings, West Highland Estates Office, 33 High Street, Fort William. Tel: (01397) 702433.	
Loch Beannachran	Glen Strathfarrar	Brown Trout	15 Mar. to 6 Oct.	Glen Affric Hotel, Cannich. Tel: Cannich 214.	Fly fishing only. 1 boat. No bank fishing.
Loch Benevean (Bheinn a' Mheadhoin)	Glen Affric	Brown Trout	15 Mar. to 6 Oct.	Glen Affric Hotel, Cannich. Tel: Cannich 214.	Fly fishing only. 6 Boats available. No bank fishing.
Loch Dochfour	Inverness	Brown Trout	15 Mar. to 6 Oct.	Dochfour Estate Office, Dochgarroch, by Inverness. Tel: (0146386) 218.	No Sunday fishing. Bank fishing only.

Water	Location	Species	Season	Permit available from	Other information
Loch Doilet	Strontian	Salmon Sea Trout Brown Trout	1 May to 31 Oct.	George Fisher, Polloch Lodge, Strontian. Tel: (01967) 402412. General Store, Strontian. Post Office, Strontian.	Average weight of fish caught: Salmon - 6lbs, Sea Trout 1lb. Popular flies: black flies. Worm and spinning permitted. No prawns. Boats available from: Jim Bannerman, (01967) 402408 or (01967) 402412.
Glen Affric Hill Lochs	Tomich Strathglass	Brown Trout	15 Mar. to 6 Oct.	Caledonian Hotel, Beauly. Tel: (01463) 782278.	Fly only. Boats available. Some salmon fishing.
Glenmoriston Hill Lochs (21)	Glenmoriston	Brown Trout	May to Oct.	Vincent Tait, (Gamekeeper), Levishie, Glenmoriston, Tel: (01320) 351219 (Eve.)	1 boat available.
Guisachan Hill Lochs	Tomich	Brown Trout	Apr. to Sept.	Tomich Hotel, Tomich, by Beauly. Tel: (01456) 415399.	Fly fishing only. Rainbow Trout on 2 lochs.
Loch Inchlaggan & Loch Garry	Invergarry	Brown Trout Arctic Char	May-Sept.	Mr. Isaacson, Garry Gualach Country Holidays, Invergarry. Tel: (01809) 511230.	Boats available. Loch Inchlaggan fly only.
Loch Insh	Kincraig	Salmon Trout Arctic Char Pike	May to September	Loch Insh Watersports, Boat House, Kincraig. Tel: (01540) 651272.	Boats are available.
Loch Lundavra	Nr. Fort William	Brown Trout	15 Apr. to 30 Sept.	Mrs. A. MacCallum, Lundavra Farm, Fort William. Tel: (01397) 702582.	Average weight of fish caught: 8oz. Popular flies: Black Pennel, Bloody Butcher, Peter Ross. Fly fishing only. 2 boats available. Bank fishing.
Loch Lungard	Glen Cannich	Brown Trout	15 Mar. to 6 Oct.	Glen Affric Hotel, Cannich. Tel: Cannich 214.	Fly fishing only. No bank fishing. Boats available from Loch Mullardoch.
Loch Mealt	North Skye	Brown Trout Arctic Char	15 Mar. to 30 Sept.	Jansport, Wentworth Street, Portree, Skye. Tel: (01478) 612559.	
Loch Monar	Glen Strathfarrar	Brown Trout	15 Mar. to 6 Oct.	Glen Affric Hotel, Cannich. Tel: Cannich 214.	Fly fishing only. Boat for hire. No bank fishing.
Loch Morar (and hill lochs)	Morar	Salmon Sea Trout Brown Trout Arctic Char	15 Mar. to 6 Oct.	The Morar District Salmon Fishery Board, Superintendant, Viv de Fresnes. Tel: (01687) 2388.	6 boats for hire, and ghillie if required.
Loch Mullardoch	Cannich	Brown Trout	15 Mar. to 6 Oct.	Glen Affric Hotel, Cannich. Tel: Cannich 214.	Fly fishing only. 4 boats. No bank fishing.

Water	Location	Species	Season	Permit available from	Other information
Loch Ness	Glenmoriston	Salmon Trout	15 Jan.	Vincent Tait (Gamekeeper), Levishie, Glenmoriston. Tel: (01320) 351219 (Eve.)	1 boat available.
Loch Ruthven	Farr	Brown Trout	15 Mar. to 6 Oct.	J. Graham & Co., 37/39 Castle Street, Inverness. Tel: (01463) 233178.	Fly fishing only.
Loch Sheil	Glenfinnan	Salmon Sea Trout	Apr.-Oct.	The Prince's House, Glenfinnan. Tel: (01397) 722246.	4 boats available with outboards. Advance bookings only.
South Skye Fishings (various lochs)	South Skye	Sea Trout Brown Trout	Apr.-Oct.	Fearann Eilean Iarmain, Eilean Iarmain, Isle of Skye. Tel: (0147 13) 266.	
Storr Lochs (and hill lochs)	North Skye	Brown Trout	1 Apr. to 30 Sept.	Jansport, Wentworth Street, Portree, Skye. Tel: (01478) 612559.	Further info: Sec., Portree Angling Assoc., Hillcroft, Treaslane, By Portree.
Whitebridge Lochs (Knockie, Bran & Killin)	Whitebridge	Brown Trout	Mar.-Oct.	Whitebridge Hotel, Stratherrick, Gorthleck, Inverness-shire. Tel: (01456) 486226.	Boats available. Fly fishing only.

Traditional Flies

Please mention this Pastime Publications guide

Constituent Area Tourist Boards

Caithness Tourist Board
Area Tourist Office,
Tourist Information Centre,
Whitechapel Road, Wick,
Caithness KW1 4EA.
Tel: (01955) 2596.

Sutherland Tourist Board
Area Tourist Officer,
Tourist Information Centre,
The Square, Dornoch,
Sutherland IV25 3SD.
Tel: (01862) 810400.

Ross and Cromarty Tourist Board
Area Tourist Officer,
Information Centre, North Kessock,
Black Isle, Ross-shire IV5 1XB.
Tel: (01463 73) 505.

RIVER PURIFICATION BOARD
HIGHLAND RIVER PURIFICATION BOARD
Graesser House,
Fodderty Way,
Dingwall IV15 9QY.
Tel: (01349) 62021.

RIVERS

Water	Location	Species	Season	Permit available from	Other information
Alness	Alness	Salmon Sea Trout	5 May to 16 Oct.	Novar Estates, Estate Office, Evanton, Ross-shire. Tel: (01349) 830208.	Fly fishing only. 6 beats on rotation. 4 rods per beat.
Beauly	Muir of Ord	Salmon Sea Trout Brown Trout	May to Sept.	Ord House Hotel, Muir of Ord. Tel: (01463) 870492.	River and loch fishing available.
Blackwater	Strathpeffer	Salmon Sea Trout	Apr. to end Sept.		Further info. from: Craigdarroch Lodge Hotel, Contin, by Strathpeffer. Tel: Strathpeffer 21265.
Brora (Lower)	Brora	Salmon Sea Trout	1 Feb. to 15 Oct.	Mr. & Mrs. Hammond, Sciberscross Lodge, Strath Brora, Rogart. Tel: (01408) 641246.	Popular flies: Orange, black, red Waddingtons, Willie Gunn.
Conon	Contin	Salmon Sea Trout	26 Jan. to 30 Sept.	Coul House Hotel, Contin, by Strathpeffer. Tel: Strathpeffer 421487.	Lower/middle/upper Brahan, lower Fairburn beats various times. Ghillies, boats. Fly (& spinning until end May).
	Maryburgh	Brown/ Rainbow Trout Pike	15 Mar. to 15 Oct.	Seaforth Highland Estate, Brahan, Dingwall. Tel: (01349) 65505.	Stocked pond. Loch fishing and river in the lower, middle and upper Conon. Fishing available in the stocked pond and loch all year round.
	Muir of Ord	Salmon Sea Trout Brown Trout	May to Sept.	Ord House Hotel, Muir of Ord. Tel: (01463) 870492.	River & loch fishing available.
	Strathpeffer	Salmon Brown Trout	1 Apr. to 30 Sept.	Further info. from: Craigdarroch Lodge Hotel, Contin, by Strathpeffer. Tel: Strathpeffer 21265.	

Water	Location	Species	Season	Permit available from	Other information
Conon cont.	Dingwall	Salmon Sea Trout	25 Jan. to 30 Sept.	The Sports & Model Shop, High Street, Dingwall. Tel: (01349) 62346.	Popular flies: Greenwell's Glory, Peter Ross, Black Pennel. Fly fishing only. Thigh waders only.
Lower Conon	Contin	Salmon Sea Trout	26 Jan. to 30 Sept.	Dingwall & District A.C., c/o Sports & Model Shop, High Street, Dingwall. Tel: (01349) 62346.	Fly only. Thigh waders only.
Doinard	Durness	Salmon Sea Trout		Cape Wrath Hotel, Durness, Sutherland. Tel: (0197 181) 274.	Please phone in advance, especially in high season.
Glass	Evanton	Brown Trout	15 Mar. to 6 Oct.	Novar Estates, Estate Office, Evanton, Ross-shire. Tel: (01349) 830208.	Fly fishing only.
Halladale Forsinard (2 mile upper beat)		Salmon	11 Jan. to 30 Sept.	Forsinard Hotel, Forsinard KW13 6YT. Tel: (016417) 221.	Fly fishing only (spate river).
	Forsinard to Melvich Bay	Salmon	11 Jan. to 30 Sept.	Mrs. J. Atkinson, 8 Sinclair Street, Thurso, Caithness.	Fly fishing only. Lodge also available.
Helmsdale	Helmsdale	Salmon Sea Trout	11 Jan. to 30 Sept.	Strathullie Crafts & Fishing Tackle, Dunrobin Street, Helmsdale KW8 6AH. Tel: (0143 12) 343.	Association beat. Fly fishing only.
Kirkaig	Lochinver	Salmon	1 May to 15 Oct.	Inver Lodge Hotel, Lochinver IV27 4LU. Tel: (015714) 496.	
Kyle of Sutherland	Bonar Bridge	Salmon Sea Trout	1 June to 30 Sept.	Dunroamin Hotel, Bonar Bridge IV24 3EB. Tel: (01863) 766236.	
Okyel	Sutherland	Salmon Sea Trout	End June to 30 Sept.	Inver Lodge Hotel, Lochinver IV27 4LU. Tel: (015714) 496.	2 top beats only (3 miles).
Thurso	Thurso/ Halkirk	Salmon Trout	11 Jan. to 5 Oct.	Thurso Fisheries Ltd., Estate Office, Thurso East, Thurso. Tel: (01847) 63134.	Fly fishing only. Twelve 2 rod beats in rotation.
Ullapool	Ullapool	Salmon Sea Trout Brown Trout	May to 30 Sept.	Ullasports, West Argyle Street, Ullapool. Tel: (01854) 612621.	
Wester	by Wick	Salmon Sea Trout Brown Trout	1 Mar. to 31 Oct.	Mrs. G. Dunnet, Auckhorn Lyth, by Wick KW1 4UD. Tel: (0195583) 208. Hugo Ross, Tackle Shop, 56 High Street, Wick. Tel: (01955) 604200.	
Wick	Wick	Salmon Sea Trout Brown Trout	11 Feb. to 21 Oct.	Hugo Ross Tackle Shop, 56 High Street, Wick. Tel/Fax: (01955) 604200.	Fly/worm fishing. Spate river with good holding pools.

Water	Location	Species	Season	Permit available from	Other information
LOCHS					
Loch A'chroisg	Achnasheen	Brown Trout Pike Perch	No close season	Ledgowan Lodge Hotel, Achnasheen. Tel: (01445) 720252.	Free to customers.
Loch a'Ghriama	Overscaig	Brown Trout	30 Apr. to 30 Sept.	Overscaig Lochside Hotel, Loch Shin, by Lairg IV27 4NY. Tel: (0154 983) 203.	Boats available. No Sunday fishing.
Loch an Ruthair	by Kinbrace	Brown Trout	Apr. to end Sept.	Head Keeper, Achentoul Estate, Kinbrace. Tel: (014313) 227.	Average weight of fish caught: 8 to 12oz. Popular flies: Soldier Palmer, Black pennel. Bait fishing and spinning allowed. 2 boats available.
Loch Achall	by Ullapool	Salmon Sea Trout Brown Trout	1 May to 30 Sept. 15 Mar.- 6 Oct.	Ullasport, West Argyle Street, Ullapool. Tel: (01854) 612621.	Popular flies: Soldier Palmer, Butcher, Grouse & Claret. 3 boats available. Bank fishing.
Lochs Airigh Leathaid	By Westerdale, Halkirk	Brown Trout	Apr. to Sept.	Ulbster Arms Hotel, Halkirk.	Fly only. Average Weight: 1lb 2oz.
Loch Ascaig	Helmsdale	Salmon Sea Trout Brown Trout	1 June to 30 Sept. 15 Mar.- 6 Oct.	M. Wigan, Borrobol, Kinbrace KW11 6UB. Tel: (01431) 831264.	Popular flies: Loch Ordie, Soldier Palmer, Fly fishing only. 3 boats available.
Loch Badagyle	Nr. Achiltibuie	Sea Trout Brown Trout Arctic Char	1 Apr. to 30 Sept.	Polly Estates Ltd., Inverpolly, Ullapool IV26 2YB. Tel: (0185 482) 452.	Fly fishing only. No Sunday fishing. Boats with or without motors are available.
Loch Badanloch (& other hill lochs)	Kinbrace	Brown Trout	15 Mar. to 6 Oct.	Richard McNicol, Badanloch, Kinbrace, Sutherland. Tel: (0143 13) 232.	Average weight of fish caught: 8oz. Popular flies: Loch Ordie, Black Pennel, Soldier Palmer. 6 boats. Fly only. Sunday fishing.
Loch Beannach	Lairg	Brown Trout	30 Apr. to 30 Sept.	Boat permits: R. Ross (Fishing Tackle), Main Street, Lairg IV27 4DB. Tel: (01549) 2239.	Average weight of fish caught: 1lb. Popular flies: Kate McLaren, Loch Ordie. strictly fly fishing only. Boats available from above.
Bad an Scalaig	Nr. Gairloch	Brown Trout Pike	Mar. to Oct.	Wildcat Stores, Gairloch.	Spinning allowed for Pike. 2 boats are available.
Loch Bad na H-Achlaise (Green Loch)	Nr. Achiltibuie	Brown/Sea Trout	1 Apr. to 30 Sept.	Polly Estates Ltd., Inverpolly, Ullapool IV26 2YB. Tel: (0185 482) 452.	Fly fishing only. No Sunday fishing.

Water	Location	Species	Season	Permit available from	Other information
Loch Bad na H Erba	Sciberscross	Wild Brown Trout	1 Apr. to 15 Oct.	Mr. & Mrs. Hammond, Sciberscross Lodge, Strath Brora, Rogart IV28 3YQ. Tel: (01408) 641246.	Average weight of fish caught: 12oz. Popular flies: Black Pennel, Ke-He, Loch Ordie, Dunkeld. Boats are available.
Black Loch	Nr. Achiltibuie	Brown Trout	1 Apr. to 30 Sept.	Polly Estates Ltd., Inverpolly, Ullapool IV26 2YB. Tel: (0185 482) 452.	Fly fishing only. No Sunday fishing. Boat available.
Loch Borralan	Ledmore	Brown/ Rainbow Trout Arctic Char	15 Mar. to 6 Oct.	The Alt Bar, The Altnacealgach, Ledmore, by Lairg. Tel: (01854) 666220.	Any legal method permitted. Boat & bank fishing.
Loch Borralie	Durness	Brown Trout	Apr. to End Sept.	Cape Wrath Hotel, Durness, Sutherland. Tel: (0197 181) 274.	Limestone loch. Fly fishing only. Boats available. Please phone in advance, especially in high season.
Loch Broom	by Ullapool	Salmon Sea trout	Apr. to Oct.	Ullasport, West Argyle Street, Ullapool. Tel: (01854) 612621.	
Loch Brora	Brora	Salmon Sea Trout Brown Trout	Apr. to Oct.	Rob Wilson Rods & Guns, Rosslyn Street, Brora. Tel: (01408) 621373.	Boats available.
		Salmon Sea Trout Brown Trout Char	1 May to 15 Oct.	Mr. & Mrs. Hammond, Sciberscross Lodge, Strath Brora, Rogart IV28 3YQ. Tel: (01408) 641246.	Popular flies: General Practitioner, Stoats Tail, Dunkeld. Boats available with outboard, if required.
Loch Buidhe	by Bonar Bridge	Brown Trout	1 Mar. to 30 Sept.	Dunroamin Hotel, Bonar Bridge IV24 3EB. Tel: (01863) 766236.	1 boat available. No restrictions.
Loch Caise	Forsinard	Brown Trout	1 May to 30 Sept.	Forsinard Hotel, Forsinard. Tel: (016417) 221.	
Loch Caladail	Durness	Brown Trout	Apr. to End Sept.	Cape Wrath Hotel, Durness, Sutherland. Tel: (0197 181) 274.	Limestone loch. Fly fishing Only. Boats available. Please phone in advance, especially in high season.
Loch Calder	Thurso	Brown Trout	15 Mar. to 6 Oct.	Harper's Fishing Tackle, 57 High Street, Thurso. Tel: (01847) 63179.	Average weight of fish caught: 12oz to 1lb (fish upto 7lbs). Popular flies: Bibio, Black Pennel, Kate McLaren. Spinning & bait fishing permitted, but fly fishing preferred. Boats available.
Caol Loch	Forsinard	Brown Trout	1 May to 30 Sept.	Forsinard Hotel, Forsinard. Tel: (016417) 221.	Boat & bank fishing. Use standard pattern loch flies.
Cape Wrath & hill lochs (30 plus)	Durness	Brown Trout	Apr. to End Sept.	Cape Wrath Hotel, Durness, Sutherland. Tel: (0197 181) 274.	Please phone in advance, especially in high season.

Please mention this Pastime Publications guide   119

Water	Location	Species	Season	Permit available from	Other information
Cherigal Loch	By Westerdale, Halkirk	Brown Trout	Apr. to Sept.	Ulbster Arms Hotel, Halkirk.	Fly only. Average weight: 12 oz.
Col Loch Beg		Wild Brown Trout	1 Apr. to 15 Oct.	Garvault Hotel, by Kinbrace. Tel: Kinbrace 224.	Average weight of fish caught: 8oz. Popular flies: Loch Ordie, Black Spider, Black Pennel. Fly fishing only.
Col Loch Mhor		Wild Brown Trout	1 Apr. to 15 Oct.	Garvault Hotel, by Kinbrace. Tel: Kinbrace 224.	Average weight of fish caught: 8oz. Popular flies: Loch Ordie, Black Spider, Black Pennel. Fly fishing only.
Loch Cracail	By Bonar Bridge	Brown Trout	May to 31 Oct.	Dunroamin Hotel, Bonar Bridge, Sutherland. Tel: (018632) 236.	1 boat available.
Loch Craggie	Tongue	Wild Brown Trout (occ. Salmon)	15 Mar. to 6 Oct.	Ben Loyal Hotel, Tongue. Tel: Tongue 216. Post Office, Tongue. Tel: Tongue 201.	Fly fishing only. Boat available.
		Brown Trout	Mar. to Sept.	Altnaharra Hotel, By Lairg IV27 4UE.	Average weight of fish caught: 8oz to 1lb. Popular flies: Pennel, Goats Toe, Zulu. Boat available.
Loch Croispol	Durness	Brown Trout	Apr. to End Sept.	Cape Wrath Hotel, Durness, Sutherland. Tel: (0197 181) 274.	Limestone loch. Fly fishing only. Boats available. Please phone in advance, especially in high season.
Loch Culag (and numerous other lochs)	Lochinver	Brown Trout	Mid-May to 6 Oct.	Inver Lodge Hotel, Lochinver, Sutherland. Tel: Lochinver 496.	7 lochs with boats. 2 lochs for residents of hotel only. (Check for details).
The Dam Lochs	Nr. Ullapool	Brown Trout	15 Mar. to 6 Oct.	Ullasport, West Argyle Street, Ullapool. Tel: (01854) 612621.	Fly fishing only.
Loch Doir na H-Airbhe (Stac Loch)	Nr. Achiltibuie	Brown/Sea Trout	1 Apr. to 30 Sept.	Polly Estates Ltd., Inverpolly, Ullapool IV26 2YB. Tel: (0185 482) 452.	Fly fishing only. No Sunday fishing.
Dornoch & District A.C. (7 lochs)	Dornoch	Salmon Sea Trout Brown Trout	15 Mar. to 6 Oct.	Dornoch & District A.A., William A. McDonald, Castle Street, Dornoch. Tel: (01862) 810301.	No Sunday fishing. Fly fishing only. 7 boats available.
Lochan Dubh na H-Amaite	Sciberscross	Wild Brown Trout	1 Apr. to 15 Oct.	Mr. & Mrs. Hammond, Sciberscross Lodge, Strath Brora, Rogart IV28 3YQ. Tel: (01408) 641246.	Average weight of fish caught: 1lb. Popular flies: Black Pennel, Ke-He, Loch Ordie, Dunkeld. Boats are available.
Dubh-nan-Geodh	By Westerdale, Halkirk	Brown Trout	Apr. to Sept.	Ulbster Arms Hotel, Halkirk.	Fly only. Average Weight: 1lb 10oz.

Water	Location	Species	Season	Permit available from	Other information
Dunnet Head Loch	Dunnet Head (B855)	Brown Trout	May to Oct.	Dunnet Head Tearoom, Brough Village, Dunnet Head. Tel: (0184 785) 774.	Loch well stocked. Fly from bank only. No Sunday fishing. Sea fishing from rocks.
Eileanach Loch	By Westerdale, Halkirk	Brown Trout	Apr. to Sept.	Ulbster Arms Hotel, Halkirk.	Fly only. Average weight: 9oz.
Eun Loch	By Westerdale, Halkirk	Brown Trout	Apr. to Sept.	Ulbster Arms Hotel, Halkirk.	Fly only. Average Weight: 1lb 8oz.
Forsinard Loch (& many others)	Forsinard	Brown Trout	1 May. to 30 Sept.	Forsinard Hotel, Forsinard, Sutherland. Tel: (016417) 221.	Fly fishing only. Bank & boat fishing (5 boats). Sea trout up to 3.5lbs.
	Kyle of Tongue	Salmon Sea Trout Sea Bass	11 Feb. to 31 Oct.	Ben Loyal Hotel, Tongue. Tel: Tongue 216. Post Office, Tongue. Tel: Tongue 201.	No Sunday fishing. Bank fishing only.
Gainaimh Loch	By Westerdale, Halkirk.	Brown Trout	Apr. to Sept.	Ulbster Arms Hotel, Halkirk.	Fly only. Average weight: 7oz.
Loch Ganneigh		Wild Brown Trout	1 Apr. to 15 Oct.	Garvault Hotel, by Kinbrace. Tel: Kinbrace 224.	Average weight of fish caught: 8oz. Popular flies: Loch Ordie, Black Spider, Black Pennel. Fly fishing only.
Loch Glascarnoch	Aultguish	Brown Trout Pike	Mar to Sept. All year	Tel: (019975) 254 to obtain permission.	
Loch Glass	Head of River Glass	Brown Trout	15 Mar. to 6 Oct.	Novar Estates, Estate Office, Evanton, Ross-shire. Tel: (01349) 830208.	Bank fishing only. Any legal method.
Garbh Loch	Forsinard	Brown Trout	1 May to 30 Sept.	Forsinard Hotel, Forsinard. Tel: (016417) 221.	Bank & boat fishing. Popular flies: Black Pennel, Ke-He, Invicta.
Golspie A.C. Waters (Loch Brora Loch Lundie Loch Horn Loch Buidhe)		Salmon Sea Trout Brown Trout	1 Apr. to 15 Oct.	Golspie A.C., Lindsay & Co., Main Street, Golspie. Tel: (01408) 633212.	Fly fishing only. Bank & boat fishing. No Sunday fishing.
Loch Heilan	Castletown	Brown Trout	May to Sept.	H.T. Pottinger, Greenland Mains, Castleton, Thurso. Tel: (01847) 82210.	Bank & Boat fishing.
Loch Hempriggs	South of Wick	Brown Trout	14 Mar.to 14 Oct.	Thrumster Filling Station. Tel: (01955) 85252. Hugo Ross Fishing Tackle Shop, 56 High Street, Wick. Tel/Fax: (01955) 604200.	Average weight of fish caught: 12oz to 1lb.
Hill Lochs (32)	Around Assynt	Brown Trout	15 Mar.to 6 Oct.	Tourist Information Centre, Lochinver. Tel: (01571) 844330.	Mainly fly fishing, there are 6 lochs where spinning or bait can be used. Bank fishing only.

Please mention this Pastime Publications guide

Water	Location	Species	Season	Permit available from	Other information
Loch Hope	Nr. Tongue	Salmon Sea Trout	Mid-Apr.to Sept. June to Sept.	Altnaharra Hotel, by Lairg IV27 4UE.	Average weight of fish caught: Salmon - 8lbs, Sea Trout - 3lbs. Popular flies: Salmon - Invicta, Pennel. Sea Trout - Peter Ross. Other baits: Toby, sprat. 6 boats are available.
Lochs Kernsary Tournaig Goose	Gairloch	Brown Trout	15 Mar. to 6 Oct.	National Trust for Scotland, Inverewe Visitor Centre, Poolewe, Ross-shire. Tel: (0144 586) 229.	
Kyle of Tongue & local lochs	Tongue & Farr	Salmon Sea Trout Brown Trout		Tongue Stores & P. Office, Main Street, Tongue. Tel: (0184 755) 201.	Sunday fishing for brown trout only. Boats available from: Ben Loyal Hotel, Tongue.
Loch Lagain	By Bonar Bridge	Brown Trout	May to 31 Oct.	Dunroamin Hotel, Bonar Bridge, Sutherland. Tel: (01863) 766236.	1 boat available.
Loch Laro	By Bonar Bridge	Brown Trout	May to 31 Oct.	Dunroamin Hotel, Bonar Bridge, Sutherland. Tel: (01863) 766236.	
Leckmelm Hill Lochs	Ullapool	Brown Trout	May to Sept.	Leckmelm Holiday Cottages, Leckmelm, Ullapool. Tel: (01854) 2471.	Bank fishing only. No Sunday fishing.
Loch Loyal	Tongue	Salmon Sea Trout Wild Brown Trout	15 Mar. to 6 Oct.	Ben Loyal Hotel, Tongue. Tel: Tongue: 216. Post Office, Tongue. Tel: Tongue 201.	Fly fishing only. Bank or boat fishing. (2 boats available).
		Brown Trout	Mar. to Sept.	Altnaharra Hotel, By Lairg IV27 4UE.	Average weight of fish caught: 8oz to 1lb. Popular flies: Pennel, Goats Toe, Zulu. 1 boat available.
Loch Lurgainn	Nr. Achiltibuie	Brown/Sea Trout	1 Apr. to 30 Sept.	Polly Estates Ltd., Inverpolly, Ullapool IV26 2YB. Tel: (0185 482) 452.	Fly fishing only. No Sunday fishing. Boats with or without motors available.
Loch Maree	Wester Ross	Salmon Sea Trout Brown Trout	May-Oct.	Loch Maree Hotel, Achnasheen IV22 2HL. Tel: (0144 584) 288.	Several boats available.
				Kinlochewe Holiday Chalets, Castlegate House, Castlegate, Ceres, Fife. Tel: (0144584) 256.	2 boats available. Fly only - end June onwards.
Meadie Loch	By Westerdale, Halkirk	Brown Trout	Apr. to Sept.	Ulbster Arms Hotel, Halkirk.	Fly only. Average weight: 10oz.
Loch Meadie	Tongue	Brown Trout	Mar. to Sept.	Altnaharra Hotel, By Lairg IV27 4UE.	Average weight of fish caught: 8oz to 1lb. Popular flies: Pennel, Goats Toe, Zulu. 1 boat available.

Water	Location	Species	Season	Permit available from	Other information
Loch Merkland	Overscaig	Brown Trout	30 Apr. to 30 Sept.	Overscaig Lochside Hotel, Loch Shin, by Lairg IV27 4NY. Tel: (0154 983) 203.	Boat available. Fly only. No Sunday fishing.
Loch Migdale	By Bonar Bridge	Brown Trout	May to 31 Oct.	Dunroamin Hotel, Bonar Bridge, Sutherland. Tel: (01863) 766236.	1 boat available.
More Loch	By Westerdale, Halkirk	Brown Trout	Apr. to Sept.	Ulbster Arms Hotel, Halkirk.	Fly only. Average weight: 9oz.
Loch More	N.W. Sutherland	Salmon Sea Trout Brown Trout	1 May to 15 Oct.	Scourie Hotel, Scourie IV27 4SX. Tel: (01971) 502396.	Fly fishing only. Boats available.
Loch Morie	Head of River Alness	Brown Trout	15 Mar. to 6 Oct.	Novar Estates, Estate Office, Evanton, Ross-shire. Tel: (01349) 830208.	Bank fishing only. Any legal method.
Loch na Dail (Polly Loch)	Nr. Achiltibuie	Brown/Sea Trout	1 Apr. to 30 Sept.	Polly Estates Ltd,. Inverpolly, Ullapool IV26 2YB. Tel: (0185 482) 452.	Fly fishing only. No Sunday fishing. Boat available.
Loch nan Clar		Wild Brown Trout	1 Apr. to 15 Oct.	Garvault Hotel, by Kinbrace. Tel: Kinbrace 224.	Average weight of fish caught: 8oz. Popular flies: Loch Ordie, Black Spider, Black Pennel. Fly fishing only.
Loch Navar		Salmon Brown Trout	March to End Sept.	Altnaharra Hotel, By Lairg IV27 4UE.	Average weight of fish caught: Salmon - 8lbs, Brown Trout - 8oz. Popular flies: Trout - Pennel, Zulu, Peter Ross. Salmon - Invicta, Pennel. Other baits: toby and sprat. 3 boats available.
Loch Palm		Wild Brown Trout	1 Apr. to 15 Oct.	Garvault Hotel, by Kinbrace. Tel: Kinbrace 224.	Average weight of fish caught: 8oz. Popular flies: Loch Ordie, Black Spider, Black Pennel. Fly fishing only.
Loch Rangag	Latheron	Brown Trout	1 Apr. to 30 Sept.	John Anderson, Lochend Cottage, Latheron, Caithness. Tel: (015934) 230.	Average weight of fish caught: 12oz. Fly fishing only. Boats are available.
Rhiconich (50 lochs)	Nr. Kinlochbervie	Salmon Sea Trout Brown Trout	15 Feb. to 15 Oct.	Rhiconich Hotel, Kinlochbervie. Tel: (01971) 521224.	Fly fishing only. 7 boats available.
Loch Rhifail		Wild Brown Trout	1 Apr. to 15 Oct.	Garvault Hotel, by Kinbrace. Tel: Kinbrace 224.	Average weight of fish caught: 8oz. Popular flies: Loch Ordie, Black Spider, Black Pennel. Fly fishing only.

Water	Location	Species	Season	Permit available from	Other information
Loch Rhimsdale		Wild Brown Trout	1 Apr. to 15 Oct.	Garvault Hotel, by Kinbrace. Tel: Kinbrace 224.	Average weight of fish caught: 8oz. Popular flies: Loch Ordie, Black Spider. Fly fishing only.
Loch Rhuard	Latheron	Brown Trout	1 Apr. to 30 Sept.	John Anderson, Lochend Cottage, Latheron, Caithness Tel: (015934) 230.	Average weight of fish caught: 12oz. Fly fishing only. Boats are available.
Loch Rossail		Wild Brown Trout	1 Apr. to 15 Oct.	Garvault Hotel, by Kinbrace. Tel: Kinbrace 224.	Average weight of fish caught: 8oz. Popular flies: Loch Ordie, Black Spider, Black Pennel. Fly fishing only.
Loch Ruith a Phuil	by Strathpeffer	Brown Trout Rainbow Trout	15 Mar.-6 Oct. All year	The Tarvie Lochs Trout Fishery, Tarvie, by Strathpeffer IV14 9EJ. Tel: (01997) 421250.	Average weight of fish caught: Rainbow - 1lb 8oz, Brown - 12oz. Popular flies: Black Pennel, Zulu, Invicta, Sedge. Any legal baits or methods permitted. Bank fishing only. Open all year, except Xmas.
Loch St. Johns	Caithness	Wild Brown Trout	7 Apr. to 31 Sept.	Hugo Ross Fishing Tackle, 56 High Street, Wick. Tel/Fax: (01955) 604200.	Boats are available from above.
Sarclet Loch	Thrumster	Brown Trout	15 Mar.to 14 Oct.	Thrumster Filling Station. Tel: (01955) 85252.	Average weight of fish caught: 8oz to 1lb and + Popular Flies: Cocky Bundu, Soldier Palmer, Loch Orpy, Black Pennel.
Scourie Lochs	N.W. Sutherland	Salmon Sea Trout Brown Trout	1 May to 15 Oct.	Scourie Hotel, Scourie IV27 4SX. Tel: (01971) 502396.	Fly fishing only. Boats available.
Loch Sgeirach		Wild Brown Trout	1 Apr. to 15 Oct.	Garvault Hotel, by Kinbrace. Tel: Kinbrace 224.	Average weight of fish caught: 8oz. Popular flies: Loch Ordie, Black Spider, Black Pennel. Fly fishing only.
Loch Shin	Overscaig	Brown Trout Ferox Trout	30 Apr. to 30 Sept.	Overscaig Lochside Hotel, Loch Shin, by Lairg IV27 4NY. Tel: (0154 983) 203.	Boats and outboards available.
Lairg		Brown Trout Char	15 Apr. to 30 Sept.	Bank permits: R. Ross (Fishing Tackle), Main Street, Lairg IV27 4DB. Tel: (01549) 2239.	Average weight of fish caught: 7oz. Popular flies: Kate McLaren. Spinning & worm permitted, fly preferred. Boats and engines available from boathouse from 1 June.

Water	Location	Species	Season	Permit available from	Other information
Loch Sionascaig (& 9 other lochs)	Ullapool	Brown Trout	1 Apr. to 30 Sept.	Polly Estate Office, Inverpolly, Ullapool IV26 2YB. Tel: (0185 482) 452.	Boats & outboards available. No Sunday fishing. Fly fishing only, trawling for ferox permitted. Noted for large ferox.
Skyline Loch	Forsinard	Brown Trout	1 May to 30 Sept.	Forsinard Hotel, Forsinard. Tel: (016417) 221.	Popular flies: Black Zulu, Silver Butcher.
Loch Sletill	Forsinard	Brown Trout	1 May to 30 Sept.	Forsinard Hotel, Forsinard, Sutherland. Tel: (016417) 221.	Fly fishing only. Bank & boat fishing.
Loch Stack	N.W. Sutherland	Salmon Sea Trout Brown Trout	1 May to 15 Oct.	Scourie Hotel, Scourie IV27 4SX. Tel: (01971) 502396.	Fly fishing only. Boats are available. Ghillie mandatory on loch.
Loch Staink	Tongue	Brown Trout	Mar. to Sept.	Altnaharra Hotel, By Lairg IV27 4UE.	Average weight of fish caught: 8oz to 1lb. Popular flies: Pennel, Goats Toe, Zulu. 1 Boat available.
Loch Stemster	Latheron	Brown Trout	1 Apr. to 30 Sept.	John Anderson, Lochend Cottage, Latheron, Caithness. Tel: (015934) 230.	Average weight of fish caught: 12oz. Fly fishing only. Boats are available.
Loch Strath-Kinaird	by Ullapool	Salmon Sea trout	Apr. to Oct.	Ullasport, West Argyle Street, Ullapool. Tel: (01854) 612621.	
Tarvie Lochs	By Contin	Brown/ Rainbow Trout (stocked)		Sports & Model Shop, High Street, Dingwall. Tel: (01349) 62346.	Main loch: Fly fishing only. Boat available. Troutmaster water.' Small loch only: coarse methods.
Loch Tarvie	by Strathpeffer	Brown/ Rainbow Trout	15 Mar.-6 Oct. All year	The Tarvie Lochs Trout Fishery, Tarvie, by Strathpeffer IV14 9EJ. Tel: (01997) 421250.	Average weight of fish caught: Rainbow - 2lbs 4oz, Brown - 1lb 12oz. Popular flies: Black Pennel, Zulu, Invicta, Sedge. Fly fishing only. Boat fishing only. Open all year, except Xmas.
Tongue Lochs (8)	Tongue	Wild Brown Trout	15 Mar. to 6 Oct.	Ben Loyal Hotel, Tongue. Tel: Tongue 216. Post Office, Tongue. Tel: Tongue 201.	Fly fishing only. Boats available on some.
Loch Uidh Tarraigean (Upper Polly Lochs)	by Achiltibuie	Brown Trout	1 Apr. to 30 Sept.	Polly Estates Ltd., Inverpolly, Ullapool IV26 2YB. Tel: (0185 482) 452.	Fly fishing only. No Sunday fishing.
Ulbster Estate Lochs (9 hill lochs)	Halkirk	Brown Trout	15 Mar. to Sept.	Ulbster Arms Hotel, Halkirk, Caithness. Tel: (0184783) 206.	No Sunday fishing. Fly fishing only. 1 boat on each of 5 lochs.

Please mention this Pastime Publications guide

Water	Location	Species	Season	Permit available from	Other information
Loch Watenan	Ulbster	Brown Trout	1 May to 30 Sept.	Mr. J. Swanson, Aspen Bank, Banks Road, Watten. Tel: (0195582) 208.	Fly fishing only. 1 boat available.
Loch Watten	Watten Village	Brown Trout	1 May to 31 Sept.	Hugo Ross Fishing Tackle, 56 High Street, Wick. Tel/Fax: (01955) 604200.	Boats for hire from tackle shop. Fish min. size 10". No Sunday fishing. Fly only.
		Brown Trout	1 May to 1 Oct.	J.A. Barnetson, Lynegar Farm, Watten. Tel: (0195582) 205/308.	Average weight of fish caught: 12oz. Popular flies: March Brown, Butcher, Peter Ross. Fly fishing only. 3 boats available.
	(A882) Between Wick & Thurso	Stocked Brown Trout	1 May to 30 Sept.	John F. Swanson, Aspen Bank, Banks Lodge, Watten. Tel: (0195582) 326/208.	Average weight of fish caught: 12oz to 1lb. Fly fishing only. 4 boats are available.
Loch Wester	by Wick	Salmon Sea Trout Brown Trout	1 Mar. to 31 Oct.	Mrs. G. Dunnet, Auckhorn Lyth, by Wick KW1 4UD. Tel: (0195583) 208. Hugo Ross, Fishing Tackle, 56 High Street, Wick. Tel: (01955) 604200.	Fly fishing only. Boats available: 1 July to 31 Oct.
Yarrows Loch	Thrumster	Brown Trout	15 Mar.to 14 Oct.	Thrumster Filling Station. Tel: (01955) 85252.	Average weight of fish caught: 12oz to 1lb (heavier fish have been caught). Popular Flies: Black Pennel, Cinnamon & Golf, Peter Ross, Soldier Palmer. Boats are available - ask at Thrumster Filling Station.

FOR MAPS TURN
TO PAGE 171

Area Tourist Boards
Area Tourist Board
Western Isles Tourist Board,
Area Tourist Officer,
Western Isles Tourist Board,
26 Cromwell Street, Stornoway,
Isle of Lewis PA87 2XY.
Tel: (01851) 703088.

RIVER PURIFICATION AUTHORITY
WESTERN ISLES ISLAND AREA
(No formal Board constituted)

RIVERS

Water	Location	Species	Season	Permit available from	Other information
LEWIS River Blackwater	13m West of Stornoway	Salmon Sea Trout Brown Trout	1 Jul.-14 Oct. 15 Mar. to 30 Sept.	The Manager, Garynahine Estate Office, Isle of Lewis. Tel: (01851) 621314.	Fly fishing only from bank.

LOCHS

Water	Location	Species	Season	Permit available from	Other information
LEWIS Beag-Na-Craoibhe	Stornoway	Brown Trout	15 Mar. to 6 Oct.	Sportsworld, 1-3 Francis Street, Stornoway. Tel: (01851) 705464.	Bank fishing. 1 boat available.
Loch Bruiche Breivat	Nr. Stornoway	Brown Trout Arctic Char	15 Mar. to 30 Sept.	Estate Office, Scaliscro, Timsgarry, Isle of Lewis. Tel: (01851) 75 325.	Popular flies: Brown Muddler, Invicta, Soldier Palmer. Boats are available.
Breugach	Stornoway	Brown Trout	15 Mar. to 6 Oct.	Sportsworld, 1-3 Francis Street, Stornoway. Tel: (01851) 705464.	Bank fishing. Two boats available.
Loch Coirigeroid	Nr. Stornoway	Brown Trout Arctic Char	15 Mar. to 30 Sept.	Estate Office, Scaliscro, Timsgarry, Isle of Lewis. Tel: (01851) 75 325.	Popular flies: Brown Muddler, Invicta, Soldier Palmer. Boats are available.
Loch Fhir Mhaoil	Nr. Stornoway	Salmon Sea Trout Brown Trout	June to 15 Oct.	Estate Office, Scaliscro, Timsgarry, Isle of Lewis. Tel: (01851) 75 325.	Spinning and worm fishing permitted. Boats are available.
Keose (and other lochs in Keose Glebe fishings	10 mls South of Stornoway	Brown Trout	15 Mar. to 30 Sept.	M. Morrison, Handa', 18 Keose Glebe, Lochs, Isle of Lewis PA86 9JX. Tel: (0185 183) 334. Sportsworld, 1-3 Francis Street, Stornoway. Tel: (01851) 705464. Tourist Office, 26 Cromwell Street, Stornoway. Tel: (01851) 703088.	Two boats, rods, tackle, life jackets. No Sunday fishing.
Loch Langavat	Nr. Stornoway	Salmon Sea Trout Brown Trout Arctic Char	15 Mar. to 15 Oct.	Estate Office, Scaliscro, Timsgarry, Isle of Lewis. Tel: (01851) 75 325.	Spinning and worming permitted. boats are available.
Loch MacLeod	Nr. Stornoway	Salmon Sea Trout Brown Trout	1 Jul.-14 Oct. 15 Mar. to 30 Sept.	The Manager, Garynahine Estate Office, Isle of Lewis. Tel: (01851) 621314.	

Water	Location	Species	Season	Permit available from	Other information
Loch na Craoibhe	Achmore	Brown Trout	15 Mar. to 6 Oct.	Sportsworld, 1-3 Francis Street, Stornoway. Tel: (01851) 705464.	Bank fishing. 1 boat available.
Loch nam Falcag	Achmmore	Brown Trout	15 Mar. to 6 Oct.	Sportsworld, 1-3 Francis Street, Stornoway. Tel: (01851) 705464.	Bank fishing. 1 boat available.
Loch nan Culaidhean	Nr. Stornoway	Salmon Sea Trout Brown Trout	1 Jul.-14 Oct. 15 Mar. to 30 Sept.	The Manager, Garynahine Estate Office, Isle of Lewis. Tel: (01851) 621314.	
Lochs Sgibacleit, Shromois, Airigh Thormaid	Nr. Stornoway	Salmon Sea Trout Brown Trout	May to 30 Oct.	Estate Office, Scaliscro, Timsgarry, Isle of Lewis. Tel: (01851) 75 325.	Spinning & worm fishing permitted. Boats are available,
Loch Tarbart	Nr. Stornoway	Salmon Sea Trout Brown Trout	1 Jul.-14 Oct. 15 Mar. to 30 Sept.	The Manager, Garynahine Estate Office, Isle of Lewis. Tel: (01851) 621314.	
Loch Tungavat	Nr. Stornoway	Brown Trout	15 Mar. to 15 Oct.	Estate Office, Scaliscro, Timsgarry, Isle of Lewis. Tel: (01851) 75 325.	Average weight of fish caught: 6 to 8oz Popular flies: Soldier Palmer, Butcher, Invicta. Boats are available.
Vatandip	Stornoway	Brown Trout	15 Mar. to 6 Oct.	Sportsworld, 1-3 Francis Street, Stornoway. Tel: (01851) 705464.	Bank fishing. 1 boat available.
BENBECULA Loch Eilean Iain	Benbecula	Brown Trout	Mar. to Sept.	South Uist Estates Ltd., Estate Office, South Uist.	Average weight of fish caught: 1 to 3lbs. Popular flies: Soldier Palmer, Black Pennel, Ke-He, Worm Fly. 1 boat available.
Loch Hermidale	Benbecula	Brown Trout		South Uist Estates Ltd., Estate Office, South Uist. Colin Campbell Sports, Benbecula. Tel: (01870) 602236. Bornish Stores, Bornish, South Uist. Tel: (018785) 366.	Average weight of fish caught: 12oz to 1lb. Popular flies: Black Spider, Blue Zulu, Peter Ross, Invicta. 1 boat is available.
South Langavat (Heorovay - Olavat) and numerous other lochs	Benbecula	Brown Trout	15 Mar.- 30 Sept.	Bornish Stores, Tel: (08785) 366. Colin Campbell Sports Ltd., Balivanich. Tel: (01870) 602236.	Fly only. Boats available.
Loch Olavat (East, West, North)	Benbecula	Brown/ Sea Trout		South Uist Estates Ltd., Estate Office, South Uist.	Popular flies: Black Pennel, Invicta, Peter Ross, Grouse & Claret. 2 boats are available.

Water	Location	Species	Season	Permit available from	Other information
SOUTH UIST **Loch Druim** **an Lasgair**	South Uist	Brown Trout	15 Mar. to 6 Oct.	South Uist Estates Ltd., Estate Office, South Uist.	Average weight of fish caught: 12oz to 1lb. Popular flies: Soldier Palmer, Butchers, Black Spider.
East Loch **Bee**	South Uist	Brown Trout	Mar. to Sept.	South Uist Estates Ltd., Estate Office, South Uist. Colin Campbell Sports, Benbecula. Tel: (01870) 602236. Bornish Stores, Bornish, South Uist. Tel: (018785) 366.	Average weight of fish caught: 12oz to 1lb 8oz. Popular flies: Black Pennel, Ke-He, Bloody Butcher. 2 boats are available.
All hill and **Machair** **Lochs**	South Uist	Salmon Sea Trout Brown Trout	Jul. to Oct. Apr.-End Sept.	Resident Manager, Lochboisdale Hotel, Lochboisdale, South Uist. Tel: (018784) 332. South Uist Estates Ltd., Estate Office, South Uist.	Fourteen boats available on lochs. Fly fishing only.
Loch Snaid	South Uist	Brown Trout		South Uist Estates Ltd., Estate Office, South Uist.	Average weight of fish caught: 12oz to 1lb. Popular flies:: Grouse & Claret, Black Pennel, Black Spider, Butchers.
NORTH UIST **Lochs & Sea** **Pools in** **North Uist**		Salmon Sea Trout Brown Trout	25 Feb.-15 Oct. 15 Mar.-31 Oct. 15 Mar.- 30 Sept.	The Manager, Lochmaddy Hotel, North Uist. Tel: (01876) 500331.	Average weight of fish caught: Salmon - 5lbs 5oz, Sea Trout - 2lbs 5oz, Brown Trout - 8oz. Fly fishing only. No Sunday fishing. Boats are available on most lochs.
ISLE OF **HARRIS** **Laxdale** **System**	Isle of Harris	Salmon Sea Trout Brown Trout	15 Mar. to 15 Oct.	Tony Scherr, Borve Lodge Estates, Isle of Harris. Tel: (01859) 550202.	Fly fishing only. Permits cannot be reserved in advance.

Please mention this Pastime Publications guide

Area Tourist Boards

Orkney Tourist Board,
Information Centre,
6 Broad Street, Kirkwall,
Orkney KW15 1NX.
Tel: (01856) 872856.

Shetland Islands Tourism
Area Tourist Officer,
Shetland Islands Tourism,
Information Centre,
Market Cross, Lerwick,
Sheltand ZE1 0LU.
Tel: (01595) 3434.

PURIFICATION AUTHORITY
ORKNEY ISLANDS AREA
SHETLAND ISLANDS AREA
(No formal Boards constituted)

LOCHS

Water	Location	Species	Season	Permit available from	Other information
ORKNEY Boardhouse	Mainland	Brown Trout	15 Mar.-6 Oct.	None required	Boats available locally. All legal methods permitted. Anglers are recommended to join Orkney Trout Fishing Association, Kirkwall, who make facilities available to visitors.
Harray	Mainland	Brown Trout	15 Mar.-6 Oct.	Merkister Hotel. Loch Harray, Orkney. Tel: (0185 677) 366.	See Orkney for further information.
Hundland	Mainland	Brown Trout	15 Mar.-6 Oct.	None required	See Orkney for further information.
Kirbister	Mainland	Brown Trout	15 Mar.-6 Oct.	None required	See Orkney for further information.
Stenness	Mainland	Sea Trout Brown Trout	25 Feb.-31 Oct. 15 Mar.-6 Oct.	None required.	See Orkney for further information.
Swannay	Mainland	Brown Trout	15 Mar.-6 Oct.	None required	See Orkney for further information.
SHETLAND 1000 lochs & voes	Shetland Islands	Sea Trout Grilse Brown Trout	25 Feb. to 31 Oct. 15 Mar.-6 Oct.	Shetland Anglers Association, A. Miller, Hon. Sec., 3 Gladstone Terrace, Lerwick. Shetland Tourist Info. Centre, Market Cross, Lerwick. Anderson & Co., Market Cross, Lerwick.	Average weight of fish caught: Brown Trout - 1 to 1lb 8oz, Sea Trout & Grilse - 2 to 8lbs. Popular flies: all dark flies - Black Pennel, Grouse & Claret, Ke-He, Invicta, Blue Zulu (sizes 10 & 12). Other baits: spinning where permitted with mepps spoons and toby lures. Association boats available on 5 popular lochs: Spiggie, Benston, Tingwall, Clousta, Eela Water.

Water	Location	Species	Season	Permit available from	Other information
Various	Yell Island	Brown Trout	15 Mar. to 6 Oct.	No permit required, fishing free.	Average weight of fish caught: 8oz to 8lbs+ Popular flies: Bibio, Silver Invicta. Spinning permitted. 1 boat on Littlestar Loch, Burravoe. Boat permit available from Old Haa Museum.
Huxter Loch	Isle of Whalsay	Brown Trout	15 Mar. to 6 Oct.	Brian J. Poleson, Sheardaal, Huxter, Symbister, Whalsay.	Average weight of fish caught: 12oz. Fly fishing only. 1 boat available.
Ibister Loch	Isle of Whalsay	Brown Trout	15 Mar. to 6 Oct.	Brian J. Poleson, Sheardaal, Huxter, Symbister, Whalsay.	Average weight of fish caught: 10 to 12oz. Fly fishing only. 1 boat available.

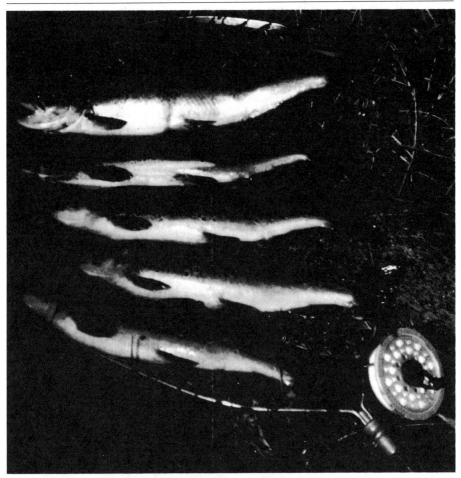

5 splendid trout taken during the evening rise.

Please mention this Pastime Publications guide

TYING THE TRADITIONAL HIGHLAND FLIES

BY

LESLEY CRAWFORD

Though I have fished on and off for over 30 years my serious interest in fly tying only really started about 10 years ago when I came North from Glasgow to the wild and beautiful fishing County of Caithness. Albeit I had been brought up with largely traditional loch style techniques with trusted wet fly patterns, in reckless youth I somehow never found the patience or the time to construct my own flies. This was to change when my husband, perhaps out of pity for a listless out of season fisher, bought me a starter fly tying kit and a vice and let me get on with it. After many breaks of thread, spilling of varnish, considerable myopia and much back strain I at last began to achieve some consistency and lo and behold the next season the fish even liked the results! And therein lies the rub for in the end the only real judge of your fly is the trout who takes it. You may tie the most exquisite of Greenwells Glory's or the neatest of nymphs yet they can be studiously ignored in preference to a dog eared, thoroughly chewed Ke He or a scrunched up Black Pennel.

Trout will take the artificial fly either because they think its a piece of food or because they are almost playfully curious or because it stimulates an aggressive response, so we anglers will want to know what does the trick and what does not. I offer now some simple guidelines for tying flies successfully for Highland lochs, they are by no means fail safe, fish are cantankerous beasts but usually they work. For a start the pattern you tie should have a good shape, trout see suggestions of outlines first then think about whether the wing

is too short or long after. To me the fly should at least try and copy an insect, nymph, mollusc, crustacean or a small fish, if it ends up looking like a hefty woolly clump like my very first attempts, don't use it. The fly should be scruffy yet lightly and securely tied (wild trout often strip the hackle off when caught, they fight so hard) and it should move well in the water. Good flies pulse or dance on the loch, poor ones plop like a stone. I like scruffy but not overly dressed flies as I want light to come through the hackles making them look like struggling legs of an insect or shrimp, overly dressed flies look like black blobs though trout will take them now and then when actively feeding. The effective use of good 'combination' colours cannot be overemphasised, that is colours which are best seen in our often peat stained waters. The top combination without fail for Highland waters is black and red and there are endless wet fly patterns using these - Zulus, Bibio's, Watsons Fancy and all their variations. Flies of brown and red are next and Soldier Palmers, Ke He and Red Invicta are extremely successful. Browns and golds are good as are browns and black. Colours you will see little of in my box are lurid pinks, fluorescent greens or yellows, peach and purple, I give them all a wide berth as do a number of the trout. It is difficult to know exactly why the wild trout prefers the darker colours though it is almost certainly due to the peculiarities of the trouts eyesight and the way light is transmitted through our Northern waters. So when you are tying think of shape, colour and movement and you will not go far wrong.

I am often asked if I have an ultimate favourite fly, a fly which does everything and means all things to all trout. The simple answer to that is not really but I would offer now a deadly trio of patterns which will usually work somewhere, somehow and at sometime in the fishing day! First the old favourite the Zulu and its variations. The Black Zulu is my most commonly used fly and I tie it traditionally with black wool body, silver rib, palmered black hackle and red wool tail. It is not a difficult one to tie but make sure the tail does not bulge much over the bend of the hook and that the hackle is lightly palmered down the hook rather than bunched at the head like some shop bought versions. It is not very clear what the Zulu was tied to represent for it looks anything from a struggling insect to a snail to a small fish fry depending on how you move it through the water. One thing is certain however, the brown trout and the sea trout relish it wet or when dabbed with floatant, it's just as effective dry. Secondly there is that other wonderful multi purpose fly the Soldier Palmer. This fly (also known as the Red Palmer) seems to have been around in some form or other since Medieval times when the Mummers dressed themselves in palms and twigs for an ancient ceremony, hence the name 'palmer' loosely meaning wrapped around. Tying this fly is relatively simple and I use a red floss or wool body, red wool tail (again not too long over the hook bend) gold wire rib, reddish brown hen hackle palmered down the body and tied in with the gold

wire for security. The Soldier Palmer is such a versatile fly it can be added to in a variety of ways, for example, by using a pearl maraflash along with the traditional rib or adding in another shade of brown hackle at the head for extra bounce. Fish take this fly as a shrimp or a struggling sedge and it can be fished wet or dry almost always eliciting a strong take from the trout.

The Invicta completes the trio and this fly is extremely effective as a general representation of sedges, various other winged insects, nymphs or small fish. There are a number of variants involved with this pattern including the Silver, Orange and Red Invicta. The traditional tying is probably the most used and involves a yellow seals fur body, oval gold rib, palmered red cock hackle, hen pheasant wing, blue jay throat hackle and a few yellow strands of golden pheasant for the tail. I like a straggly Invicta rather than a neatly dressed one and the wing should not be over heavy. The most effective dressing for both brown and sea trout in the Far North is in my opinion the Red Invicta which is the standard dressing plus dyed red hen hackle at the neck. This is very deadly when fished deeper than usual on a slow retrieve and I assume trout take it as a fish in difficulty.

Fly tying is rather like fishing. You need deftness of touch, patience and an understanding of why the fish take the particular pattern you are tying. Experiment as much as you like once reasonably competent and if you visit the North as we hope you will do, have the aforementioned patterns in your box!

TURN TO PAGE 58
FOR GAME ANGLING
GAZETTEER

SCOTTISH FEDERATION FOR COARSE ANGLING

The Federation was formed in 1975 to promote and encourage the sport of Coarse Angling in Scotland. It is recognised by the Scottish Sports Council as being the governing body for Coarse Angling throughout Scotland.

Objects and Functions
To obtain waters for coarse angling.
To assist with fisheries management.
To assist with stocking of waters.
To promote and develop coarse angling in Scotland.
To promote and organise competitions and league matches.
To provide team representation at the World Championships (CIPS-FIPS-ED).
To organise international events for Scottish anglers.

Members
At present, 12 clubs are affiliated to the Federation. Individual membership of the Federation is available although it is preferred that individuals join clubs affiliated to the Federation. The annual subscription for Club Membership of the SFCA is £35 with a joining fee of £17.50. Individual membership is offered at £3.

Coaching and Courses
Some SFCA member clubs hold in class' coaching sessions for novice anglers, while others operate on the bank' instruction thus providing knowledge under varying conditions.

Committee Structure
The affairs of the Federation are at present conducted by a Management Committee comprising the Chairman, Hon. Secretary, Hon. Treasurer and Club representatives. A development and a Match Angling Committee also exist to deal with specific projects.

Office Bearers
Chairman
Ralston McPherson,
17 Barrhill Court,
Rosebank,
Kirkintilloch G66 3PL.
Secretary
David Charlton,
26 Hawthorn Drive,
Banknock,
Stirlingshire FK4 1LF.
Treasurer
Robert Crossan,
2 Quarryknowe Place,
Bellshill ML4 2AW.
National Team Manager
George Glen,
29 Riverside Grove,
Edinburgh EH12 5QS.
Match Committee Secretary
Stephen McCavney,
165 Airbles Street,
Motherwell,
Strathclyde ML1 1UH.
Development Committee Secretary
Frank Gibbons,
32 Clark Street,
Motherwell ML1.

Avon Coarse Angling Club
William McClymont, 85 Horatius Street,
Motherwell, Strathclyde ML1 3RS.

Barochan Angling Club
A.H. Keir, Tigh Na Fleur,
Mill O'Gryffe Road, Bridge of Weir.

Glasgow Match Anglers Club
Frank Revell,
93 Woodhead Crescent,
Tannochside,
Uddingston G71.

Glasgow & West of Scotland Regional Association of the Pike Anglers Club of G.B.
Ralston McPherson,
17 Barrhill Court,
Rosebank,
Kirkintilloch G66 3PL.

Kirkintilloch Match Angling Club
Drew McCluskey,
15 Locheil Drive,
Milton of Campsie,
Strathclyde G65.

Lanarkshire Colts Angling Club
M. Dunn,
47 Hamilton Street,
Carluke,
Strathclyde ML8 4HA.

Linlithgow Coarse Angling Club
David Hood,
161 Bailielands,
Linlithgow.

Monklands Coarse Angling Club
John McShane,
5 Crinan Crescent,
Townhead, Coatbridge,
Strathclyde ML25 2LG.

Milton Coarse Angling Club
John Torrance,
2 Mireton Street,
Ruchill, Glasgow.

North West Coarse Angling Club
Brian Cochrane,
30 Langa Street,
Glasgow G20.

Royal Air Force (Kincaple A.C.)

Westside Angling Group
Craig Cowan,
45 Portsoy Place,
Glasgow G13 4LN.

Competition

The S.F.C. organise a Summer and Winter league programme for competing teams of six anglers. Two divisions are involved in the Summer League programme. Within the format of both Summer Leagues, a Knockout Championship is staged. The winning teams from both divisions meet in an ultimate 'Fish-off' to establish the knockout champions.

Also staged are a number of other events for S.F.C.A. affiliated clubs and members including visiting individuals and teams.

The 'All Scotland Championships', decided on a penalty points basis, open to individuals and teams resident in Scotland.

Specifically for S.F.C.A. members, is the 'Scottish Federation Cup'. This being an individul entrant event, the result is decided upon on weight.

Open to visiting anglers is the 'Scottish Federation Open' and the 'Scottish National' catering for both individual entries and teams.

A 'Junior National Championship', is staged annually.

The 'Scottish Pole Championships',

open to both individuals and teams, entry being open to all.

The *Scottish National Team* compete in the Home Internationals against England, Ireland and Wales. This event in 1995 is hosted by Scotland. Scotland continue to gain respect on the World stage and will continue to compete at World level and are optimistic for the future.

Many S.F.C.A. member clubs stage their own match programmes throughout the year, enjoying the absence of a 'closed season', and are very receptive to new members and enquiries are welcomed.

THE S.F.C.A. COARSE ANGLER'S COUNTRY CODE

1. Never throw away hooks, line or shot.
   Take them home and get rid of them properly.

2. Plastic bags can kill.
   Take away all rubbish from your spot,
   even if it was there before.

3. Know the fishery rules and return all coarse fish,
   including pike and eels, unharmed.

4. Help protect wildlife, plants and trees.
   Fish well away from birds' nesting places.

5. Place your keepnet to hold your fish properly.
   Stake it out if you can.

6. Use barbless hooks when you can.
   Take care when casting.

7. Park cars away from entrances.
   Keep to paths and close all gates.

8. Carbon rods conduct electricity.
   Keep well away from overhead power lines.

9. Don't light fires.
   Report any sign of pollution.

10. Keep dogs under control.
    Don't disturb the peace of the countryside.

DEFEND YOUR SPORT
JOIN THE SCOTTISH FEDERATION FOR COARSE ANGLING

SCOTTISH FRESHWATER FISH RECORDS

Bream   8lbs, 1oz (3.629kg) Castle Loch, Lochmaben D. Beattie 1990

Carp   26lbs, 2oz (11.849kg) Duddingston S. Killen 1990

Dace   1lb, 3oz, 8dr (0.553kg) River Tweed, Coldstream G. Keech 1979

Eel   5lbs, 8oz (2.495kg) Loch Ochiltree T. May 1987

Goldfish   1lb, 9oz (0.709kg) Forth & Clyde Canal B. Stevenson 1978

Grayling   2lbs, 14oz, 2dr (1.308kg) Lyne Water R. Brown 1987

Perch   4lbs, 14oz (2.210kg) Loch Ard J. Walker 1989

Pike   47lbs, 11oz (21.631kg) Loch Lomond T. Morgan 1947

Roach   2lbs, 11oz (1.219kg) Strathclyde stillwater P. Russell 1987

Tench   6lbs, 00oz, 4dr (2.729kg) Lanark Loch A. Gardner 1991

No record exists for the following species, however qualifying weights are as follows:

Barbel	1lb	**Rudd**	2 lbs
Bleak	2oz	**Ruffe**	4oz
Chub	4lbs	**S/Bream**	8oz
Gudgeon	4oz	**Zander**	1lb
Orfe	2 lbs		

How to claim a record:

1. No claims will be considered for dead fish. All fish must be returned to the water alive.

2. The claim should be made on a form available from the Development Committee who must be satisfied by the evidence that the fish was correctly identified and weighed, and was captured by fair angling.

3. New claims will be considered subject to the following minimum requirements:

   a) Photographs of the fish must be available.

   b) The scales must be certified as being accurate.

   c) Witnesses will assist the claim and if possible these should be experienced anglers.

   In the case of a fish over the British record weight please telephone either Peterborough (01733) 54084 (day) or 25248 (night) for advice.

COARSE FISHING

BORDERS

RIVERS

Water	Location	Species	Season	Permit available from	Other information
Eden	Kelso (Ednam East Mill)	Grayling	1 Apr to 30 Sept	Dr. & Mrs. Poole, Ednam East Mill, Kelso.	Fly only.
Kale Water	(above Easter Wooden) Bowmont (above Primside Mill), Oxnam (above Bloody-laws).	Grayling	All year	Mr. D.Y. Gray, 17 Mainsfield Avenue, Morebattle. Templehall Hotel, Morebattle. Garage, Morebattle.	No ground fishing. No Sunday fishing.
	1.5 miles from Junction with Teviot upstream	Grayling	15 Mar to 30 Sept	Mr. A. Graham, Loch Keeper, The Cottage, Eckford. Tel: (018355) 255. R.B. Anderson ws, Royal Bank Buildings, Jedburgh. Tel: (01835) 863202.	No Sundays.
Leader Water		Grayling	1 Jan to 30 Sept	Pollards, Newsagent, Earlston. G. Birbeck, Grocer, Earlston. E & M Browne Newsagent, Earlston. Black Bull, Earlston. Red Lion Hotel, Earlston. White Swan Hotel, Earlston. Anglers Choice, Melrose. Wilsons, The Saddlers, Dalkeith.	Permit also covers trout during trout season. No Sundays. Full details on permits.
Leet Water	Coldstream (North bank to main road bridge)	Grayling Dace Gudgeon Eel Roach	All year	Crown Hotel, Market Square, Coldstream. Coldstream Guardian, 60 High Street, Coldstream.	Normal methods. No spinning.
Teviot	(Ale, Borthwick, Rule and Slitrig)	Grayling	1 Jan to end Sept	Pet Shop, 1 Union Street, Hawick. Club Premises, 5 Sandbed, Hawick. Lindsays, Denholm.	All rules and regulations on ticket.
	Kelso	Grayling	1 May to 31 Aug & 1 Dec to 31 Jan	Forrest & Sons, 35 The Square, Kelso. Springwood Caravan Park. Intersport, 43 The Square. Kelso. Border Temperance Hotel. Tweedside Tackle, 36-38 Bridge Street, Kelso.	No Sundays. Restrictions on spinning. No maggots or ground bait. No trout or coarse fishing above Roxburgh Viaduct between 14th Sept & 30th Nov - both banks.

Water	Location	Species	Season	Permit available from	Other information
Teviot cont.	2.5 miles: Oxnam Mouth to Nine Wells, both banks in places. 1.5 miles Chesters Estate Boundary - A68 Road Bridge Cleikimin S bank only	Grayling	1 Dec to 31 Mar	Jedforest Angling Assoc. J.T. Renilson, 72 Howdenburn Court, Jedburgh. Sanford's, 6/8 Canongate, Jedburgh. W. Shaw, Canongate, Jedburgh.	No Sundays. Bait fishing allowed. No spinning. No Minnow fishing.
Tweed	Horncliffe 8 miles from Island above Horncliffe Village to Sea at Berwick	Grayling Roach Perch Dace Eel	All year	Free fishing	
	Kelso	Grayling	1 May to 31 Aug & 1 Dec to 31 Jan	Forrest & Sons, 35 The Square, Kelso. Intersport, 43 The Square, Kelso. Springwood Caravan Park. Tweedside Tackle, 36-38 Bridge Street, Kelso. Border Temperance Hotel.	South side: Junction pool to Kelso Bridge and Mellendean Burn to top of Broase Stream. North side: Kelso Cauld to top of Broase Stream except 2 private stretches. No Sunday fishing. Spinning restrictions. No maggots or ground bait.
	Ladykirk Norham Bridge to Horncliffe	Grayling Roach Perch Dace	19 Mar to 8 Oct	Ladykirk & Norham Angling Assoc., Mason's Arms, Norham. Tel: (01289) 82326. Victoria Hotel, Norham. Tel: (01289) 82237. Mace Shop, Norham. Tel: (01289) 382205.	No spinning. No ground baiting. Fly only above Norham Bridge to West Ford. No Sundays.
	Melrose	Grayling	Dec & Jan only	Anglers Choice, 23 Market Square, Melrose. Tel: (0189 682) 3070.	
	Norham Dean Burn at West Newbiggin	Grayling Roach Gudgeon Eel Dace	15 Mar to 6 Oct	Farm House, West Newbiggin, Norham, Berwick-on-Tweed.	Fly and worm fishing. No Sunday fishing.

Water	Location	Species	Season	Permit available from	Other information
Tweed cont.	Peebles	Grayling	1 Apr to 30 Sept	Peeblesshire Trout Fishing Assoc., D.G. Fyfe, 39 High Street, Peebles. Tel: (01721) 720131. Tweeddale Tackle Centre, 1 Bridgegate, Peebles. Tel: (01721) 720979. Sonnys Sports Shop, 29 High Street, Innerleithen. Tweed Valley Hotel, Walkerburn. Tel: (0189 687) 220. John Dickson & Son, 21 Frederick Street, Edinburgh. F & D Simpson, 28 West Preston Street, Edinburgh. Crook Inn, Tweedsmuir. Green Tree Hotel, Peebles.	(Stanhope-Thornielee, excluding Burgh Water and certain private stretches.) No spinning, no bait fishing April and September. No Sunday fishing. Tickets also cover Lyne Water. Waders desirable. Fly only on Tweed from Lynefoot upstream. Limit of 6 fish per day during April.

LOCHS

Water	Location	Species	Season	Permit available from	Other information
Alemoor Loch	nr. Hawick	Perch Pike		Secretary, Hawick Angling Club, R. Sutherland, 20 Longhope Drive, Hawick.	All rules and regulations detailed on ticket.
Hellmoor Loch	nr. Hawick	Perch Pike	15 Mar to 30 Sept	Secretary, Hawick Angling Club, R. Sutherland, 20 Longhope Drive, Hawick. Pet Shop, Union Street, Hawick. Club Premises, 5 Sandbed, Hawick.	No competitions. Key for gate at Club Premises.
St. Mary's Loch & Loch of the Lowes	Selkirk	Pike Perch Eels	1 Apr to 30 Sept	St. Mary's Loch A.C. Secretary, J. Miller, 25 Abbotsford Court, Colinton Road, Edinburgh. Tel: 0131-447 4187. The Glen Cafe, Cappercleuch. Tibbie Shiels Inn, St. Mary's Loch. Anglers Choice, 23 Market Square, Melrose. Keeper, Henderland East Cottage, Cappercleuch. Tel: (01750) 42243. Sonny's Sports Shop, 29 High Street, Innerleithen. Gordon Arms Hotel, Yarrow. Tweeddale Tackle Centre, 1 Bridgegate, Peebles.	Spinning and bait after 1 May only. Club fishing - apply in writing to Secretary. Sunday fishing allowed. Weekly permits are obtained only from the keeper. Permits must be obtained before commencing to fish. Boats from keeper only. Special boat seat is available for disabled angler by prior arrangement with keeper. 9am till 1 hour after sunset.

DUMFRIES & GALLOWAY

Water	Location	Species	Season	Permit available from	Other information
Cairnhouse Farm Loch	Newton Stewart	Perch Rudd Roach Tench	All Year	Palakona Guest House, 30 Queen Street, Newton Stewart. Tel: (01671) 402323.	Club water. Yearly permits available. Barbless hooks. No keep-nets.
Castle Loch	Lochmaben	Bream Roach Pike		Castle Filling Station, Lochmaben.	Scotland's premier Bream water - fish to 9lbs. Excellent night fishing.

Please mention this Pastime Publications guide 139

Water	Location	Species	Season	Permit available from	Other information
Craichlaw Loch	Newton Stewart	Carp Tench Roach Bream Rudd	Open all Year	Palakona Guest House, 30 Queen Street, Newton Stewart. Tel: (01671) 402323.	Night fishing by arrangement. Non toxic weights. 28 platformed pegs. Good access for disabled.
Culscadden Farm Pond	Garlieston	Roach Rudd Perch Carp Tench Bream	Open all year	Palakona Guest House, 30 Queen Street, Newton Stewart. Tel: (01671) 402323.	Baits: Maggot, Corn, Bread. 4 anglers max. Barbless hooks. No cans.
Dabton Loch	Thornhill	Perch	No close season	The Buccleuch Estates Ltd., Drumlanrig Mains, Thornhill DG3 4AG. Tel: (018486) 283.	Average weight of fish: 8oz. Baits: Worm, Maggot. Bank fishing. Sunday fishing. Overnight fishing by arrangement.
Drumrae Loch	Nr. Port William	Roach Tench Rudd Perch Bream Carp	All year	Palakona Guest House, 30 Queen Street, Newton Stewart. Tel: (01671) 402323.	Club water. Yearly permits available. Barbless hooks. No keep-nets.
Glendarroch Loch	Newton Stewart	Roach Rudd Perch Carp Tench Bream		Palakona Guest House, 30 Queen Street, Newton Stewart. Tel: (01671) 402323.	Baits: Maggot, Bread, Corn. 14 platformed pegs. Barbless hooks. No cans.
Loch Heron	Nr. Newton Stewart	Perch Roach Pike	Open all Year	Palakona Guest House, 30 Queen Street, Newton Stewart. Tel: (01671) 402323. Three Lochs Caravan Park, Newton Stewart.	Any legal method. Pike matches held regularly.
Loch Ken	(West Bank)	Roach Perch Pike	Open all Year	Shops & hotels in New Galloway	Long range tactics pay off early in year.
	(Glenlaggan)	Roach Perch Pike		On bank	Best known match pegs. Fish beyond shelf at 60-70 yds.
Loch Maberry	Drumlamford Estate	Coarse	Open all year	The Keeper, The Kennels, Drumlamford Estate, Barrhill. Tel: (0146 582) 256.	Spinning & bait allowed. Boats available.
Morton Pond	Thornhill	Tench	No close season	The Buccleuch Estates Ltd., Drumlanrig Mains, Thornhill DG3 4AG. Tel: (018486) 283.	Average weight of fish: 2lbs. Baits: Bread, Sweetcorn. Bank fishing. Sunday fishing. Overnight fishing by arrangement.
Loch Murray	Creetown	Roach Rudd Perch Tench Carp	Open all Year	Castle Cary Holiday Park, Creetown, Newton Stewart.	Baits: Bread, sweetcorn. 7 days. Pub & parking etc.

Water	Location	Species	Season	Permit available from	Other information
Loch Ronald	Nr. Newton Stewart	Pike Perch Roach	No close season	Palakona Guest House, 30 Queen Street, Newton Stewart DG8 6JL. Tel: (01670) 402323.	Any legal method permitted. Matches held regularly.
Loch Rutton	Lochfoot	Bream Roach Perch Pike	Open all Year		Excellent tip venue.
Loch Stroan	Castle Douglas	Pike Perch	Mar. to Oct.	Forest Enterprise, 21 King Street, Castle Douglas. Tel: (01556) 503626. Ticket machines both ends Raiders Road Forest Drive.	Bank fishing only. Any legal method. Sunday fishing.
White Loch of Myrton	Nr. Port William	Roach Rudd Perch Pike	All Year	Palakona Guest House, 30 Queen Street, Newton Stewart. Tel: (01671) 402323. On bank	Excellent pike fishing. All fish must be returned alive.
Woodhall Loch	Mossdale, Nr. New Galloway	Pike Perch Roach Brown Trout	Open all year	Mossdale Post Office, Mossdale, Castle Douglas DG7 2NF. Tel: (016445) 281.	Any legal method permitted.

Strathclyde

Water	Location	Species	Season	Permit available from	Other information
Auchinstarry Quarry	Kilsyth	Pike Perch Roach Tench Rudd	Open all year	Free fishing	
Castle Semple Loch	Lochwinnoch	Roach Perch Pike	No close season	New Visitor Centre, Castle Semple Loch, Lochwinnoch. Tel: (01505) 842882.	Shallow loch fishing at distance can pay of. Day permits for bank fishing.
River Clyde	Glasgow Green	Dace Roach occas. Bream Gudgeon	Open all year		Very deep winter venue
	Swanston Street, Glasgow.	Dace Roach	Open all year		Excellent pole and tip venue.
	Dalmarnock Bridge, Glasgow	Dace Roach Eels	Open all year		
	Belvedere, Glasgow	Dace Roach Eels	Open all year		Waggler and stick float pegs.

Water	Location	Species	Season	Permit available from	Other information
Forth & Clyde Canal	Bowling	Roach Perch Pike Tench Carp Eels	Open all year	British Waterways, Applecross Street, Glasgow.	Carp to 20lb.
	Dalmuir	Roach Perch Pike Tench Carp Eels	Open all Year	British Waterways, Applecross Street, Glasgow.	Specimen Roach and Eels.
	Westerton	Roach Perch Pike		British Waterways, Applecross Street, Glasgow.	Many big Perch and Roach.
	Firhill Basin, Maryhill	Roach Pike Perch Tench		British Waterways, Applecross Street, Glasgow.	Good summer Tench venue.
	Lambhill	Roach Perch Pike		British Waterways, Applecross Street, Glasgow.	Rarely fished, holds specimen fish.
	Bishopbriggs	Roach Bream Tench Perch Pike		British Waterways, Applecross Street, Glasgow.	Attractive tree lined stretch.
	Torrance to Glasgow Bridge	Roach Bream Carp Tench Perch Pike		J.B. Angling, 37 Eastside, Kirkintilloch.	Heavily stocked club stretch.
	Glasgow Bridge to Kirkintilloch.	Roach Bream Carp Tench Perch Pike		J.B. Angling, 37 Eastside, Kirkintilloch.	Excellent winter venue.
	Hillhead Basin, Kirkintilloch.	Tench Roach Bream Pike		British Waterways, Applecross Street, Glasgow.	Superb winter Tench venue.
	Auchinstarry, Kilsyth	Tench Roach Perch Pike		British Waterways, Applecross Street, Glasgow.	Early morning summer venue nets to 70lbs recorded.
	Dullatur	Roach Perch Tench Bream Pike Eels		British Waterways, Applecross Street, Glasgow.	Quality Perch and Roach in summer.
	Kelvinhead	Roach Perch Tench Bream Pike		British Waterways, Applecross Street, Glasgow.	Tench to 5lb +. Roach to 2lb in late summer.

Water	Location	Species	Season	Permit available from	Other information
Forth & Clyde Canal cont.	Wyndford	Tench Roach		British Waterways, Applecross Street, Glasgow.	Shallow stretch. Good Tench bags possible.
	Castlecary	Roach Perch Tench Pike		British Waterways, Applecross Street, Glasgow.	Attractive tree lined sections.
Hogganfield Loch	Millerston	Carp Roach Pike Perch Bream		Free fishing	Carp to double figures
Lanark Loch	Lanark	Carp Tench Perch	Open all year	On bank	
Linfern Loch	Straiton	Pike	No close season	Mr. R. Heaney, Tallaminnoch, Straiton. Tel: (0165 57) 617.	Sunday fishing. 1 May to mid-June no permits are available.
Monklands Canal	Coatbridge	Carp Roach Bream Dace Tench Gudgeon		On bank Monklands C.A.C.	Excellent summer venue
Strathclyde Country Park (Park Loch)	Motherwell	Roach Perch Bream Eels Carp	Open all year	Booking Office, Watersports Centre.	Summer method float Winter swimfeeder.
(River Avon)	Motherwell	Dace Roach Gudgeon Grayling		Booking Office, Watersports Centre.	Good Winter sport.
(River Clyde)	Motherwell	Dace Roach		Booking Office, Watersports Centre.	Method swimfeeder

FORTH & LOMOND

Water	Location	Species	Season	Permit available from	Other information
Duddingston Loch	Edinburgh	Carp Perch	Open all year	Historic Scotland, Sgt. McQueen, Royal Park Constabulary, Holyrood Park, Edinburgh.	Bird Sanctuary. Bank fishing. Restricted area. No lead weights.
River Endrick	Drymen	Dace Chub Roach Eels	Mat.-Oct.	White House, Drymen Bridge.	Fishes from Spring to Autumn.

Water	Location	Species	Season	Permit available from	Other information
Endrick cont.	Croftamie	Dace Chub Roach Perch Eels	15 Mar.- 30 Oct.	James D. Bilsland, Spittal Farm, Croftamie. by Glasgow. Tel: (01360) 60264.	Good Dace shoals. Odd Chub.
Loch Lomond	Balloch to Ardlui	Pike Perch Roach		Local shops. Tackle dealers.	
Union Canal		Roach Pike Perch Bream	Open all year	Lothian Regional Council, George IV Bridge, Edinburgh. Tel: 0131-229 9292 Ext. 3286 Tourist Office, Linlithgow. Tel: (01506) 844600.	Shallow canal fish fine.

Perch

SCOTTISH FEDERATION OF SEA ANGLERS
OFFICIALS

President
David Neil,
30 Woodfield Road, Ayr KA8 8LZ.
Tel: (01292) 266549.

Vice-Presidents
George Kinnear,
9 Killoch Drive, Barrhead, Renfrewshire
G78 2HX. Tel: 0141-881 4127.
Francis Jefferson,
No. 1 Sheshader Point, Isle of Lewis
PA86 0EW. Tel: (01851) 870214.

Hon. Treasurer
Robert Keltie,
76 Stewart Avenue, Bo'ness, West Lothian
EH51 9NW. Tel: (01506) 826274

Hon. Fish Recorder/
Conservation Officer
Gordon Morris, 8 Burt Avenue, Kinghorn,
Fife KY3 9XB. Tel: (01592) 890055

Coaching Co-ordinator
Henry Hamilton-Willows,
15 Carrick Drive, North Mount Vernon,
Glasgow G32 0RW. Tel: 0141-778 4454.

Public Relations
Officer/Sponsorship
Brian Burn,
Flat 2, 16 Bellevue Road, Ayr KA7 2SA.
Tel: (01292) 264735.

Office
S.F.S.A.,
Caledonia House, South Gyle,
Edinburgh EH12 8DQ. Tel: 0131-317 7192

REGIONAL SECRETARIES

Clyde & Western
Mr. John Taylor,
1/1, 6 Tower Terrace, Paisley, Renfrewshire
PA1 2JT. Tel: 0141-887 0314.

Central
Mrs. Margaret McCallum,
58 Pottery Street, Kirkcaldy KY1 3EU.
Tel: (01592) 651710

West
Mr. William Clark,
4 Fullarton Street, Kilmarnock, Ayrshire.

North East
Mr. Stan Eggie,
137 Glenclova Terrace,
Forfar DD8 1NT. Tel: (01307) 465355.

Eastern
Mr. Gary Wilson,
8 Maderia Place,
Edinburgh EH6 4AN. Tel: 0131-553 7645.

Highlands & Islands
Mr. Willie Mackintosh,
Schiehallion', 16 Glengarry Road, Inverness
IV3 6NJ. Tel: (01463) 235850.

Western Isles
Mr. Francis Jefferson,
No. 1 Sheshader, Point, Isle of Lewis
PA86 0EW. Tel: (01851) 870214.

SCOTTISH BOAT AND SHORE (rod and line caught)
MARINE FISH RECORDS

B - Boat Records   S - Shore Records   Spec. - Specimen Qualifying Weight

Species		lb.	oz.	dm.	kg.	Place of Capture	Angler	Year	Spec. lb.
ANGLERFISH	B	45	0	0	20.412	Sound of Mull	D. Hopper	1978	20
Lophius piscatorius	S	38	0	0	17.237	Blairmore Pier Loch Long	L. C. Hanley	1970	15
ARGENTINE	B		5	3	0.147	Arrochar	I. Millar	1978	4oz.
Argentina sphyraena	S	OPEN AT ANY WEIGHT							
BARRACUDINA	B	OPEN AT ANY WEIGHT							any
(Paralepis coreganoides borealis	S	0	1	14	0.054	Newton Shore	D. Gillon	1987	1½oz.
BASS	B	8	14	3	4.025	Balcary Bay	D. Shaw	1975	6
Dicentrarchus labrax	S	13	4	0	6.010	Almorness Point	G. Stewart	1975	6
BLACKFISH	B	3	10	8	1.658	Heads of Ayr	J. Semple	1972	2½
Centrolophus niger	S	OPEN AT ANY WEIGHT							any
BLENNY, SHANNY	B	OPEN AT ANY WEIGHT							any
Blennius pholis	S	0	1	10	0.046	Carolina Port Dundee Docks	M. S. Ettle	1983	1oz.
BLENNY, TOMPOT	B	OPEN AT ANY WEIGHT							any
Blennius gattorugine	S		2	12	0.078	Portpatrick	G. Dods	1977	2oz.
BLENNY, VIVIPAROUS	B		10	0	0.283	Craigendoran	T. Lambert	1977	7oz.
Zoarces viviparus	S		11	3	0.317	Craigendoran	D. Ramsay	1975	7oz.
BLENNY, YARREL'S	B	OPEN AT ANY WEIGHT							any
Chirolophis ascanii	S		2	1	0.059	Gourock	D. McEntee	1979	1½oz.
BLUEMOUTH	B	3	2	8	1.431	Loch Shell	Mrs A. Lyngholm	1976	2½
Helicolenus dactylopterus	S	OPEN AT ANY WEIGHT							any
BREAM, BLACK	B	2	9	0	1.162	Kebock Head Lewis	T. Lumb	1974	1
Spondyllosoma cantharus	S	2	2	8.5	0.979	Mull of Galloway	B. Robbins	1992	1
BREAM, GILTHEAD	B	OPEN AT ANY WEIGHT							any
Sparus aurata	S	2	6	4	1.084	Dunnet Head	C. Toplis	1992	1
BREAM, RAYS	B	6	3	13	2.829	West of Barra Head	J. Holland	1978	4
Brama brama	S	6	6	8	2.905	Portobello	G. Taylor	1973	4
BREAM RED	B	4	10	0	2.097	Ardnamurchan	R. Steel	1969	1
Pagellus bogaraveo	S	OPEN AT ANY WEIGHT							any
BRILL	B	1	4	0	0.567	Portpatrick	J. Dickson	1984	1
Scophthalmus rhombus	S	1	2	0	0.510	Killintrinnan Lighthouse	P. Baisbrown	1971	1
BULL HUSS	B	20	3	8	9.171	Mull of Galloway	J. K. Crawford	1971	15
scyliorhinus stellaris	S	15	8	0	7.031	West Tarbet Mull of Galloway	A. K. Paterson	1976	10
BUTTERFISH	B	OPEN AT ANY WEIGHT							any
Pholis gunnellus	S		1	2	0.032	Gourock	D. McEntee	1978	1oz.
CATFISH, COMMON	B	13	12	11	6.256	Burnmouth	D. Brown	1985	7
Anachichas lupus	S	12	12	8	5.797	Stonehaven	G. M. Taylor	1978	4
COALFISH	B	28	4	0	12.814	Eyemouth	L. Gibson	1982	12
Pollachius virens	S	11	7	8	5.202	Loch Long	S. Mather	1976	7
COD	B	46	0	8	20.879	Gantocks	B. Baird	1970	25
Gadus morhua	S	40	11	8	18.470	Balcary Point	K. Robinson	1988	15
DAB	B	2	12	4	1.254	Gairloch	R. Islip	1975	1½
Limanda limanda	S	2	5	0	1.049	Cairnryan	A. Scott	1969	1½

B - Boat Records   S - Shore Records   Spec. - Specimen Qualifying Weight

Species		lb.	oz.	dm.	kg.	Place of Capture	Angler	Year	Spec. lb.
DAB LONG ROUGH	B		6	6	0.180	Helensburgh	J. Napier	1984	4oz.
Hippoglossoides platessoides	S		5	8	0.155	Coulport	I. McGrath	1975	4oz.
DOGFISH BLACK-MOUTHED	B	2	13	8	1.288	Loch Fyne	J. H. Anderson	1977	1½
Galeus melastromus	S	OPEN AT ANY WEIGHT							any
DOGFISH LESSER-SPOTTED	B	3	15	12	1.807	Portpatrick	R. I. Carruthers	1987	3
Scyliorhinus caniculus	S	4	15	3	2.246	Abbey Burnfoot	S. Ramsay	1988	3
DRAGONET COMMON	B		5	0	0.142	Gareloch	T. J. Ashwell	1985	4oz.
Callionymus lyra	S		5	0	0.143	Loch Long	J. Crawford	1985	4½
EEL, COMMON	B	1	13	7	0.834	Gareloch	P. Fleming	1976	1½
Anguilla anguilla	S	3	0	0	1.360	Ayr Harbour	R. W. Morrice	1972	2
EEL, CONGER	B	48	1		21.820	Largs	R. Bond	1985	30
Conger conger	S	63	8	0	28.803	Balcary	B. Ford	1991	25
FLOUNDER	B	2	13	11	1.295	Portnockie	K. F. Mackay	1985	2½
Platichthys flesus	S	4	11	8	2.140	Musselburgh	R. Armstrong	1970	2½
GARFISH	B	1	11	8	0.799	Brodick	R. Stockwin	1970	1
Belone belone	S	1	11	0	0.764	Bute	Miss McAlorum	1971	1
GOBY BLACK	B		1	4	0.035	Cairnryan	J. Price	1976	1oz.
Gobius niger	S		2	4	0.063	Inveraray	F. O'Brien	1980	1oz.
GURNARD, GREY	B	2	7	0	1.105	Caliach Point	D. Swinbanks	1976	1¾
Eutrigla gurnardus	S	1	5	0	0.595	Peterhead	A. Turnbull	1973	1
		1	5	0	0.595	Port William	J. W. Martin	1977	1
GURNARD, RED	B	2	8	8	1.148	Tobermory	D. V. Relton	1985	1½
Aspitrigla cuculus	S	1	4	9	0.584	Dunure	J. Williamson	1993	12oz.
GURNARD STREAKED	B		10	10	0.301	Isle of Mull	J. Duncan	1985	any
Trigloporus lastoviza	S	1	6	8	0.637	Loch Goil	H. L. Smith	1971	1
GURNARD, TUB	B	5	5	0	2.409	Luce Bay	J. S. Dickinson	1975	3½
Trigla lucerna	S	1	1	12	0.503	Terally Bay	L. Green	1993	12oz.
HADDOCK	B	9	14	12	4.501	Summer Isles	M. Lawton	1980	6
Melanogrammus aeglefinus	S	6	12	0	3.061	Loch Goil	G. B. Stevenson	1976	3
HAKE	B	18	5	8	8.321	Shetland	B. Sinclair	1971	10
Merluccius merluccus	S		11	7	0.324	Gourock	S. Moyes	1979	8oz.
HALIBUT	B	234	0	0	106.136	Scrabster	C. Booth	1979	50
Hippoglossus hippoglossus	S	OPEN AT ANY WEIGHT							any
HERRING	B	1	2	0	0.510	Loch Long	R. C. Scott	1974	14oz.
Culpea harengus	S		11	11	0.331	Port Logan	R. Smith	1984	10oz.
LING	B	57	8	0	26.082	Stonehaven	I. Duncan	1982	20
Molva molva	S	12	4	0	5.557	Scrabster	A. Allan	1984	6
LUMPSUCKER	B	4	11	4	2.133	Innellan	G. T. Roebuck	1976	3
Cyclopterus lumpus	S	5	12	10	2.626	Cruden Bay	M. Rennie	1987	3
MACKEREL	B	3	12	0	1.701	Ullapool	E. Scobie	1965	2
Scomber scombrus	S	2	5	9	1.063	Wick	W. Richardson	1969	2
MEGRIM	B	3	12	8	1.715	Gareloch	P. Christie	1973	2
Lepidorhombus whiffiagonis	S		11	6	0.325	Loch Ryan	C. N. Dickson	1989	any
MULLETT, GOLDEN GREY	B	OPEN AT ANY WEIGHT							any
Lisa aurata	S		11	0	0.312	Fairlie	I. McFadyen	1972	8oz.

Species		lb.	oz.	dm.	kg.	Place of Capture	Angler	Year	Spec. lb.
MULLET, THICK LIPPED GREY	B	3	15	4	1.793	Girvan Harbour	M. Kelman	1992	3
Crenimugil labrosus	S	6	14	14	3.143	Ayr Harbour	T. Parker	1992	4½
NORWAY HADDOCK	B	1	10	5	0.750	Eyemouth	P. Skala	1988	14oz.
Sebastes viviparus	S	OPEN AT ANY WEIGHT							any
PIPEFISH GREATER	B	OPEN AT ANY WEIGHT							any
Sygnathus acus	S	0	1	13	0.052	Loch Goil	J.C. Ogilvie	1992	any
PLAICE	B	10	3	8	4.635	Longa Sound	H. Gardiner	1974	5
Pleuronectes platessa	S	5	8	0	2.494	Arrochar	A. Holt Jnr.	1971	3½
POLLACK	B	18	0	0	8.165	Scrabster	N. Carter	1971	10
Pollachius pollachius	S	13	14	0	6.293	Furnace	J. Arthur	1974	8
POOR COD	B	1	4	0	0.567	Arbroath	F. Chalmers	1969	1
Trisopterus minutus	S	1	0	0	0.453	Loch Fyne	F. Johnstone	1970	12oz.
POUTING	B	3	8	0	1.587	Gourock	J. Lewis	1977	2
Trisopterus luscus	S	3	3	7	1.458	Kirkcudbright	R. Cartwright	1984	1½
RAY BLONDE	B	26	11	0	12.105	Caliach Point	B. Swinbanks	1977	15
Raja brachyura	S	OPEN AT ANY WEIGHT							any
RAY CUCKOO	B	5	4	4	2.388	Gairloch	A. Bridges	1979	4
Raja naevus	S	4	11	0	2.126	Gourock	R. A. H. McCaw	1973	3¾
RAY SPOTTED	B	8	3	14	3.739	Isle of Whithorn	G. Brownlie	1989	4
Raja montagui	S	5	12	0	2.608	Cairnryan	G. C. Styles	1975	4
RAY THORNBACK	B	29	8	10	13.399	Luce Bay	A. McLean	1982	15
Raja clavata	S	21	12		9.866	Kirkcudbright	S. Ramsay	1985	4
ROCKLING, FIVE BEARDED	B	OPEN AT ANY WEIGHT							any
Ciliata mustela	S		7	0	0.198	Balcarry Point	K. Greason	1988	4½oz
ROCKLING, FOUR BEARDED	B		1	7	0.040	Gourock	S. Hodgson	1981	1¼oz.
Rhinomenus cimbrius	S	OPEN AT ANY WEIGHT							any
ROCKLING SHORE	B	OPEN AT ANY WEIGHT							any
Gairdropsarus mediterraneus	S		14	8	0.411	Loch Long	A. Glen	1982	7oz.
ROCKLING, THREE BEARDED	B	2	10	8	1.205	Gruna/Vementry	P. Georgeson	1993	1¼
Gairdropsaus vulgaris	S	3	1	12	1.410	Holburn Head	W. Crowthers	1992	1½
SANDEEL, GREATER	B		8	0	0.227	Caliach Point	T. J. Ashwell	1984	6oz.
Hyperoplus lanceolatus	S	0	6	4	0.177	Isle of Lewis	S. Macleod	1993	3oz.
SCAD (HORSE MACKEREL)	B	1	7	0	0.652	Loch Sheil	D. MacNeil	1976	1
Trachurus trachurus	S	3	0	14	1.384	Cockenzie	R. Dillon	1981	1
SEA SCORPION, LONGSPINED	B		3	6	0.096	Rhu Narrows	C. Heath	1985	2½oz.
Taurulus bubalis	S		5	9	0.157	Aberdeen	T. J. Ashwell	1982	2½oz.
SEA SCORPION SHORTSPINED	B	2	3	0	0.992	Kepple Pier	R. Stevenson	1973	1¾
Myoxocephalus scorpius	S	2	3	0	0.992	Cloch, Gourock	W. Crawford	1979	1½
SHARK, BLUE	B	85	8	0	38.781	Stornoway	J. Morrison	1972	50
Prionace glauca	S	OPEN AT ANY WEIGHT							any
SHARK PORBEAGLE	B	507	0	0	230.00	Dunnet Head	C. Bennet	1993	300
Lamna nasus									300

B - Boat Records   S - Shore Records   Spec. - Specimen Qualifying Weight

Species		lb.	oz.	dm.	kg.	Place of Capture	Angler	Year	Spec. lb.
SKATE, COMMON	B	227	0	0	102.967	Tobermory	R. Banks	1986	100
Raja batis	S	154	0	0	69.854	Achiltibuie	M. J. Traynor	1971	50
SMELT	B	OPEN AT ANY WEIGHT							any
Osmerus Eperlanus	S		5	4	0.149	Riverside, Dundee	M. Ettle	1988	4½oz.
SMOOTHHOUND	B	OPEN AT ANY WEIGHT							any
STARRY									
Mustelus asterias	S	7	12	14	3.540	Kirkcudbright	M. Roberts	1987	5
SOLE, DOVER	B	1	12	0	0.793	Killintrinnon	W. Hannah	1974	1
Solea Solea	S	2	0	8	0.922	Balcary	W. Lees	1989	8oz.
SOLE LEMON	B	2	2	0	0.963	Lochgoilhead	J. Gordon	1976	1
Microstomus kitt	S	1	6	2	0.627	Peterhead	B. N. Davidson	1982	12oz.
SPURDOG	B	18	14	0	8.560	Tobermory	J. Bean	1988	14
Squalus acanthias	S	15	3	0	7.139	Loch Etive	P. de Looze	1991	8
TADPOLE FISH	B		14	14	0.421	Firth of Clyde	R. Donnelly	1981	8oz.
Raniceps raninus	S	1	3	0	0.538	Dunbar	W. Dickson	1977	10oz.
TOPE	B	74	11	0	33.877	Loch Ryan	P. Marsland	1989	45
Galeorhinus galeus	S	54	4	0	24.606	Loch Ryan	D. Hastings	1975	30
TOPKNOT	B	OPEN AT ANY WEIGHT							any
Zeugopterus punctatus	S		8	8	0.241	Peterhead	G. M. Taylor	1975	6oz.
TORSK	B	15	7	2	7.006	Pentland Firth	D. J. Mackay	1982	8
Brosme brosme	S	OPEN AT ANY WEIGHT							any
TRIGGER FISH	B	OPEN AT ANY WEIGHT							any
Balistes Carolinesis	S	1	12	5	0.804	Newton Shore	J. Murphy	1989	1
TURBOT	B	25	4	0	11.453	Mull	I. Jenkins	1982	15
Scophthalmus maximus	S	2	13	12	1.300	Cairnryan	G. Calderwood	1989	1
WEAVER, GREATER	B	OPEN AT ANY WEIGHT							any
Trachinus draco	S	1	1	14	0.508	Mull of Galloway	W. Allison	1984	1
WHITING	B	6	8	0	2.948	Girvan	A. M. Devay	1969	3
Merlangius merlangus	S	3	0	0	1.360	Gourock	D. McTehee	1970	2
WHITING, BLUE (POUTASSOU)	B	1	12	0	0.793	Loch Fyne	J. H. Anderson	1977	8oz.
Micromesistius poutassou	S	OPEN AT ANY WEIGHT							any
WRASSE BALLAN	B	4	12	4	2.161	Calgary Bay, Mull	K. F. J. Hall	1983	3½
Labrus bergylta	S	5	0	0	2.268	Girvan	T. McGeehan	1971	3½
WRASSE, CORKWING	B	OPEN AT ANY WEIGHT							any
Crenilabrus melops	S		6	3	0.175	Wigton	I. Wilson	1989	4oz.
WRASSE, CUCKOO	B	3	0	0	1.361	Scrabster	Mrs H. Campbell	1969	1¼
Labrus mixtus	S	1	2	0	0.510	Neist Point, Skye	Q. A. Oliver	1972	12oz.
WRASSE	B	0	0	12	0.021	Lochaline	D. D. Morrison	1983	1oz.
GOLDSINNY	B		2	8	0.071	Lunderston Bay	J. Baillie	1990	1½oz.
Ctenolabrus rupestris	S		1	13	0.051	Loch Goil	T. Lambert	1977	1½oz.
			1	13	0.051	Mull of Galloway	G. V. R. Griffiths	1985	1½oz.
WRASSE SMALL MOUTHED ROCK COOK	B	OPEN AT ANY WEIGHT							any
Centrolabrus exoletus	S		2	0	0.056	Achiltibuie pier	D. F. McKendrick	1985	1½oz.
WRASSE, SCALE RAYED	B	0	10	15	0.310	Tobermory	J. T. Bishop	1986	8oz.
Acantholabrus palloni	S	OPEN AT ANY WEIGHT							any

The above records are based on information received up to 10th September 1993, by the S.F.S.A. Honorary Fish Recorder, G.T. Morris, 8 Burt Avenue, Kinghorn, Fife.

SCOTTISH FEDERATION OF SEA ANGLERS
SCOTTISH BOAT & SHORE (rod caught) RECORD
AND SPECIMEN MARINE FISH
RULES OF PROCEDURE

1.   (a)   The Claimant should contact the Fish Recorder. Advice will then be given concerning preservation, identification and claims procedure.

        (b)   Notification of claim or intention to claim a record or specimen must be made within 10 days of capture of the fish; a further period of 21 days being allowed for the return ol the completed claim form and relevant documents.

2.   Claims must be made in writing to the Fish Recorder, stating:
        (a)   The species of fish and the weight.
        (b)   The date and place of capture and the tackle used, and whether boat or shore caught.
        (c)   The names and addresses of reliable witnesses both as to capture by the claimant and the weight, who will be required to sign the forms supporting the claim. If no witnesses to the capture are available, the claimant must verify his claim by affidavit.

3.   No claim will be accepted unless the Committee is satisfied as to the species, method of capture and weight. The Committee reserves the right to reject any claim if not satisfied on any matter which it may think in the particular circumstances to be material.

4.   IDENTIFICATION OF SPECIES

    (i)   **for Record Claims**
        (a)   To ensure the correct identification, it is essential that claimants should retain the fish and immediately contact The Fish Recorder who will advise as to production of the fish for inspection on behalf of the Committee.
        (b)   No claims will be considered unless the fish in its natural state, dead or alive, is available for inspection.
        (c)   All carriage costs incurred in production of the fish for inspection by the Committee must be borne by the claimant.
    (ii)   **for Specimen Claims**
        Claims should be accompanied by a clear detailed photograph or transparency of the fish in close-up which shows the fish in lateral view with the fins spread. In the case of sharks, a sample of the teeth and a photograph of these in position should be submitted.

5.   METHOD OF CAPTURE

    (a)   Fish caught at sea will be eligible for consideration for record or specimen status if they have been caught from a shore within the political boundary of Scotland, or from a boat, if that boat has set out from and returned to a port within Scotland, without having first called at any port outside Scotland. Fish caught in the territorial waters of other countries will not be eligible.
    (b)   Claims can only be accepted in respect of fish whlch are caught by fair angling with rod and line. Fair angling is defined by the fish taking the baited hook or lure into its mouth
    (c)   BOAT caught includes those fish caught from any man made structure which may be moored but not permanently anchored to the sea bed. SHORE caught means those fish caught from a natural shore or any man made structure permanently secured to the sea bed.
    (d)   Fish must be caught on rod and line with any legal hook or lure and hooked and played by one person only. No one other than the angler playing the fish may touch any part

of the tackle e.g. to adjust the reel clutch, but he may be given assistance in putting on a harness. Assistance to land fish (i.e. gaffing, netting) is permitted provided the helper does not touch any part of the tackle other than the leader.

6. WEIGHT

(a) The fish must be weighed on land using scales or steelyards which can be tested on behalf of the Committee. Where possible, commercial or trade scales which are checked regularly by the Weights and Measures Department should be used. The sensitivity of the scales should be appropriate to the size of the fish i.e. small fish should be weighed on finely graduated scales and the weight claimed for the fish should be to a division of weight (ounces, dram, gramme) not less than the smallest division of the scales.

(b) A Weights and Measures Certificate must be produced certifying the accuracy of the scales used and indicating testing at the claimed weight.

(c) The weight must be verified by two independant witnesses who for example should not be relations of the claimant or a member of his club or party.

Note: Specimen tope and common skate may be weighed on board a boat when this is possible so that they may be returned to the water alive to conserve stocks.

7. Claims can be made for species not included in the Committee's Record Fish List.

8. A fish for which a record is claimed must be normal and not obviously suffering from any disease by which the weight could be enhanced.

9. The activities of the Committee are voluntary and claims are considered and adjudication upon, only on the basis that the Committee shall be under no obligation whatsoever to claimants, that its decisions shall be final and it shall not be obliged to give reasons for its decisions.

The body of the fish should, whenever possible, be kept in a deep freeze until required for identification. If this is not possible, then it should be kept in a solution of one tablespoon of formalin (40% solution of formaldehyde) to a pint of water.

When sending fish for inspection please:

(a) notify the Recorder or the person appointed by him that the fish is being sent for identification

(b) attach a label to each fish forwarded for identification or inspection giving the captor's name and address, date and place of capture, and weight of fish

(c) send deep frozen specimens by express post or rail, first wrapping them In cotton polythene before parcelling them.

(d) wrap specimens preserved in formalin in a cloth wrung out in the solution before parcelling them.

S.F.S.A. RULES FOR FISHING EVENTS (3/93)

A.   ORGANISATION OF EVENTS

1.   The organisers shall publish the fee for participating in an event and shall detail the same as being the sum of:

(a) An entry fee   (b) boat fee
(c) daily S.F.S.A. Festival Levy.

2.   The organisers will issue official entry cards prior to the start of the event and these shall bear the name and registration number of the entrant and in the case of boat events, the name or number of the boat to which the entrant is allocated.

3.   The allocation of boat places is to be made in public.

4.   The organisers will publish, prior to the event, the times for Registration, departure, fishing, return and weigh-in. (Departure and fishing times must be such that all anglers have the same opportunity of getting to the fishing grounds before the start of fishing.)

5.   The organisers will publish, prior to the event, definable limits within which the event will be fished. In shore events, boundaries apply to stance not to direction of cast.

6.   Stewards, whose task is to enforce the rules, will be appointed by the organisers and will be identified by official badges.

7.   (a) **Shore Events:**   All Sections of a shore event will be stewarded.
(b) **Boat Events:**   All boats will carry an official steward.

8.   The organisers shall have the right to:
(a) refuse to accept the entry of any applicant.
(b) inspect all tackle and items of equipment belonging to any entrants.

9.   The organisers will have all weighing machines checked for accuracy and suitability prior to the weigh-in.

10.   **Disputes:** Any dispute or complaint arising will be investigated by an adjudicating committee made up of a minimum of three (3) members of the organising committee and an equal number of neutral entrants, together with a neutral, non-voting, chairman who shall have casting vote only. The chairman will be the official representative of the S.F.S.A. if he is not involved as an organiser of the event.

11.   In boat events the number of anglers carried in a boat of any particular size will comply with the Department of Trade Recommendations.

12.   In shore events, the minimum distance between anglers will be 5 metres (5.5 yards).

13.   A JUNIOR is a person who is under sixteen (16) years of age on 1st January.

14.   **Tope and Skate Festivals:** The organisers shall provide each boat (or shore section) with a set of tested scales in all events designated as TOPE or SKATE festivals to enable all fish of these species to be weighed immediately after their capture then returned to the water. The boat steward or boat skipper together with one angler, or in a shore event a steward and one angler, shall act as weighmasters.

B. FISHING RULES

1. Entrants must be in possession of an entry/weigh-in card which must be produced on demand by a steward or official.

2. Fishing is only to take place in the times and within the limits laid down by the organisers.

3. Fishing will be with rod, reel and line only.

4. Participants may fish with only one rod fully fitted up. Spare rods and reels with terminal tackle not fitted may be carried.

5. Rods shall have a minimum length of 1 .52m. (5ft.). The maximum length for boat fishing will be 3.04m. (10ft.) (from March 1992). A limit on maximum length for shore fishing is not imposed.

6. Hydraulic, electric and double handed reels are not permitted.

7. The running line is not to be more than 50lbs. BS for multi-strand types (Dacron etc.) and more than 0.75 mm. diameter for monofilament types. (Rule 7 does not apply for events designated as special events for tope, conger, skate, shark or halibut).

8. A maximum of three (3) single hooks may be used. Treble hooks count as three (3) hooks and a double hook as two (2) hooks.

9. Artificial lures may be of any type and size but may only be fitted with hooks whose gape does not exceed 25mm.

10. Only fish fairly hooked from inside the mouth and landed with the hook in the mouth may be presented for weigh-in.

11. Fish hooked fairly in the mouth by more than one angler will not be eligible for weighing-in.

12. Anglers may only receive the help of other persons to gaff or lift a fish.

13. The rod is not to be rested on boat-gunwhales, capstans or rod seat, etc., while playing a fish. Hand lining is only permitted when the terminal trace can be used for that purpose.

14. Competitors with physical handicaps may receive help in casting provided they obtain permission in writing from the organisers prior to the event.

15. Contravention of any of these fishing rules may result in disqualification.

C. MINIMUM QUALIFYING SIZES OF FISH PRESENTED FOR WEIGH-IN FROM 1 JANUARY 1994.

1. Bass (Dicentrarchus labrax)   36 cm.   (14.2 in.)
    Brill (Scophthalmus rhombus)   30 cm.   (11.8 in.)
    Coalfish (Pollachius virens)   35 cm.   (13.8 in.)
    Cod (Gadus morhua)   35 cm.   (13.8 in.)
    n.b. In U.K. Fishery area V11a from 1st October to
         31 December the minimum size for Cod will be   45 cm.   (17.7 in.)
    Dab (Limanda limanda)   23 cm.   (9.06 in.)
    Dogfish – all species (Scyliorhinus, Squalius sp)   35 cm.   (13.8 in.)
         Eel Common (Anguilla anguilla)   35 cm.   (13.8 in.) **
    Eel Conger (Conger conger)   58 cm.   (22.8 in.)
    Flounder (Platichthys flesus)   25 cm.   (9.8 in.)
    Haddock (Melanogrammus aeglefinus)   30 cm.   (11.8 in.)
    Hake (Merluccius merluccius)   30 cm.   (11.8 in.)
    Halibut (Hippoglossus hippoglossus)   50 cm.   (19.5 in.)
    Ling (Molva molva)   70 cm.   (27.625 in.) **
    Mackerel (Scomber scombrus)   30 cm.   (11.8 in.)
                                 (North Sea only)
    Megrim (Lepidorhombus wiffiagonis)   25 cm.   (9.8 in.)
    Mullets (Grey)   30 cm.   (11.8 in.)
    Pollack (Pollachius pollachius)   35 cm.   (13.8 in.)
    Plaice (Pleuronectes platessa)   27 cm.   (10.6 in.)
    Rays (Raja sp)   35 cm.   (13.8 in.)
    Seabream, Red (Pagellus bogaraveo)   25 cm.   (9.8 in.)
    Seabream, Black (Spondyliosoma cantharus)   23 cm.   (9.05 in.)
    Skates (Raja batis, alba, oxyrinchus sp)   11.35 kg.   (25 lbs.)
    Sole Lemon (Microstomus kitt)   25 cm.   (9.8 in.)
    Sole (Solea solea)   24 cm.   (9.4 in.)
    Tope (Galeorhinus galeus)   9.10 kg.   (20 lbs.)
    Turbot (Scophthalmus maximus)   30 cm.   (11.8 in.)
    Wrasse Ballan   25 cm.   (9.8 in.)
    Whiting (Merlangius merlangus)   27 cm.   (10.6 in.)
    Witches (Glyptocephalus gynoglossus)   28 cm.   (11.0 in.)
    All other species   20 cm.   (7.9 in.)

    **These sizes may be altered when the European Community determine the new limit for the species.

2. A maximum of three mackerel and three herring may be presented for weigh-in.

3. TOPE AND SKATE: Common (R. batis); long-nosed (R. oxyrhinchus) or white (R. alba) are not to be brought ashore during events designated as TOPE or SKATE competitions. They are to be weighed immediately after capture and returned to the sea. (This rule does not apply to potential national record fish which must be brought ashore for weighing.) In designated TOPE competitions no minimum size for weighing will be applied as long as fish are weighed on board and returned alive.

4. Any obviously undersized fish presented for weigh-in will result in the entrant being disqualified.

THE GOLDEN POLLACK

BY

JIM MCLANAGHAN

The calm oily surface of the sea was suddenly broken as a beautiful golden pollack flashed into the air, somersaulted and splashed back down, stripping off yards of line in a headlong dive for the sanctuary of the kelp beds. The time - November, the place - Portpatrick, but it could have been any one of ten thousand venues along Scotland's indented shoreline.

We had anchored our boat only 100 yds from the cliffs and using conventional spinning rods up to 10ft long, I was having one of my most memorable days afloat with some magnificent pollack, the best of which were 14 lbs. Such is the sporting value of the pollack that a great number of sea anglers are now specialising in them and tackle has become more sporty and specialised.

One look at these beautiful slab sided fish with their huge eyes readily confirms them as predators and this fact mainly dictates the methods used to take them. Movement is all important when pollack fishing and all the successful lures have some sort of vibratory or swimming action, the most successful being redgills and the Mister Twister range of "rubberised" eels.

For the real giants one must get afloat and over a wreck, and by giants we can mean fish as large as 25 lbs! Being one of our most sporting fish, they possess great speed and are capable of stripping line off in searing runs which can be almost heart stopping. When wreck fishing and the chances of a big fish are high, one is torn between the risk of losing a fish on "sporting" tackle and over gunning a fish on the heavier gear which may be needed to drag it clear of the wreck.

Whatever the choice of tackle, the lure or bait and its presentation will almost certainly be the same, either a rubber eel or king ragworm. Artificial eels are lowered or cast across a wreck and allowed to settle almost into it, as near as can be judged, and a very slow retrieve started. Since the fish can be at any level above the wreck, most anglers start counting the turns on the reel in order that they can ascertain feeding depth and be prepared for that gut wrenching take. The same technique also applies when ragworm are being used. The actual take usually is a sudden thump with the rod tip being dragged almost to the water, or an initial tentative tap, which the angler should ignore and carry on winding. This generally incites the fish to hit or take in a more positive and forceful manner, giving one of the most satisfying hook ups in angling. Some anglers are combining both small jigheads and ragworms, which on light tackle can outfish just about any other bait on the day, but this method is most effective in shallower water.

I have hooked pollack of only 8 lbs which in their initial surges made me think I had hooked a tope, such was the power and duration of the runs!

How long a battle with a pollack will last will obviously be governed by how large the fish is, the tackle used, depth of water and tide. One thing is almost certain whether fishing a wreck or reef, if the fish reaches back into cover it is 99% lost, the chances of its retrieval are very slim indeed.

Whilst the really biggest pollack will

mainly come from wrecks, a growing number of people are taking advantage of inshore reefs which are still capable of producing fish to 20lbs or more.

Such was the position we were in off the Mull of Galloway and sport was hectic. With only 3 people in the boat, we could cast with total safety and accuracy. Using 10ft spinning rods and Mister Twisters on lead jigheads we had a field day and we also had the luxury of having time and space to experiment. Varying colours, speed of retrieve, depth, we tried them all but no difference was discernible, the fish were on the feed - hard.

With the water depth being in the region of 10 metres, it was impossible to keep fish from reaching the kelp and the occasional loss was inevitable but we had an impressive array of fish - one at 2lbs - the rest ranging from 6lbs to 14lbs on light tackle. The heaviest fish took almost 20 minutes to subdue. The bonus for us was the sport and to help ensure it would be there for the future, all fish were returned alive with the exception of a seven pounder for the pan.

Some pollack can be so voracious on the feed they defy belief. One day whilst shark fishing with whole mackerel as baits, four of our floats suddenly went under and line was dragged off our large reels. On retrieving our baits imagine our surprise to haul up no sharks but a quartet of 8lbs pollack!

Some of our longer casts were actually bouncing off the cliffs, so the spot we were fishing was equally available to the shore angler, which is a big plus for pollack fishing. Spinning from the shore with a rubber eel is just as effective as from a boat and a float fished ragworm can be absolutely deadly, particularly towards evening. Scotland is rich in areas giving access to deep water and there are many well known pollack hot spots, all the way up the east coast from Eyemouth to Arbroath and Aberdeen. The rugged north along the Pentland and down the west coast through the Isles all have some prodigious areas. I spoke to one chap in Skye who told me his biggest shore pollack in a week's fishing had gone 20lbs and he had lost what he thought were bigger fish! The prospects are there and if the salmon's not biting or there's "nae watter" in the rivers, try some pollack fishing, the tackle's the same - even try fly fishing!

The only frustrating aspect of pollack angling is that fish can suddenly come onto the feed, go hard at it for a few hours - or minutes - then switch off completely. Whether this is triggered by tide, food or time of day no-one knows but one thing for sure - get it right and you'll have the time of your life.

Most of the areas likely to produce pollack will be rocky exposed headlands or cliff venues where anglers are exposed to the elements. Please be careful, keep an eye out for rogue waves, particularly if a large ship or boat has just passed. The wake of a ship can take as long as half an hour to reach shore and can swamp the unwary - and never go alone.

One final plea - any fish of any size not wanted for consumption - please return them alive.

TO BOOK YOUR SEA ANGLING TRIP TURN TO PAGES 11, 12, & 13

SEA ANGLING

BORDERS

The Scottish Borders provide some of the best sea angling in the UK. Based on Eyemouth, which has the largest fishing fleet in the South of Scotland, and the smaller fishing villages of Burnmouth and St. Abbs, the clear unpolluted waters are well stocked with a wide variety of sea fish. So clear is the water that one of the first Marine Reservations has been established off Eyemouth. The rugged coastline with its unique fauna make a spectacular background to your day's fishing. It should be noted that sea angling is not permitted off St. Abbs Head National Reserve (Petticowick – Long Carr).

Eyemouth is only nine miles north of Berwick-upon-Tweed, just off the A.1. Its colourful boats, fish auction and sandy beach make it a popular resort during the summer. Well known for its excellent rock fishing, the town is also a useful point of access to shoreline to the north and south. Boat fishing has developed over the years due to the efforts of Eyemouth Sea Angling Club who now run a number of shore and boat competitions throughout the season.

The club operates the coast from Burnmouth harbour in the south to the harbour at St. Abbs in the north.

Types of fish: Shore – cod, mackerel, coalfish, flounder, plaice, sole, haddock, whiting, catfish, ling and wrasse. Boat – the same species can be caught as on shore but larger specimens.

Boats: A large number of fishing boats are usually available from Eyemouth, St. Abbs and Burnmouth for parties of anglers at weekends.

DUMFRIES AND GALLOWAY

Solway Firth to Isle of Whithorn
The area is renowned for its strong tides which can create difficulties for boat angling in the wrong conditions. Local advice should be sought before sailing and as a further safety measure the Coastguard should be advised of any intended trips. If a boat trip is cancelled or an angler prefers

shore fishing, the coastline abounds with excellent shore marks which produce a great diversity of species. Summer months are undoubtedly the most productive but the winter cod fishing can also be very good with many large fish being taken.

Kippford
Better known as a yachting centre, Kippford still offers good angling opportunities. Shore marks around Kippford yield bags of flatfish and dogfish in the summer with the occasional bass. The area excels in the winter with catches of big cod. The Scottish shore caught record cod came from here. Boat fishing during the summer tends to give more variety with mackerel, thornback and dogfish, both spur and spotted featuring in the catches.
Bait: Lug and ragworm can be dug locally and cockles and mussels picked from the shore.
Season: May to September for comfort and variety. November to February for big cod but wrap up well!

Kirkcudbright
About 5 miles from the open sea on the Dee estuary, Kirkcudbright is at the centre of an excellent shore fishing area. Rocky points in Kirkcudbright bay along the Dundrennan shore to the east and Borgue to the west, give good varied fishing especially during the summer. Dogfish feature heavily in local club matches with the occasional conger, bull huss and thornback. Settled conditions and clear water give good bags of pollack and garfish and mullet are attracted to ground bait. The estuary produces bags of plaice, dabs and flounders with flounders, eels and coalfish giving good sport at the harbour. The bay also fishes well for cod and whiting in the winter. Boat fishing can be good with launching sites at the harbour, Ross Bay and Brighouse but these are restricted by the tides. One charter boat operates from Kirkcudbright. Boat catches are as varied as the shore, but there is always the chance of a tope.
Bait: Lug and ragworm are available locally along with cockles and mussels. Mackerel and herring can be bought in the town.
Tackle: A limited amount available from: Watson Mckinnel in Kirkcudbright.

A better selection from: "Patties", 109 Queensberry Street, Dumfries. "Reel em In", Friars Vennel, Dumfries.
Charter Boat: "Howzat" - Howard Williams, Tel: (01557) 30367.
Further Information:
Information Centre, Kirkcudbright. Tel: (01557) 30494.

Garlieston & The Isle of Whithorn
Situated on the east side of the Machars Peninsula, the area is sheltered from the prevailing westerly winds giving good shore and boat fishing. Rock marks give good bags of dogfish, pollack and wrasse with conger and mullet also being taken. Burrow Head gives good fishing when the weather is fine. The summer months are the best for both shore and boat fishing. Boats can be launched from both habours on a suitable tide and charter boats operate from the Isle of Whithorn. The biggest attraction for boat anglers is tope which can sometimes be caught in numbers. Some big fish are caught every year and most are released. Spurdog and thornback sometimes take bait meant for tope.
Tackle: Some available locally from: A. Mcghie, Radio Shop, George Street, Whithorn.
J.M. William, Grocer & Harbour Master, The Harbour, Isle of Whithorn. Tel: (019885) 246.
Bait: Lug, rag and shellfish available locally.
Boats: Craig Mills, Main Street, Isle of Whithorn DG8 8LN. Tel: (019885) 393 - (Manu Kea). Rab McCreadie - (Crusader).
Local Clubs: Kirkcudbright & District SAC, Stuart Ross, "Fanore", 53 St. Cuthbert Street, Kirkcudbright. Tel: (01557) 30845.
Peever Sea Anglers, Jack McKinnel, 20 Merse Strand, Kirkcudbright. Tel: (01557) 31505.

Luce Bay
There are some good shore marks, namely Sandhead Sands for Flatfish, Dogfish and Bass in season, Terrally Bay for these species plus Codling, Whiting, Spurdogfish. Around East and West Tarbet bays at the Mull of Galloway good rock fishing may be had for Lesser Spotted Dogfish, Bull Huss, Spurdogfish, Conger Eels, Wrasse, Whiting, Pollack,

Coalfish, Flatfish and Mackerel in season, normally from late April to December.

Boats: W. Carter, Castle Daly Angling Centre, Auchenmalg, Glenluce. Tel: 0158 15 250. (Self drive boats for hire & hotel accommodation).

Bait: Lug can be dug in most sandy bays around Luce Bay, especially at Sandhead. Some shellfish available, mussels and cockles with razorfish on spring tides.

Launching Sites: Difficult to launch without four wheel drive vehicle.

Sites: Yacht Club at Drummore - high water only. Cailiness Road picnic site. Back of harbour Drummore. East Tarbet Bay - usually necessary to rope the trailer over shingle.

Safety: Dinghy anglers should be aware of the strong tides in the area, especially around the Mull of Galloway area.

Port William

Port William is situated on the east side of Luce Bay and has a good though tidal harbour. It is the starting point for many anglers wishing to fish the lower part of Luce Bay. The once famous shore mark of Monreith Bay, still a good bass beach, lies just to the south of Port William.

Types of fish: Tope, spurdog, rays, cod, pollack, flatfish from boats. Bass, wrasse, codling and pollack from the shore.

Tackle: Available in village.

Bait: Lugworm, shellfish an molluscs along beach. Mackerel in bay.

Season for fishing: May- October.

Drummore

Drummore, the main port for anglers wishing to fish the western side of Luce Bay lies 5 miles north of the Mull of Galloway. Hotels and guest houses cater for anglers. There are many good shore marks on sandy beaches north of Drummore, while the Mull of Galloway provides excellent shore fishing over rocky ground. The Mull, the most southerly part of Scotland, is an area of very strong tides and is not recommended as a fishing area to anglers with small boats incapable of at least 10 knots, especially during ebb tides.

Types of fish: Pollack, wrasse from rocky shores, flatfish, bass, mullet and rays from sandy beaches. Pollack, coalfish, cod, whiting, wrasse, lesser, spotted dogfish, bullhuss, spurdog, tope, rays, conger from boats.

Boats: On yer Marks" Ian or Sue Burrett, Cardrain Cottage, Drummore. Tel: (01776) 84 346.

Charter Boats:

Ian Hutton - Tel: (01776) 86981. Stuart Aylott - Tel: (01776) 84226.

Bait: All types available on shore at low tide. Mackerel from Mull of Galloway shore marks.

Port Logan

Port Logan is the small community which is situated about 7.5 miles north of the Mull of Galloway on the west side of the Galloway Peninsula. An area with many good shore marks both to the north and south of the village. It is one of the few relatively easy launching sites on this coastline south of Portpatrick. A good alternative for the angler with his own boat when easterly winds prevent fishing in Luce Bay. Like the Mull of Galloway an area of strong tides, especially off Crammoc Head, to the south of Port Logan Bay.

Types of fish: As for the southern part of Luce Bay with occasional haddock. Herring in June and July. Ideal to launch dinghies at Port Logan from concrete slipway onto hard sand where two wheel drive vehicles can run onto beach. Slack water occures 1.5 hours before high and low water.

Boats: Ian Burrett, Cardrain Cottage, Drummore. Tel: (01776) 84346.

Portpatrick

The small fishing port and holiday resort of Portpatrick lies on the west coast of Wigtownshire, 8 miles from Stranraer. There is good shore fishing from the many rocky points north and south of the resort, the best known being the Yellow Isle, 0.5 mile north of the harbour. Sandeel Bay, a little further north, and Killintringan Lighthouse are also worth fishing.

Types of fish: Pollack, coalfish, plaice, flounder, codling, mackerel, dogfish, conger, wrasse, and tope occasionally.

Boats: Peter & Martin Green, 2 Eastcliff, Portpatrick. Tel: (01776) 81 534. Brian Tyreman, Pinminnoch Cottage, Portpatrick DG9 9AB. Tel: (01776) 81468 - "Cornubia".

Bait: None sold locally. Lugworm and some ragworm can be dug east of the railway pier, Stranraer.

Season for fishing: May-December.

Further information from: Mr R. Smith, 24 Millbank Road, Stranraer. Tel: (01776) 3691.

Stranraer & Loch Ryan

Stranraer, at the head of Loch Ryan, offers the angler, as a rail and bus terminal, a good stepping off point for many sea angling marks and areas in this part of Scotland, with Sandhead on Luce Bay (8 miles) to the south, Portpatrick (8 miles) to the west and Lady Bay (8 miles) on the west side of Loch Ryan with Cairnryan (6 miles) and Finnart Bay (10 miles) on the opposite side of the loch. Best Shore marks being Cairnryan Village, South of Townsend Thoresen ferry terminal. Old House Point and Concrete Barges north of Cairnryan Village, Finnart Bay on East Mouth of Loch, Wig Bay, Jamiesons Point and Lady Bay on west side of Loch Ryan. Boats may be launched at Wig Bay Slipway, Lady Bay and at Stranraer Market Street.

Access Safety: Most landowners will grant permission to cross lands to fish if this is requested and will advise best routes to avoid crossing crops. Most rock marks are safe but caution is needed in wet conditions as they may become slippy. In Lochryan anglers fishing from rocks or beaches should be aware of the wash from ferries and seacat as these can be dangerous if caught in the drive up the beaches or rocks.

Please note: No fishing is allowed on the jetty at Cairnryan at any time and the owners are going to take legal action against anglers who break through the boundary fence to obtain access. The jetty is unsafe and no insurance is in force.

Types of fish: taken from shore - pollack, codling, coalfish, plaice, dabs, wrasse, whiting, conger eel, lesserspotted dogfish, flounder, with spurdog, thornback ray and bull huss at times. Occasional tope. Taken from boat: Pollack, codling, coalfish, plaice, dabs, wrasse, whiting, conger eel, lesserspotted dogfish, flounder with spurdog thornback ray and bull huss at times. Turbot, monkfish and spotted and cuckoo ray in the deeper water.

Boat: Mike Watson, Main Street, Stranraer. Tel: (01776) 85 3225.

Tackle: The Sports Shop, George Street, Stranraer, Tel: (01776) 2705, (frozen bait stocked).

Bait: Lugworm can be dug in most sandy bays, with the cockle shore at Stranraer the most popular. Loch Ryan Sea Angling Association has a lease on the cockle shore at Stranraer to restrict bait digging and the conditions are that anglers are only allowed to dig sufficient bait for one day's fishing. Ragworm can be dug in places. Cultured ragworm on sale at sports shop in Stranraer along with a good assortment of frozen baits. Mussel can be obtained on most beaches. Mackerel caught from shore and boat in season.

Season: Sea fishing is carried out all year but from May to October the best for daylight with a lot of night fishing giving better results.

Local Clubs: Lochryan Sea Angling Association, Paul Paterson, 46 Antrim Avenue, Stranraer. Tel: (01776) 3529. Sealink S.A.C., Niven Dickson, Seabank Road, Stranraer. Tel: (01776) 4895.

Further information from above or: Mr. R. Smith, 24 Millbank Road, Stranraer. Tel: (01776) 3691.

STRATHCLYDE SOUTH

Loch Ryan to Ardrossan
The angling potential of much of the coast between Loch Ryan and Girvan remains unknown, the many rocky shores, small headlands and sandy beaches probably only attracting the anglers in an exploratory mood, or those seeking solitude in pursuit of their hobby.

Girvan
Girvan has a sheltered port and is a family holiday resort. From the end of the pier good fishing can be had for fair-sized plaice, flounders and spotted dog. Night fishing is good for rock cod. Just one mile to the south of the town lies the noted Horse Rock', only about 50 yards from the main Stranraer road. Access to the rock may be gained from about half-tide. Except during very high tides and during storms it is a good shore mark providing access to water of about 20 feet on the sea-side even at low tide.

Types of fish: Plaice, codling, rays, flounder, pollack and ling, whiting, and gurnard (mostly from boat). (Mullet in harbour during the summer months).

Boats: M. McCrindle, 7 Harbour Street, Girvan KA26 9AJ. Tel: (01465) 3219. Tony Wass, 22 Templand Road, Dalry KA24 5EU. Tel: (01294) 833724.

Baits: Lugworm and ragworm can be dug at beach nearby or fresh mackerel from boat.

Tackle: Available from Girvan Chandlers, 4 Knockcushon Street, Girvan KA26 9AG.

Season for fishing: March to October.

Further information from: Brian Burn (S.F.S.A.), Tel: (01292) 264735.

Ayr
Ayr is a popular holiday town on the estuaries of the Rivers Ayr and Doon, 32 miles south-west of Glasgow. Good shore fishing can be had on the Newton Shore, north of the harbour for flounders and the odd doggie during summer months with a few coallies, codling and whiting throughout the winter, especially when there is a good storm. Some flounders and eels are taken from the harbour and at times excellent mullet can be caught from the tidal stretches of the river Ayr. Boat fishing in the bay can be very productive for mackerel and herring from May to October. Usually from July to November the boat fishing improves with the arrival of codling, pollack, ling, coallies, plaice, dabs, sea scorpions and spotted dogs.

Tackle: Available from Gamesport, 60 Sandgate, Ayr.

Bait: Lug and rag can be dug at the Newton shore with Doonfoot beaches producing lug and peeler crab during summer months.

Boats: Tony Medina - Tel: (01292) 285297. Graham Johnston - Tel: (01292) 281638. There is also a good public slipway for dinghies to launch from at the side of Ayr Multi Water Sports Centre (Yacht Club). Difficulty can be had on exceptionally low tides at low water.

Further information: Brian Burn (S.F.S.A.) - Tel: (01292) 264735.

Prestwick & Troon
Just north of Ayr, Prestwick and Troon offers some reasonable shore fishing at certain times of the year. Prestwick beaches fish for codling, flounders and coallies from usually November to January especially on evening tides. Flounders, the odd coallie and spotted dog can be caught throughout the summer months. The Ballast Bank at Troon can produce conger, pollack, doggies, wrasse and the odd codling throughout the summer months with the better chance of a few codling and coallies during the winter. Troon Pier is a favourite

mark for herring and mackerel during the summer and there is always the chance of a conger or two from this area.

Bait: Lug and rag can be dug on Prestwick shore and mussel beds also at Troon and Barassie beaches.

Boats: Jimmy Wilson, 27 Wallace Avenue, Troon. Tel: (01292) 313161. Dinghies can be launched from Troon Marina, however there is a launching charge.

Further Information: John Fitchett - Tel: (01292) 314057.

Irvine
Irvine on the Ayrshire coast, is a rapidly developing New Town on the River Irvine. The sea is relatively shallow, with long sandy beaches. It is a fair boat fishing area. Irvine was previously a very busy port, but now the river anchorage is used by a greater number of small craft. The estuary can produce a few dabs, flounders and common eels. South of Irvine Estuary is a small island called The Lady Isle'. In the past few years the pollack have decreased not only in number but also in size. Just off this Isle pollack can be taken with ragworm on a long flowing trace. Pollack to 6 lbs., are not an unusual sight at some club matches. For codling close inshore is best and small coloured beads are preferred to spoon and lures. The best bait by far is a cocktail of lugworm and mussels or ragworm and mussels, all of which can be obtained locally.

Types of fish: Pollack, wrasse and coallies. Small codling after May from boat.

Bait: Rag worm, lug worm from beaches and mud flats around Irvine. Mussels from harbour walls.

Boats: Donald Findlay, Bert Harris, Robin Richmond, Davie Hollis (telephone number for any of the above can be obtained from Irvine Water Sports Club - Tel: (01294) 74981. Easy access to boats from pier.

Season for Fishing: May to September boat angling.

Local Club: Irvine Sea Angling Club.

Further information: J. Falconer, 10 Rosemount Square, Pennyburn, Kilwinning KA13 6LZ.

Saltcoats & Ardrossan
Saltcoats with the neighbouring towns of Stevenston and Ardrossan, is situated on the Ayrshire coast 30 miles south-west of Glasgow. Shore fishing is possible in the South Bay and around the harbours.

Approximately 3 miles north is Ardneil Bay which can produce a few codling over the rough ground.

Types of fish: Pollack, wrasse, doggies, eels, cod, saithe, flatties and herring.

Further information: Please obey any private fishing signs within the area and remember dinghy anglers. No fishing within 50 meters of Ore Terminal.

Boats: Robert Reid - Tel: (01294) 601844.

Bait: Ragworm available from Saltcoats Harbour, Fairlie Pier. Lugworm from Ardrossan north shore and Fairlie sand flats.

Tackle: Light tackle is all you require for most species in the area. Fixed spool or multiplier, light rod - 8-10lb line, spinning or bait.

Season for fishing: May to October.

Local Club: Ardrossan & District Sea Angling Club.

Further Information from: Bud McClymont, 41 Corrie Crescent, Saltcoats KA21 6JL. Tel: (01294) 61830.

Largs

Largs is within easy reach of several good fishing banks, including the Piat Shoal, the Skelmorlie Patch and the east shore of Cumbrae.

Types of fish: Dogfish, flounders, gurnard, dragonets, pollack, mackerel, plaice, coalfish and dabs.

Boats: Are readily available from local hirers.

Tackle: Hastie of Largs Ltd, Department Store, 109 Main Street, Largs. Tel: Largs 673104

Bait: Lug, rag, cockles and mussels are available from Fairlie Flats.

Gourock

The coastline from Largs to Greenock was probably the most popular area in Scotland for shore angling, with many anglers from the Midlands of England and beyond making regular trips north. Now the fishing is generally poor. At Wemyss Bay, angling is not permitted from the pier, but odd good catches can still be had to the south, and the Red Rocks, about a mile to the north, are noted for odd codling and other species. At Inverkip there is a sandy beach around the entrance to the marina where flounders, odd dabs and eels can be taken. Cloch Point, where the Firth turns east, is well known for its fishing potential, although the current can be fierce, and because of the rough

bottom, relatively heavy lines are necessary. The coastline from Cloch along Gourock Promenade to the swimming pool car park provides fair fishing and is easily accessible. Further inland, at Greenock Esplanade, flounders, dabs, eels and coallies are among the species available, although the water here is shallower, and this area is more productive at night. This stretch of coastline provides the dinghy angler with easy access to many of the Clyde marks, including the Gantocks, where outsize cod and coalfish were taken many years ago, mainly on pirks. The bay beside the power station holds flatfish and the ground off Greenock Esplanade is popular for coallies, some pollock and dabs. Dinghy owners should note that no anchoring is permitted in the main navigation channels, and several other regulations must also be adhered to.

Types of fish: Coalfish (known locally as saithe), odd codling, conger eel, dab, dogfish, flounder, occasional ling, plaice, pollack (lythe), pouting, whiting and wrasse. Grey mullet, herring and mackerel can also be caught during the summer months.

Tackle: Inversports, 27a Kempock Street, Gourock.
Brian Peterson & Co., 12 Kelly Street, Greenock.
Findlay & Co., 58 Lynedoch Street, Greenock.

Bait: Lug, rag, mussels, cockles and crabs can all be obtained from the shoreline.

Boats: J. Crowther, Inverclyde Boat Owners Association, 164 Burns Road, Greenock. Tel: (01475) 34341 can advise.

Isle of Arran

The island of Arran, lying in the outer Firth of Clyde, may be reached from the mainland by ferries running from Ardrossan to Brodick, the largest community on the island. Good shore fishing is found around the whole of the island, much of which remains unexplored.

Lamlash

Lamlash is the main centre for sea angling on the island, probably because of its situation on the shores of Lamlash Bay, the large horse-shoe shaped bay which is almost landlocked by the Holy Isle. This gives excellent protection to the bay from easterly winds. Lamlash is also the starting point for boat trips to the excellent fishing grounds off Whiting Bay and those around Pladda to the south.

Types of fish: Codling, whiting, coalfish, pollack, conger, rays, flatfish, mackerel, dogfish, plaice, dabs, gurnard, wrasse and odd haddock.

Bait: Obtainable from many beaches.

Season for fishing: March-November.

Corrie

Corrie is situated on north east coast of the island.

Types of fish: Codling, haddock, conger, rays, dogfish, ling, pollack, gurnard, garfish, mackerel and wrasse.

Whiting Bay

This bay, which takes its name from the whiting, is very open to the sea. There are excellent fishing banks from Largiebeg Point to King's Cross Point.

Boats: Dinghies can be hired from the Jetty, Whiting Bay or by arrangement with Jim Ritchie, Tel: (017707) 382.

Bait: Cockles, mussels, lugworm, ragworm, limpets and crabs are abundant on the banks from half-tide.

Lochranza

Lochranza is situated at the northern end of the island. The loch is surrounded by hills opening out on to Kilbrannan Sound.

Types of fish: Cod, conger, wrasse and pollack from the shore. Codling, conger, some haddock, plaice and dabs from boat.

Tackle: Available from boat hirers.

Bait: Mussels, cockles, lugworm and ragworm obtainable.

Brodick

Good fishing in Brodick Bay from Markland Point to Clauchlands Point.

Types of fish: Codling, plaice and other flatfish, conger, wrasse and pollack, can be had from the shore while cod, conger, rays, dogfish, ling, pollack, gurnard, garfish and other round fish can be fished from boats.

Bait: Mussels are obtainable from the rocks around Brodick Pier or may be purchased from boat hirers.

Isle of Cumbrae, Millport

There is good fishing at a bank between the South East Point of Millport Bay (Farland Point) and Keppel Pier. Fintry Bay and Piat Shoal provide good sport. West of Portachur Point in about 15/20 fathoms and in Dunagoil Bay, S.W. Bute are good. Fairlie

Channel directly seaward of Kelburn Castle is about 12/15 fathoms. East shore northwards about 10 fathoms line.
Types of fish: Saithe, conger, coalfish, dogfish, mackerel and flatfish.
Tackle: Available locally from boat hirers.
Bait: Mussels, worms, etc. on shore. Boat hirers and local shops provide bait.

STRATHCLYDE NORTH

Helensburgh
Helensburgh is a small seaside town on the Firth of Clyde at the southern end of the Gareloch, easily reached by train or car.
Types of fish: Shore and boat – flounder, coalfish, conger, dogfish, whiting, dab, pollack and mackerel.
Tackle: Spriggs Leisure Marine. Tel: (01436) 820586.
Bait: Ragworm, lugworm, may be dug locally. Mussels and crabs can be gathered from the shore. Fresh & frozen bait can be purchased from Spriggs Leisure Marine. Tel: (01436) 820586.
Season for fishing: All year.
Further information from: Mr. M.J. Partland, Drumfork S.A.C., 142 East Clyde Street, Helensburgh G84 7AX. Tel: (01436) 71937.

Garelochhead
Garelochhead is the village at the head of the Gareloch, with the whole shoreline within easy reach. Upper and lower Loch Long and Loch Goil are only a few miles away.
Types of fish: Coalfish, pollack, dab, flounder, plaice, whiting, pouting, mackerel and lesser spotted dogfish.
Tackle: Spriggs Leisure Marine. Tel: (01436) 820586.
Bait: Garelochhead – cockles and mussels. Roseneath – lugworm, ragworm and cockles. Rhu – ragworm. Kilcreggan – ragworm. Coulport – cockles. Fresh & frozen bait can be bought from: Spriggs Leisure Marine. Tel: (01436) 820586.
Season for fishing: All year.
Further information from: Mr. M.J. Partland, Drumfork S.A.C., 142 East Clyde Street, Helensburgh G84 7AX. Tel: (01436) 71937.

Arrochar, Loch Long
The village lies at the northern end

of the loch, and has waters sheltered by the high surrounding hills.
Types of fish: Shore – conger, pollack, coalfish. Boat – whiting, dabs, conger, pollack, coalfish, mackerel, dogfish and odd rays.
Tackle: Spriggs Leisure Marine. Tel: (01436) 820586.
Bait: Fresh herring and mackerel, mussels and cockles usually available from the pier. Artificial baits, lures etc. available from shops in village. Fresh and frozen bait can be bought from Spriggs Leisure Marine. Tel: (01436) 820586.
Season for fishing: All year.
Further information from: Mr. M.J. Partland, Drumfork S.A.C., 142 East Clyde Street, Helensburgh G84 7AX. Tel: (01436) 71937.

Clynder
Clynder is the fishing centre on the sheltered west side of the Gareloch and one mile north of the popular Rhu Narrows.
Types of fish: Conger, rays, plaice, flounders, dogfish, whiting, pouting and mackerel.
Tackle: Spriggs Leisure Marine. Tel: (01436) 820586.
Boats: C. Moar (01436) 831336.
Bait: Cockles, mussels, lug, ragworm, can be dug. Fresh & frozen bait can be bought from Spriggs Leisure Marine. Tel: (01436) 820586.
Season for fishing: All year.
Further information from: Mr. M.J. Partland, Drumfork S.A.C., 142 East Clyde Street, Helensburgh G84 7AX. Tel: (01436) 71837.

Isle of Bute, Rothesay
The holiday resort of Rothesay, situated on the island of Bute, only a 30 minute crossing by roll-on/roll-off ferry from Wemyss Bay, is sheltered from the prevailing south- westerly winds. Several boat hirers cater for sea anglers. There are also many excellent shore marks. The deep water marks at Garroch Head can be productive for both shore and boat anglers.
Types of fish: Shore – cod, coalfish, pollack, plaice, mackerel, wrasse. Boat – cod, pollack, plaice, mackerel, conger, coalfish, wrasse, whiting and ling.
Tackle: Available from Bute Arts & Tackle, 94- 96 Montague Street, Rothesay, Isle of Bute, Tel: (01700) 503598.
Bait: Lugworm, ragworm, cockles and mussel can be obtained from beaches around the island, and no

angler should set forth without feathers or tinsel lures and a few good heavy spinner. Herring is also useful bait.
Season for fishing: July-October.

Kilchattan Bay
Sheltered bay waters at the south end of the Isle of Bute renowned for its good all year round fishing.
Types of fish: Cod, pollack, plaice, mackerel, conger, dogfish, wrasse, whiting.
Bait: Worm, fresh cockle available locally.
Season for fishing: July to October.

Mainland Ardentinny
Ardentinny is a small unspoiled village picturesquely situated on the west shore of Loch Long, 12 miles from Dunoon by car.
Types of fish: Cod, mackerel, from the shore. Cod, conger, haddock, ray, plaice, flounder, whiting, coalfish and mackerel from boats.
Bait: Cockles, mussels, lug and ragworm easily dug in bay.
Season for fishing: All year, winter for large cod.

Dunoon
Types of fish: Most of the shoreline around Dunoon provides catches of cod, coalfish, pollack, flounder, mackerel, plaice. Using ragworm & lugworm, cockle, mussel, razorfish & Peeler crab. Boat fishing takes mostly cod, pollack, coalfish, dogfish, dabs, plaice, flounder. Also conger over wrecks or rough ground at night.
Boats: Gourock skippers fish Dunoon waters. Approx. 3 miles from Dunoon is Holy Loch.
Bait: Can be bought at shops most of the year or obtained in East Bay shore.
Further information from: John Murray - Tel: (01475) 38241.

Tighnabruaich & Kames
Tighnabruaich, on the Kyles of Bute, is famed for its beauty and Highland scenery. Access to some good fishing banks on the west side of the Bute and around the Kyles.
Types of fish: Mackerel and coalfish from the shore. Flatfish, whiting, dogfish, pollack, gurnard and several species of wrasse. Conger fishing can be arranged.
Bait: Supplies of fresh bait (lug, cockle, mussel, clams etc.) are locally available.
Boats: Motor dinghies available for hire. Local fishermen can take parties of anglers by arrangement. Contact: Andy Lancaster, Kames

Hotel, Tel: (01700) 811489.
Season: Spring to Autumn.

Loch Fyne
This is the longest sea-loch in Scotland, penetrating into the Highlands from the waters of the lower Firth of Clyde. The depth of the water within the loch varies enormously with depth of around 100 fathoms being found not only at the seaward end but also at the head of the loch of Inveraray. Much of the shore angling potential remains unknown although access to both shores is made relatively easy by roads running down each side. Boat launching facilities are less easy to find because of the rugged shoreline. Best side is Inveraray to Furnace. Quarry is now out of bounds.
Types of fish: Mackerel, codling, pollack, flatfish, conger (at night).

Inveraray
Inveraray stands on its west shore near the head of Loch Fyne.
Types of fish: Mackerel, pollack, coalfish, ling, dogfish, conger eel and plaice.
Bait: Mussels and worms available from shore at low tide.
Season for fishing:
June-September.

Tarbert (Loch Fyne)
The sheltered harbour and the adjacent coast of the loch near the lower end of the loch on the west shore are good fishing grounds for the sea angler.
Types of fish: Mackerel, coalfish, and sea trout from the shore. Mackerel, cod, coalfish and whiting from boats.
Boats: Evening out with the boats of the herring fleet can be arranged.
Tackle: Local shops.
Bait: There is an abundance of shellfish and worms on the mud flats.
Season for fishing: June, July and August.

Oban
Good catches can be occasionally taken in Kerrera Sound near the Cutter Rock and the Ferry Rocks. Fishing is much better off the south and west coasts of Kerrera Island, particularly near the Bach Island and Shepherds Hat, Maiden Island and Oban Bay give good mackerel fishing in July and August. These places are very exposed and should only be attempted in good settled weather.
Best shore marks: Salmore Point, North Connel at road bridge,

Bonawe Quarry, rail bridge at Loch Creran, Easdale Rocks.
Types of fish: Boat & Shore – Tope, conger, whiting, codling, cod, pollack, coalfish, skate, thornback ray, spurdog, dogfish, mackerel, ling, wrasse and gurnard.
Tackle Requirements: From light spinning to beachcasters. Boat rods mainly 20lb class, but for skate 50lb class. All sea and game anglers necessities stocked at The Anglers Corner".
Boats: Ronnie Campbell, 14 Kenmore Cottages, Bonawe, Argyll. Tel: (01631) 75213 (launching for Loch Etive best at Oban).
Bait: Mussels and lugworm, etc. can be dug from the Kerrera beaches. Frozen and preserved baits can be bought from The Anglers' Corner, 2 John Street, Oban - Tel: (01631) 66374 or from Binnie Bros., Fishmongers, 8 Stevenson Street, Oban. Tel: (01631) 62503.
Local Club: North Argyll Sea Anglers, Secretary: Andy MacArthur, Craignish, Pulpit Drive, Oban. Tel: (01631) 64657.
Season for fishing:
May-November.
Further information from: Ross Binnie, Tel: (01631) 66374.

Isle of Islay
This is the southernmost of the islands. Several of the larger communities like Port Ellen and Port Askaig have good harbours.
Types of fish: Boat – cod, haddock, whiting, mackerel, dogfish, flounder, conger, rays.
Tackle: available from J. Campbell, sub-Post Office, Bridgend.
Bait: Lugworm plentiful on most beaches. Clam skirts from fish factory waste. Bait can be purchased from fishing boats at the piers.
Season for fishing: June-October.
Further information from: Bowmore Tourist Office, Tel: (0149 681) 254.

Isle of Mull (Salen)
Salen is situated on the east coast of Mull facing the Sound of Mull in a central position, 11 miles from Craignure and 10 miles from Tobermory. The village is sited between Aros River and a headland forming Salen Bay. The Sound of Mull is on the main skate marks in the Argyll area. Many 100 lbs., plus skate have now been taken. One of the contributing factors is the sheltered nature of the Sound,

which can allow practically uninterrupted angling. This area has also yielded a number of fine tope, the largest of which was a specimen of 50 lbs. It is worth noting that cod and haddock seldom frequent the sound and should not be expected. This is an area recommended for dinghy owners.
Types of fish: Coalfish, pollack, wrasse, flounder, mullet sea trout, and mackerel from the shore. Ray, skate, ling, pollack, coalfish, spurdog, tope, conger, gurnard and odd codling from boats.
Tackle: Available from the Tackle and Books, Main Street, Tobermory, 10 miles away.
Bait: Easily obtainable from shoreline. Mackerel bait from Tackle and Books, Main Street, Tobermory.
Season for fishing:
March-November.
Further information from: Mr. Duncan Swinbanks, Tackle and Books, 10 Main Street, Tobermory.

Isle of Mull (Tobermory)
The principal town on Mull, it is situated on a very sheltered bay at the north eastern tip of the island. Apart from hitting the headlines in the national press with its treasure, Tobermory has been extensively covered in the angling press. It is Scotland's most popular centre for skate fishing. Every year an average of 50 ton-up specimens are caught, tagged and returned alive. It is this thoughtful conservation that has maintained the quality of fishing in the area. Large tope of between 35 lbs., and 45 lbs., can be numerous. Ten Scottish records, red gurnard, grey gurnard, blonde ray, spotted ray, spurdogfish, angler fish, turbot, common skate and two wrasse, have come from these Mull waters. Every year catches of migratory fish can be made. Coalfish, whiting, haddock and cod are encountered.
Types of fish: Tope, skate, rays, pollack, coalfish, ling, conger, gurnard, spurdog, cod, haddock, flatfish (plaice, dabs, and turbot) and whiting from boats. Coalfish, pollack, cod, wrasse, flounder, grey mullet, sea trout, conger, thornback and mackerel from the shore.
Boats: Andrew Jackson, Laggerbay, Acharacle, Argyll PH36 4JW, Tel: (01972) 500208, has a purpose built 38 ft. sea angling boat for fishing parties with boat rods and reel available. There are 14-16 ft. dinghies for hire for fishing in and around the bay.

Tackle: A tackle shop, with a complete range of stock is on the Main Street.
Bait: Herring and mackerel available from Tackle and Books, Tobermory. Mussels and lugworms are easily obtainable from the shoreline.
Season for fishing: May-November.
Further information from: Mr. Duncan Swinbanks, Tackle and Books, 10 Main Street, Tobermory.

Isle of Coll
Coll is one of the smaller islands seaward of Mull. Fishing vessels concentrate on the Atlantic side, but good sport can be had on the Mull side and even at the mouth of Arinagour Bay where the village and hotel lie and the mail steamer calls. Fishing from rocks at several spots round the island can give good results.
Types of fish: Mackerel, coalfish, pollack, cod, conger, haddock, skate and flounder.
Boats: Dinghies with or without outboard engines can be hired from local lobster fishermen.
Tackle: Visitors are advised to bring their own.
Bait: Mussels, worms and small crabs can readily be obtained at low tide in Arinagour Bay.
Season for fishing: May to September and later depending on weather.

FORTH AND LOMOND (EAST COAST)

Anglers going afloat from Fife and Forth Harbours are advised to contact the coastguard at Fifeness for weather information. Tel: (01333) 50666 (day or night).

Tayport
Tayport, on the Firth of Tay opposite Dundee, in the northern-most part of Fife, enjoys good shore fishing in sheltered waters. There are no hotels but there is a modern caravan and camping site with showers, laundry etc.
Types of fish: Cod, flounder and plaice from shore, with occasional sea trout (permit required).
Bait: Lugworm, ragworm, mussels, cockles and crabs available locally at low water.
Season for fishing: April-January.

St. Andrews
St. Andrews is a leading holiday resort with sea angling as one of its attractions. Fishing is mainly from boats, but good sport can be had from the rocks between the bathing pool and the harbour.
Tackle: Messrs. J. Wilson & Sons (Ironmongers), 169-171 South Street, St. Andrews, KY16 9EE, Tel: (01334) 72477.
Bait: Excellent supplies of Lugworm, ragworm and large mussels can be gathered on the beach.

Boarhill and Kings Barns
Good beach fishing for cod and flatfish.

Anstruther
It is a fishing village with plenty of good boat and beach fishing. A very rocky coastline but can be very rewarding with good catches of cod, saithe, flounder, wrasse, and whiting. Be prepared to lose tackle.
Types of fish: Cod, saithe, wrasse, flounder, ling, conger and mackerel.
Boats: Plenty charter boats with local skippers who know all the hot spots.
Bait: Lug, rag, white rag, cockle, crab, mussel which can be dug locally.
Season: Boat – May-October. Beach – September-January.

Pittenweem
The nerve centre of the East Neuk with a large deep water harbour which boats can enter or leave at any stage of the tide. The European Cod Festival is now held here each year and produces large catches of cod. The harbour wall is very popular with young and old alike, with some good catches.
Types of fish: Cod, saithe, flounder, wrasse, ling, conger, whiting, mackerel from boats. Cod, saithe, flounder, wrasse and whiting from beach.
Bait: Lug, rag, can be dug locally.
Season: Beach – September-January.

Leven
A holiday resort with about 2 miles of lovely sandy beaches. Beach fishing is very popular with some very good catches.
Types of fish: Flounder, cod, bass, mullet, saithe.
Boats: No charter boats.
Bait: Lug available locally.
Season: July-January.

Buckhaven
A small town on the north side of the Firth of Forth, which is renowned for its boat and beach fishing. The Scottish Open Beach Competition is fished from Buckhaven to Dysart each year with large entries from all over Scotland.
Types of fish: Cod, saithe, flounder, whiting, mackerel from beach. Cod, saithe, flounder, whiting, ling, mackerel and wrasse from boat.
Bait: Lug available at Leven.
Boats: No charter hire.
Season: Boat – June-November. Beach – October-January.

Kirkcaldy
Beach fishing at east and west end of town.
Types of fish: Cod, flatfish, saithe, mackerel.
Bait: Beach off bus station.

Pettycur and Kinghorn
Rock and beach fishing off Pettycur Harbour and Kinghorn Beach.
Types of fish: Saithe, flatfish.
Boats: Small boats can be launched from beaches.
Bait: Plenty locally. Local caravan sites.

Burntisland
Permission required to fish the beach from harbour to swimming pool.
Types of fish: Saithe, flatfish, small cod.
Boats: None locally.
Bait: Lug available locally.

South Queensferry
A picturesque burgh overshadowed by the Forth Bridges. There are 3 launching slips in the area, but currents can be dangerous and local advice should be obtained before setting out in dinghies.
Types of fish: Cod, whiting, coalfish, mackerel, flounder from boat and shore in season.
Bait: Lugworm, ragworm, mussel, cockle, clams and crabs at low water in the area.
Season for fishing: May to October.

Edinburgh
Scotland's capital city, on the south of the Forth estuary, has several miles of shoreline. Most of this is sandy, and can produce good catches of flatfish, although codling, Ray's bream, whiting, eels and mackerel can be taken in season from the shore. Best marks are at Cramond, round the mouth of the River Almond, and the Seafield to Portobello area.
Bait: Lugworm, ragworm,

mussels, cockles and clams from most beaches at low water.
Season for fishing: All year round.

Musselburgh
This town stands on the estuary of the River Esk, 6 miles to the east of Edinburgh, overlooking the Firth of Forth. It has a small but busy harbour at Fisherrow, catering mainly for pleasure craft.
Boats: Enquiries should be made at the harbour. Best shore marks range from Fisherrow harbour to the mouth of the Esk.
Bait: Lugworm, ragworm, mussels, cockles and clams at low water.

Cockenzie
Mullet can be caught around the warm water outfall to the east of Cockenzie Power station and around the harbour. Other species include flatfish, codling and mackerel.

North Berwick
There is good boat fishing out of North Berwick and the coastline between the town and Dunbar is good for shore fishing.
Types of fish: Cod, haddock, plaice, mackerel and coalfish.
Bait: Mussels, crabs and shellfish of various types available at low water.
Further information from:
Information Centre, Quality Street. Tel: (01620) 2197 January-December.

Dunbar
The coastline from Dunbar to Eyemouth is very popular for rock and beach fishing.
Types of fish: Cod, haddock, flounder, coalfish, mackerel, wrasse and whiting.
Boats: Details can be obtained from The Tourist Information Centre, Dunbar.
Bait: Mussels, lug and ragworm available at low water, and also from tackle dealers.
Season for fishing: Best April to October.
Further information from:
Information Centre, Town House, High Street. Tel: (01368) 63353 January-December.

TAYSIDE

Arbroath
Situated on the east coast of Angus, 17 miles north-east of Dundee, Arbroath is easily

accessible by road and rail. It is the centre for commercial fishing, and famous for its smokies. Pleasure boats ply for short cruises to local sea cliffs and caves, from the harbour. There are about 10 boats between 15ft and 35ft used for lobster and crab fishing, taking out parties for sea angling.
Types of fish: Cod, coalfish, mackerel, flounder, conger, plaice, haddock and pollack.
Boats: Available through local fishermen and part time lobster and crab fishermen at reasonable prices.

Dundee
Dundee is situated on the estuary of the River Tay and has sea fishing in the city centre, while Broughty Ferry, a suburb of Dundee, Easthaven and Carnoustie, all within easy reach by road and rail, have sea fishing from rocks, piers or from boats. There are good marks around the Bell Rock about 12 miles offshore.
Types of fish: Cod, flatfish from shore plus cod, haddock, coalfish, ling, pouting and plaice from boats.
Bait: Available locally.
Season for fishing: All year.

NORTH EAST AND SPEY VALLEY

Moray Firth
The Moray Firth has always been famous for its fishing grounds and most of the towns along the south coastline depend largely on commercial fishing for their prosperity; cod, haddock, flatfish of many kings, pollack, coalfish and mackerel being landed.

Nairn
Nairn is set on the pleasant coastal plain bordering the southern shore of the Moray Firth. There is a beautiful stretch of sands to the east. Most fishing is done from two small piers at the entrance to the tidal harbour.
Types of fish: Mackerel, small coalfish, pollack, dab and cod.
Boats: One or two, privately owned, will often take a passenger out. Enquiries should be made at the harbour.
Tackle: P. Fraser, 41 High Street, Nairn. Tel: (01667) 53038.
Bait: Lugworm available on the beach at low water. Mackerel etc. mostly taken on flies.

Lossiemouth and Garmouth
Lossiemouth, a small, prosperous town, is a unique combination of white fish centre, seaside, shops and hotels. The angler will find unlimited sport of a kind probably new to him, for off the east and west beaches sea trout and finnock abound, and spinning for these into the sea, especially into the breakers, is a magnificent sport.
Types of fish: Sea trout, conger from the pier, coalfish, flatfish, 6.5 miles of shore fishing. Haddock, cod, plaice and coalfish from boats. Shore fishing – sea trout between harbour and Boar's Head Rock and at the old cement works Garmouth.
Bait: Lugworm on the west beach and the harbour at low water. Also plenty of mussels to be collected. Spinners, Pirks.
Season for fishing: Migratory fish season, October. Best months – late July, early August.

Buckie
Buckie is a major commercial fishing port on the eastern side of Spey Bay. It has become increasingly popular over the last few years as a tourist area and is well supplied with hotels, golf courses and caravan sites. It offers a varied coastline in the form of sandy beaches and quite spectacular rugged cliff formations.
Types of fish: Cod, coalfish, conger, pollack, mackerel, haddock, whiting, flatfish.
Bait: Lugworm, ragworm, mussels, cockles and crabs freely available along the shoreline eastwards.
Season for fishing: April-October. Winter months best for cod.

Cullen
M.V. Rosenberg" is a 30ft long, twin-engined cruiser providing pleasure trips and catering for sea anglers (tackle for hire or for sale). The boat is licensed by the Department of Transport and, as such, meets all its survey requirements annually. The vessel, which has all modern aids to navigation, has a certificated skipper. Details may be had from Cullen Marine Services, 27 North Deskford Street, Cullen. Tel: (01542) 840323.

Portknockie
Portknockie is a quaint little fishing village to the west of Cullen Bay. The small harbour is used by two small mackerel boats.
Types of fish: Excellent rock fishing here for cod, coalfish, and

some mackerel from the piers. Good boat fishing for haddock, ling and gurnard.

Boats: There are no boats for hire as such, although it is possible to get out in two small (18ft) mackerel boats.
Bait: Lugworm and mussels in the harbour at low water.
Further information from: Tourist Information Centre, 17 High Street, Elgin, IV30 1EG. Tel: (01343) 542666/543388.

Portsoy
One of the numerous small towns that line the Banffshire coast. It is a former seaport but the harbour is silting up.
Types of fish: Coalfish and mackerel from the small pier and some good rock fishing east and west for cod. From boats, mackerel, cod, haddock, plaice, coalfish and dab.
Bait: Some lugworm at low water mark.

Gardenstown and Crovie
These are traditional fishing villages. Mackerel are plentiful, June-September. Anglers would be well advised to follow local boats which are fishing commercially.
Types of fish: From shore – coalfish, pollack, flatfish, conger, From boats – mackerel, cod, haddock, flounder, plaice, conger, dab, catfish, gurnard and ling.
Bait: Available on beach, but local people prefer to use flies.

Fraserburgh
Situated on the north-east shoulder of Scotland, Fraserburgh has the Moray Firth to the west and north and the North Sea to the east. The Burgh was primarily given over to the herring and white fish industry, but has developed as a holiday resort with the decline of commercial fishing in the North Sea. Tickets and permits for game fishing from the beaches can be had at Weelies, Grocer, College Bounds.
Types of fish: Shore – cod, coalfish and mackerel. Boat – as shore.
Bait: Mussels and lugworm can be dug from the beach.
Season for fishing: May-October.

Peterhead
Peterhead is an important fishing port situated north of Buchan Ness, the most easterly point of Scotland. Excellent breakwaters, 1900ft and 2800ft long, are the main shore marks for holiday anglers. Access to the breakwaters

is dependent on weather conditions and can be restricted when vessels are being worked. A safety access procedure has been agreed with the North Breakwater Sea Angling Society to whom further queries should be directed. However passengers are at times taken out by private boats.
Types of fish: From the pier – mackerel, coalfish, dab and cod. From boats – cod, haddock, dabs, ling, coalfish and mackerel.
Boats: There are a number of privately owned boats which will sometimes take out passengers. Enquiries should be made at the harbour.
Tackle: Available from Robertsons Sports, 1 Kirk Street, Peterhead. Tel: (01779) 72584.
Bait: Lugworm can be dug from shore at low water while mussels can be gathered from the rocks.

Stonehaven
Stonehaven is a holiday resort 15 miles south of Aberdeen on main road and rail routes. Magnificent catches of cod and haddock are taken regularly by boat. Anglers obtain great co-operation from angling boat skippers and local professional fishermen. On either side of Stonehaven there are good rock fishing marks which should be approached with care especially during strong easterly winds.
Types of fish: Cod, haddock, pollack, coalfish, flounder, catfish and mackerel from the shore. Cod, haddock, coalfish, pollack, ling, catfish, plaice and other flatfish, ballan wrasse, cuckoo wrasse, whiting and Norway haddock from boats.
Boats: Boats are available from skipper: A. McKenzie, 24 Westfield Park, Stonehaven, Tel: (01569) 63411.
Bait: Mussels available if ordered from skippers of boats.
Season for fishing: All year.
Further information from: Information Centre, 66 Allardice Street, Tel: (01569) 62806 Easter-October.

GREAT GLEN AND ISLE OF SKYE

Isle of Eigg
The Isle of Eigg lies 5m SW of Skye.
Types of fish: Pollack, conger, spurdog, skate, cod, mackerel.
Season for fishing: Summer-Autumn.

Isle of Skye
The many lochs and bays around the beautiful Isle of Skye provide ideal facilities for sea angling. There is a great variety of fish, most of which can be caught from the shore because of the deep water found close inshore off rocky shores and headlands. Local residents are very knowledgeable about fishing in their own area. Loch-Snizort has now been found to hold a stock of large common skate and anglers could well contact these during a session there.

Isle of Skye (Portree)
Portree, the capital of Skye, is situated half way up the east coast of the island. There is a very good harbour and good fishing marks in and round it. Ample free anchorage and berthing available for visiting craft. Slipping, re-fuelling and watering facilities are easily accessible.
Types of fish: Cod, haddock, whiting, coalfish, pollack and mackerel.
Boats: Greshornish House Hotel, Edinbane, by Portree, Isle of Skye. Tel: (0147082) 266, has one boat available.
Bait: Unlimited mussels and cockles available in tidal area of Portree Bay.
Season for fishing: May-September.

Isle of Skye (Camastianavaig by Portree)
To reach this sheltered bay which lies 4 miles south east of Portree, turn off the A850 to Braes. Although local tactics are the use of feathers, bottom fishing with trace or paternoster has yielded heavy bags with skate of 62.5lbs, cod 6lbs, whiting 3lbs, haddock 3lbs, spurdog 12lbs, gurnard 2lbs, pollacks 12lbs, coalfish 14lbs, all from boats.
Types of fish: Shore – coalfish, pollack, wrasse and mackerel. Boat – cod, haddock and spurdog.
Tackle: Obtainable at Portree.
Bait: Lugworm at Broadford Bay and Balmeanac Bay. Cockles and mussels at Portree Loch.
Season for fishing: June-October.

Isle of Skye (Uig)
Uig, a picturesque village amidst some of the finest scenery in the north west, has excellent fishing on its doorstep. Loch Snizort and small islands at its entrance, together with the Ascrib Islands opposite, are well worth fishing. Fishing can be arranged as far round the coast as Score Bay,

known to some ring net fishermen as the Golden Mile'.

Types of fish: Shore – coalfish, mackerel, pollack, conger and dogfish. Boat – coalfish, mackerel, pollack, conger, whiting, haddock, dogfish, flatfish, skate, cod and gurnard.

Boats: Available locally at Uig, Waternish and Kilmuir.

Season for fishing: May-September.

Isle of Skye (Skeabost Bridge)
Skeabost Bridge is situated 5 miles from Portree at the south east end of Loch Snizort.

Types of fish: There is no shore fishing but many types of sea fish can be caught from boats.

Bait: Available locally.

Season for fishing: July-October.

Kyle of Lochalsh
The village of Kyle, on the mainland opposite Kyleakin on the Isle of Skye, is a railhead and a car ferry link with Skye and the Hebrides.

Types of fish: Conger, coalfish, pollack and whiting from the harbour. Boat – pollack, cod, coalfish, mackerel and whiting.

Tackle: Available from John MacLennan & Co., Marine Stores, Kyle of Lochalsh IV40 8AE. Tel: (01599) 4208.

Bait: Mussels from Fishery Pier and clams and cockles at spring tides.

Season for fishing: June-September.

NORTH SCOTLAND

Gairloch
Gairloch Bay is very popular with sea anglers. There is good fishing in this lovely sea loch, especially around Longa Island which lies near the entrance to the Loch.

Poolewe and Aultbea
Situated amidst magnificent scenery, the sheltered waters of Loch Ewe offer the sea angler opportunities of fine catches. Suitable accommodation is available in surrounding villages and local advice is always available.

Types of fish: Shore – pollack, coalfish, dab, codling. Boat – haddock, cod, codling, gurnard, skate, whiting, mackerel, flatfish.

Boats: Several boats available locally.

Bait: Mussels, lugworm, cockles, etc. from shore.

Season for fishing: April- October incl.

Little Loch Broom
Ten miles north east Aultbea.

Ullapool & The Summer Isles
Loch Broom and the waters encircled by the Summer Isles offer excellent sea angling. The banks can be approached from Ullapool, which is an attractive holiday village sited on a peninsula projecting into Loch Broom. The numerous banks and islands offer superb fishing and beautiful scenery in sheltered waters. Many attractions on shore via local shops; hotels and sporting facilities available throughout the season. Achiltibuie, a small village, also gives access to fishing grounds.

Types of fish: Shore – codling, coalfish, conger, pollack, mackerel, dabs, thornbacks, dogfish, flounders and plaice. Boat – as above plus haddock, whiting, wrasse, ling, megrim, gurnard, spurdog and turbot.

Season for fishing: June-October inclusive. Big skate best in autumn.

Lochinver
Lochinver is one of the major fishing ports in the north of Scotland. With a population of some 300 inhabitants it has a safe all - tides harbour with excellent shore services, including good moderately - priced accommodation and two fishing tackle shops. Excellent sea fishing within a short distance from the port, specialising in jumbo haddock, cod, skate and conger. It is one of the few areas where large halibut are caught. Boats available. A large fleet of fishing vessels operates from the harbour and bait is readily available.

Types of fish: Cod, haddock, whiting, saithe, gurnard, ling, pollack, mackerel, wrasse, conger, skate. Coalfish, pollack, cod and mackerel from the shore.

Tackle: Tackle is available from Lochinver Fishselling Co., Culag Square, Lochinver. Tel: (015714) 228/258.

Season for fishing: April-October.

Drumbeg
Seven miles north of Lochinver.

Caithness
With the prolific fishing grounds of the Pentland Firth, the north of Caithness has built up a reputation as being one of the premier sea angling areas in Scotland. It is now recognised that the chance of taking a halibut on rod and line is better in Pentland waters than anywhere else; more halibut have been taken here than in any other part of the British Isles. The presence of Porbeagle shark in these waters has been proved by the capture of two specimens, with many more hooked and lost. Among the notable fish caught were European halibut records of 194 lbs. in 1974, 215 lbs. in 1975, 224 lbs. in 1978 and 234 lbs. in 1979. This fish represented a world record catch for the species. The Scottish shore record ling of 12lbs 4oz was caught in these waters. With countless numbers of rocky coves and sandy beaches there is much for the shore angler to discover along the whole of the north coast of Scotland. Accommodation is available to suit everyone, from first class hotels, private B. & B. to caravan and camping sites with full facilities. It is also possible to have a full sea angling package holiday with full board at a hotel and all boat charges included. The number of angling boats available increases each year, but it is still advisable to book boat places in advance.

Thurso and Scrabster
Thurso is the main town on the north side of Caithness and gives access through Scrabster to the waters of the Pentland Firth, where there are first class fishing grounds. Thurso Bay and the Dunnet Head area are sheltered from prevailing winds and it is reasonably easy for anglers to get afloat to the marks. Scrabster 1.4 miles from Thurso, is the main harbour in northern Caithness. Most of the angling boats are based here. There is also some excellent rock fishing, while conger may be caught from the harbour walls.

Types of fish: Cod, ling, haddock, conger, pollack, coalfish, dogfish, spurdog, plaice, wrasse, mackerel, dab, whiting, rays, halibut, porbeagle shark.

Tackle: Harper's Fishing Services, 57 High Street, Thurso KW14 8AZ. Tel: (01847) 63179.

Bait: Mussels, lugworm can be gathered at low water, mackerel and squid from fish shops and local fishermen. Most species take lures, feather and rubber eels, etc. and most fishing done with this type of artificial bait.

Season for fishing: April-November.

Further information from: Caithness Tourist Board, Whitechapel Road, Wick, Tel: (01955) 2596 Jan-Dec.

Dunnet

Dunnet is situated 8 miles east of Thurso at the end of the famous Dunnet Sands, which are over 2.5 miles long. Few anglers fish this beach, as there is excellent boat fishing nearby. There is plenty of lugworm and the beach is well worth trying.
Types of fish: As for Thurso.
Boats and Tackle: As for Thurso.
Bait: Mussels from the rocks at low tide and lugworm all along Dunnet Sands.
Season for fishing: Shore – July and August. Boat – April-November.

Keiss

Good shore fishing is to be had around Keiss, a small fishing village between John o'Groats and Wick. It might be difficult to get out in a boat. The shore fishing is from the rocks around Keiss, and from the beach at Sinclair's Bay to the south of the village. Here some very good plaice have been taken and also anglers have caught sea trout while spinning for mackerel.
Tackle: Tackle shops at Wick.
Bait: Mussels and lugworm can be obtained at low tide.

Sutherland and Easter Ross Brora

Brora is a village situated on the A9, 12 miles south of Helmsdale. There is a small harbour and a few boats are available to sea anglers. There are rail links to Brora from the south and ample hotel accommodation and caravan facilities.
Types of fish: Cod, coalfish, cod, ling, haddock, rays and conger from boats.
Boats: Some owners are willing to take visitors at nominal costs.
Bait: Can be dug locally.
Season for fishing: July-September.

Grannies Heilan' Hame, Embo

This is a caravan holiday centre with extensive amenities 2 miles north of Dornoch.
Types of fish: Spinning for sea trout from the beach up to the mouth of Loch Fleet. Coalfish, mackerel and flatfish from the pier. The rocks provide good cod fishing. From boats, coalfish, mackerel, plaice, cod, haddock and whiting at times.
Bait: Lugworm can be dug at the ferry landing area and there are plenty of mussels and cockles near Loch Fleet.
Season for fishing: April-September.

Dornoch

Dornoch gives access to the fishing banks off the north coast of the Dornoch Firth. There is good shore fishing from the rocks at Embo, but to get afloat it is necessary to make arrangements in advance. Youngsters can enjoy good fishing from Embo Pier.
Types of fish: Sea trout from shore. Flat fish, haddock and cod from boats.
Boats: Boats are difficult to hire but there are one or two in Embo which is three miles from Dornoch.
Season for fishing: April-September.

Tain

Tain lies on the south side of the Dornoch Firth and gives access to excellent sea trout fishing, both shore and boat, in sheltered waters of the Firth.
Types of fish: Shore – wrasse, flatfish, pollack, mackerel. Boat – haddock, cod, skate, mackerel.
Boats: Available in Balintore, 6 miles from Tain and Portmahomack.
Bait: Available from the shore.

Balintore

The village of Balintore, near Tain, has over the past 4 years increased in status and is now one of the recognised centres for big catches. Catches of up to 1,000lbs of cod and ling have been made (8 anglers) in a single morning's fishing.
Types of fish: Cod, ling, wrasse, pollack and mackerel. Season from mid-April to beginning of November.

Portmahomack

This fishing village is well situated in a small bay on the southern shore of the Dornoch Firth, 9 miles east of Tain and 17 miles from Invergordon to the south. There is a well-protected harbour and a good, safe sandy beach.
Types of fish: Cod from the shore. Haddock and cod from boats.
Tackle: Available at Tain.
Season for fishing: Spring to Autumn.

North Kessock, Avoch and Fortrose

These villages lie along the north-west side of the Moray Firth north of Inverness. This sheltered sea loch provides good fishing.

WESTERN ISLES

The Western Isles

The Western Isles form a north-south chain of islands off the west coast of Scotland. Separated from the mainland by the Minches, much of their rod and line fishing remains to be discovered, not only due to a lack of boats in the area, but also due to a lack of communications between and within the islands. Car ferries run from Oban and Ullapool on the mainland and Uig on Skye. Regular air services to Barra, Stornoway, for Lewis and Harris and Benbecula for the Uists.

Isle of Harris (Tarbert)

The largest community on the southern part of the largest of the Hebridean islands, Tarbert stands on a very narrow neck of land where the Atlantic and the Minch are separated by only a few hundred yards of land. It is the terminal for the car ferry from Uig on Skye and Lochmaddy on North Uist.
Types of fish: Boat – mackerel, ling, coalfish, cod, rays, pollack and conger. Shore – plaice, haddock and flounder.
Boats: Check with Tourist Information Centre, Tarbert. Tel: (01859) 2011.
Bait: Mussels available on the shore, lugworm, cockles.
Season for fishing: May-October.
Further information from: Tourist Centre, Tarbert. Tel: (01859) 2011.

Isle of Lewis (Stornoway)

Stornoway, the only town in the Outer Hebrides, is easily accessible by air from Glasgow Airport (1 hour) and Inverness (25 mins.); there is also a drive-on car ferry service from Ullapool (3.5 hours crossing). Another ferry service connects Uig (Skye) to Tarbert (Harris), which is only an hour's drive from Stornoway. Stornoway is now recognised as a mecca for sea angling in Scotland. There is an enthusiastic sea angling club with club boats and licensed premises which overlook the harbour. Each August the club runs the Western Isles (Open) Sea Angling Championships. Many skate over the ton' have been caught, the heaviest so far being 192 lbs. The Scottish blueshark record of 85.5 lbs. was off Stornoway in August 1972. Visiting anglers may become temporary members of the Stornoway Club (one minute from the town hall) and can make arrangements for fishing trips with club members in the club boats. Accommodation can be arranged through the Wester Isles Tourist Board, Administration and Information Centre, 4 South Beach Street, Stornoway Tel: (01851) 3088.

Types of fish: Conger, cod, skate, rays, ling, pollack, whiting, dabs, bluemouth, flounder, dogfish, wrasse, haddock.

Bait: Mussels in harbour area; mackerel from local boats.

NORTHERN ISLES

Orkney
The waters around Orkney attract many sea anglers each year as big skate, halibut and ling are there for the taking. Ling of 36 lbs. skate of 214 lbs. taken by Jan Olsson of Sweden and the former British record halibut (161.5lbs.) taken by ex-Provost Knight of Stromness provide the bait which attracts anglers to these waters. The Old Man of Hoy, Scapa Flow and Marwick Head are well-known names to sea anglers. The Brough of Birsay, Costa Head and the Eday and Stronsay Firths are equally well known as marks for big halibut and skate. Fishing from Kirkwall or Stromness, there is easy access to Scapa Flow where wrecks of the German Fleet of the First World War provide homes

for large ling and conger. In the fish rich sea surrounding Orkney the angler will find some excellent shore fishing, nearly all of which remains to be discovered. Furthermore, skate of over 100 lbs. are still common while specimens of 200 lbs. have been recorded. More halibut have been caught in the waters to the south separating Orkney from the mainland than elsewhere in the U.K. Shark have also been sighted and hooked but none so far have been landed. Around the islands, in bays and firths, there is excellent sport for the specimen fish hunter and the Orcadians are eager to help sea anglers share the sport they enjoy. There is a regular car ferry service from Scrabster (Thurso) to Orkney and daily air services from Edinburgh, Glasgow and other points of the U.K.

Types of fish: Sea trout, plaice, pollack and coalfish, mackerel, wrasse from the shore. Skate, halibut, ling, cod, pollack, haddock, coalfish, plaice and dogfish from the boats.

Tackle: available from Stromness and Kirkwall.

Bait: Available from most beaches and piers.

Season for fishing: June-October.

Shetland
Shetland offers the best skate fishing to be had in Europe; during the years 1970-74 more than 250 skate over 100 lbs. were caught. These included a European record

of 226.5lbs., and 12 other skate over 190 lbs. During the same period, Shetland held nine British records, ten Scottish records and six European records, giving some indication that the general fishing is of no mean standard. Halibut and porbeagle of over 300 lbs. have been taken commercially in the Sumburgh area with porbeagle shark now being landed by anglers from this area. The Scottish record porbeagle shark of 450 lbs. has been landed here and bigger fish have been taken by commercial boat. Shore-fishing remains for the most part to be discovered.

Types of fish: Shore – coalfish, pollack, dogfish, mackerel, dabs, conger and cod. Boat – skate, halibut, ling, cod, tusk, haddock, whiting, coalfish, pollack, dogfish, porbeagle shark, Norway haddock, gurnard, mackerel, cuckoo and ballan wrasse.

Boats: Many boats available for hire throughout the islands. Boats can also be arranged through the Shetland Islands Tourism, Market Cross, Lerwick, Shetland.

Tackle: Available from J.A. Manson, 88 Commercial Street, Lerwick and Cee & Jays, 5 Commercial Road, Lerwick.

Bait: Fresh, frozen or salted fish bait available from fishmongers. Worm bait, crabs, etc. from beaches.

Season for fishing: Limited to May to October by weather conditions.

Tackle and Angler under strain

218lbs Porbeagle Shark caught Feb. 1994 (Thurso)

Please mention this Pastime Publications guide   169

SCOTLAND FOR FISHING
A Pastime Publication

I/We have seen your advertisement and wish to know if you have the following vacancy:

Name ....

Address ....

....

Dates from pm ....

Please give date and day of week in each case ....

To am ....

Number in Party ....

Details of Children ....

(*Please remember to include a stamped addressed envelope with your enquiry.*)

SCOTLAND FOR FISHING
A Pastime Publication

I/We have seen your advertisement and wish to know if you have the following vacancy:

Name ....

Address ....

....

Dates from pm ....

Please give date and day of week in each case ....

To am ....

Number in Party ....

Details of Children ....

(*Please remember to include a stamped addressed envelope with your enquiry.*)

MAPS

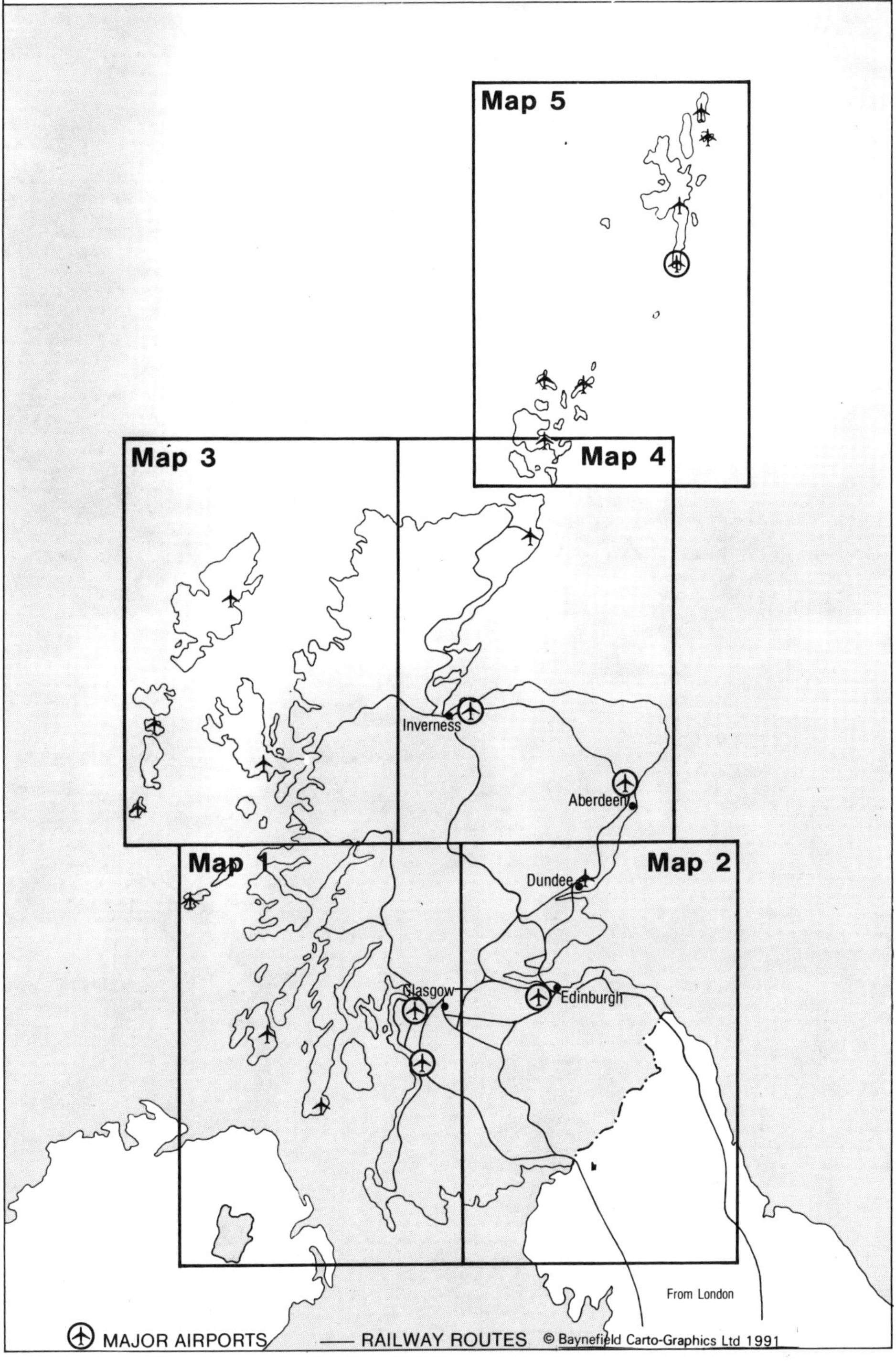

Map 5

Map 3

Map 4

Inverness

Aberdeen

Map 1

Dundee

Map 2

Glasgow

Edinburgh

From London

✈ MAJOR AIRPORTS   —— RAILWAY ROUTES   © Baynefield Carto-Graphics Ltd 1991

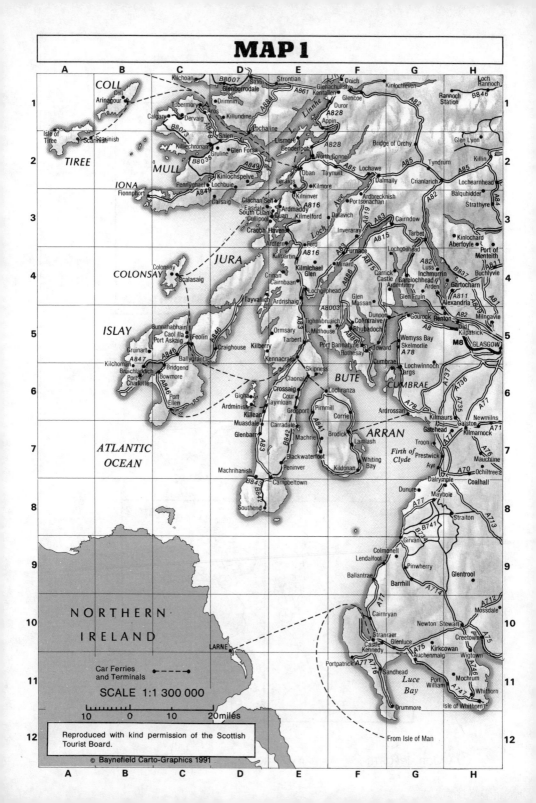

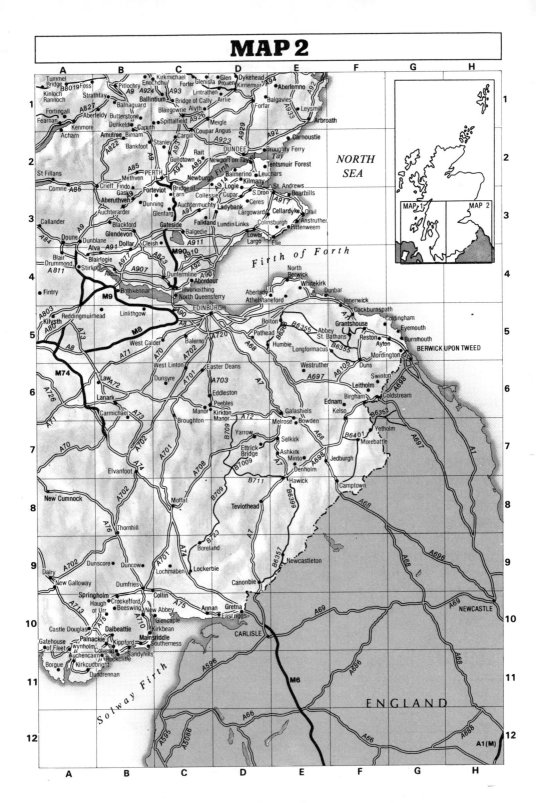

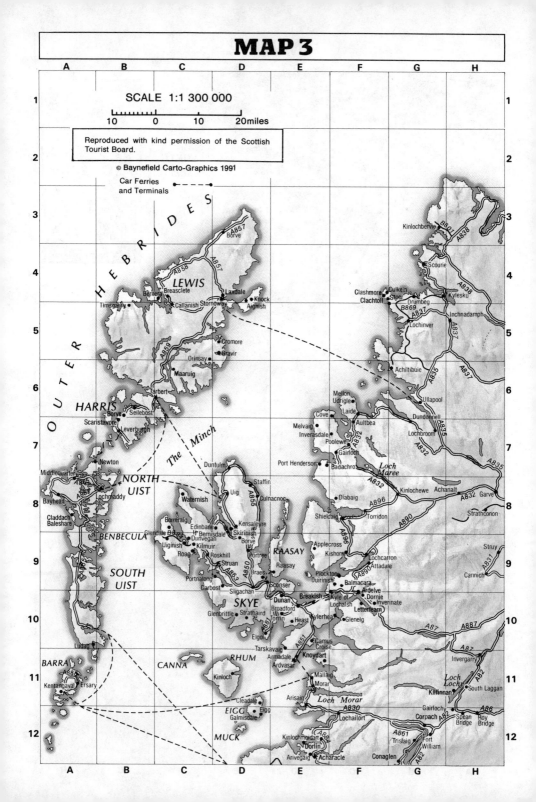

MAP 4

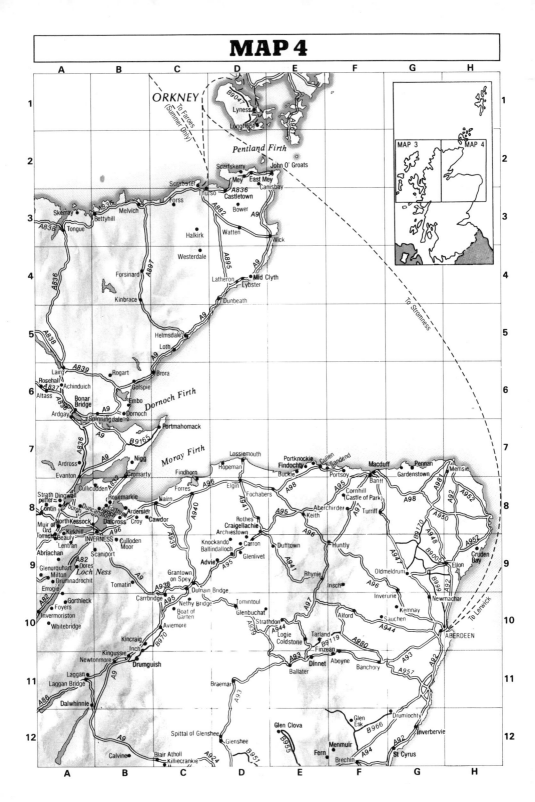

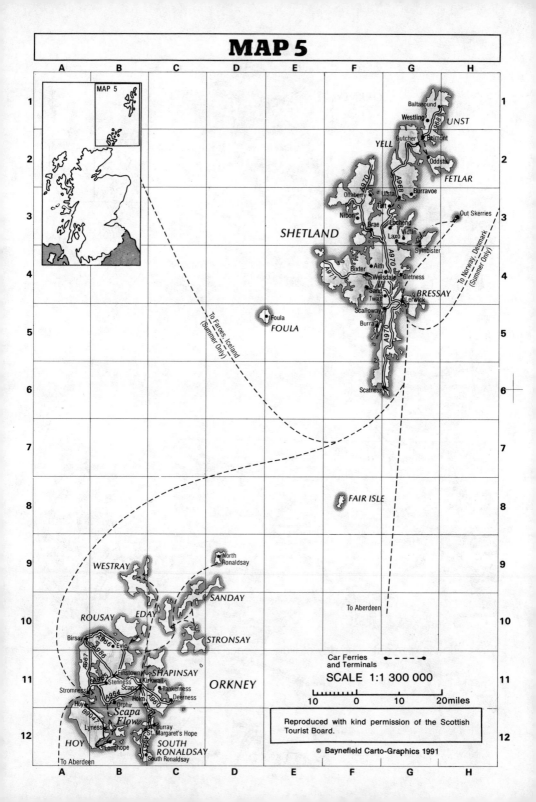

MAP 5

MAP 5

Baltasound
Westing
UNST
YELL
Gutcher
Belmont
Oddsta
FETLAR
Ollaberry
Ufsta
Burravoe
Toft
Nibon
SHETLAND
Brae
Lochend
Vidlin
Out Skerries
Laxo
Symbister
To Norway, Denmark
(Summer Only)
Bixter
Aith
Weisdale
Gletness
BRESSAY
Sand
Twatt
Lerwick
Scalloway
Burra

To Faroes, Iceland
(Summer Only)

Foula
FOULA

Scatness

FAIR ISLE

To Aberdeen

WESTRAY
North
Ronaldsay
SANDAY
ROUSAY
EDAY
STRONSAY
Birsay
Evie
SHAPINSAY
Finstown
Stenness
Kirkwall
ORKNEY
Stromness
Orphir
Scapa
Tankerness
Deerness
Holm
Hoy
Scapa
Flow
Burray
St. Margaret's Hope
Lyness
SOUTH
HOY
Longhope
RONALDSAY
To Aberdeen
South Ronaldsay

Car Ferries
and Terminals
SCALE 1:1 300 000
10   0   10   20miles

Reproduced with kind permission of the Scottish
Tourist Board.

© Baynefield Carto-Graphics 1991

SCOTLAND FOR FISHING
A Pastime Publication

I/We have seen your advertisement and wish to know if you have the following vacancy:

Name ....

Address ....

....

Dates from pm ....

Please give date and day of week in each case ....

To am ....

Number in Party ....

Details of Children ....

(*Please remember to include a stamped addressed envelope with your enquiry.*)

SCOTLAND FOR FISHING
A Pastime Publication

I/We have seen your advertisement and wish to know if you have the following vacancy:

Name ....

Address ....

....

Dates from pm ....

Please give date and day of week in each case ....

To am ....

Number in Party ....

Details of Children ....

(*Please remember to include a stamped addressed envelope with your enquiry.*)

PASTIME GUIDES FOR 1995

Pastime Publications Ltd is one of the leading Holiday Guide Publishers for U.K. Bed & Breakfast, Self Catering and Farm & Country Holidays as well as Activity and Motoring Holidays in Scotland.

The following publications are useful guides and make wonderful gifts throughout the year.

Whilst our guides are available in leading bookshops and Tourist Board Centres for your convenience we will be happy to post a copy to you or send books as a gift for you. We will post overseas but have to charge separately for post or freight.

The inclusive cost of posting and packing your selection of guides to you and your friends in the U.K. is as follows:

❑ **Farm & Country Holidays**
This guide gives details of over 300 farms, many of them working with livestock, as well as activity holidays. **£4.50**

❑ **Bed & Breakfast Holidays**
A comprehensive guide to over 300 hotels, guesthouses, farms and inns throughout Britain. **£4.50**

❑ **Self Catering Holidays**
Includes details of hundreds of houses, chalets, boats, caravans, cottages, farms and flats throughout Britain. **£4.50**

❑ **Scotland for Fishing**
Permits, fishing rights, boat hire, season/dates, rods, fly fishing and spinning . . . it's all here. **£4.50**

❑ **Scotland Home of Golf**
Over 400 golf clubs featured. Also places to stay. Editorial by well-known celebrities. **£4.50**

❑ **Scotland for the Motorist**
Over 1,000 places of interest plus road maps and where to stay. **£4.50**

❑ **Scotland Activity Holidays**
The finest walks and trails as well as hill walking, cycling, skiing, yachting, canoeing and trekking.
£4.50

Tick your choice and send your order and payment to:
Pastime Publications Ltd., 6 York Place, Edinburgh EH1 3EP.
Telephone: 0131-557 8092.
Deduct 10% for 2 or 3 titles and 20% for 4 or more titles.

Send to: NAME . . . .

ADDRESS . . . .

. . . . POST CODE . . . .

I enclose Cheque/Postal Order for £ . . . .

SIGNATURE . . . . **DATE** . . . .

"Described as

'The definitive reference guide to the salmon and sea-trout waters of Scotland,'

the claim is entirely justified ... Does seem to have thought of everything when it comes to the information the salmon fisher requires ... The whole thing builds into a very fisher-friendly Filofax and is heartily recommended to anyone wishing to book fishing." **Trout & Salmon (1994 edition)**

The Directory of Scottish Salmon Waters

The easiest way to find & book salmon fishing

Details of **over 450** salmon & sea-trout waters, including:

Contacts	*Catches & Averages*	**Nearby Tackle Shops**
Locations	**River Width & Depth**	*Dogs Policy*
Prices	*Currents & Wading*	**OS Maps**
Best Methods	**Best Flies & Rod Sizes**	*Accessibility*
Rod Availability	*Methods Allowed*	**Walking Distances**
Fishing Season	**Huts, Boats & Ghillies**	*Accommodation*

To Find Out More

Ask for a free information pack. Phone or post this coupon FREEPOST to: Durham Ranger Publishing, FREEPOST, Newcastle-upon-Tyne NE3 1BR. Tel. (0191) 284 7629.

Mr/Mrs/Ms _____ Address _____

_____ Post Code _____

PP